HONOR
AND
SACRIFICE

The Montagnards of Ba Cat

Anthony J. Blondell

Hellgate Press
Central Point, Oregon

Honor and Sacrifice: The Montagnards of Ba Cat

© 2000 by Anthony J. Blondell
Published by Hellgate Press

Hellgate Press
a division of PSI Research
P.O. Box 3727
Central Point, OR 97502-0032

(541) 245-6502
(541) 245-6505 *fax*
info@psi-research.com *e-mail*
www.psi-research.com/hellgate.htm

Editor: Kathy Marshbank
Book designer and compositor: Constance C. Dickinson
Cover designer: J. C. Young

Blondell, Anthony J., 1922–
    Honor and sacrifice : the Montagnards of Ba Cat, Vietnam / Anthony J. Blondell.
    p. cm.
    ISBN 1-55571-533-8 (cloth)
    1. Vietnamese Conflict, 1961–1975—Personal narratives, American. 2. Montagnar
(Vietnamese people). 3. United States. Army. Special Forces. 4. Blondell, Anthony J.
1922– 5. Ba Cat (Vietnam)—History. I. Title.

DS559.5.B55 2000
959.704'3'092—dc21   00-0529€

Printed and bound in the United States of America
First edition 10 9 8 7 6 5 4 3 2 1

 Printed on recycled paper when available.

Contents

Introduction

For more than 30 years, the author, a retired Green Beret master sergeant, has lived with deep feelings of sorrow and guilt because of fateful actions of his while serving in Vietnam. He was responsible for the death of many Montagnards, those small primitive men who lived in the mountains near the Vietnam-Laos border.

This account is the author's attempt to construct a Vietnam Memorial for those innocent men whose trust in us was so complete that they gave their all to support our mission, which was to "close with and destroy the enemy."

A powerful combat patrol was ordered into enemy-contested terrain. The astute reader will follow the sequence of events preceding the launching of the patrol to a point where he will say, "I'm not a Monday-morning quarterback, but I can tell this patrol is heading for disaster."

In kindness to the author one might say, "He did not start the war in Vietnam and neither did he order its rules of engagement." Some of those rules were downright ridiculous, for example, "When receiving hostile fire from out of a village, first get the village chief's permission before returning the fire." Another order that had a direct bearing on the patrol said, in effect, "Cambodia and Laos are neutral countries, so any incoming artillery your men received from those countries did not happen. Just bury your dead, call for medical evacuation for your wounded, and do not go after those guns."

The reader can decide if there is justification for lying, cheating, and disobeying orders to accomplish the mission.

The author is an old man now and will soon lie safely buried where pangs of guilt can no longer hurt him.

Chapter 1

Black Face

Above the jungle I heard the flop-flop sound of helicopter blades. A U.S. Army Low Altitude Observation Helicopter (LAOH usually pronounced Loach) hovered over us, and above it were two Cobra gunships. I knew instantly that they had seen us and recognized me as a European.

Quickly I flashed my stainless steel signal mirror at the LAOH. It circled twice, then dived down as if it were going to crash. Inches from the ground it stopped and flattened the grass as it hovered noisily. The LAOH canted slightly and swerved to within a few feet of us.

The Cobras also came closer with every gun barrel trained on the area surrounding us. Their mini-guns, rocket pods, and sharp-nosed antennas pointed directly at us. They looked like two giant machines of death.

"Just don't shoot," I whispered to myself.

The LAOH's observer leaned out and signaled for me to approach him. He smiled from ear to ear, for he had identified me as an American.

"Welcome home," the observer hollered. "You okay?"

"Yeah, we're okay, but need a taxi."

"We've got you covered, partner. Me and the Cobras." He pointed to the two Cobras that were close to us, but were searching the surrounding brush for possible enemies.

"We'll stay with you until some Huey shows up. You're in good hands now, Sergeant." He handed me three candy bars and a pack of cigarettes.

"Need water?" he asked.

"We're okay, thanks," I answered. Ding and Mo tore away at the cigarette pack and as usual ate a cigarette, paper and all.

"We spotted a VC unit not far from here," the observer mentioned as a matter of small importance. "Did you run into them?"

"No, we came out of the mountains."

"Just the three of you?" he asked incredulously.

"No....about 250 I had at one time. We're all that are left.

"Wow!" said the pilot. "You're not that patrol that went into Laos after the guns, are you?" As I nodded, he pushed his microphone away from his lips the better to speak to me.

"Wow," he said again. "We have been on the lookout for you, but expected a large body of men." He leaned even further out of the chopper so that he could hear every word that I said. "Another force of ours was trapped by a NVA regiment near the village of Attapue. Do you know about them?"

"That was us, too," I told him. I saw the pilot and the observer both transmitting the information over their radios.

"Gee, Sergeant, that was some battle. We heard it over the air. The Navy, Air Force, and we all begged to go in after you and your men, but could not get the okay until almost at the end. Man — you are a VIP as far as we're concerned."

He stuck his hand out for me to take. I could tell by his handshake that he meant what he said.

"Honored to shake your hand, Sergeant, and the Cobra pilots also want us to tell you that should they get a chance they'll buy the drinks."

I looked up at the Cobras. By that time they had come so close to us that I could see the pilots' rank insignias. They waved a salute to me and made the okay sign with their fingers.

"You've upset some people in high headquarters, though," the observer added with a warm smile. "But you've also made some powerful friends in the same high headquarters. Those NVA guns had long been a sore to us. Just about every pilot has at one time or another begged for a chance to go after them."

Under normal circumstances I would have been elated at being in the safe folds of our professionals, men who cared, men who believed in our

United States. They fought for freedom without weighing the odds first or thinking about a safe haven in Canada or Sweden, or finding ways to dodge the draft while organizing demonstrations against our country.

"There is your taxi. You'll have a hot meal within the hour!"

With that goodbye, the Loach backed away to let the Huey sit down next to us. We climbed aboard. The Cobras swerved up a little and again lined their guns on the surrounding fields. I knew that they would follow every move we made and insure our safety.

While I looked at the Cobras, a sign I had seen flashed through my mind: "Try us again, you Commie bastards."

Bitter reflections hit me and my mind reeled away from reality. How far away and how many lives ago? The faces of Tom, Mock, the kind-hearted Doc, and a parade of hundreds of toothless smiles passed through my mind. I let the wind blow the teardrops from my eyes.

Our period of hell had started three bitter weeks earlier with the orders,"Fire for effect!" Immediately a deafening blast split the night as four U.S. Army eight-inch, self-propelled artillery pieces rocked backward in their tracks and shook the earth around them. Each gun recoiled in a cloud of smoke as it hurled a 240-pound high-explosive shell into the night sky. The shells looked like four balls of fire grouped together, before they swirled out of sight and arched toward a target 20 miles away near the Laotian border. Sixteen more shells were blasted into the black sky before the first battery volley exploded on the mountain named Black Face. The triple-canopy jungle growth, which for centuries had silently hidden the mountain's face, disappeared in the holocaust.

The mountain changed shape. Its round top was flattened completely, hollowed out, blown away, only to receive the same terrible pounding over again. The shelling did not stop. Volley after volley compounded a dreadful error brought about by that day's myopic enemy intelligence estimate.

To the young Americans who fed the guns that night, it was just one more fire mission that robbed them of sleep, as night after night they manipulated the levers to blast an unseen enemy many miles away.

Circling high above the target and well out of antiaircraft fire range was the light aircraft of the artillery forward observer. The young lieutenant directing firing from the air could not see the large cloth red cross which the North Vietnamese soldiers had hastily spread open over the ground by way of signaling for a cease fire on humanitarian grounds. A few secondary explosions that were observed from the air caused the order for delayed-action fuses to be set on the shells. The airborne forward observer became excited when he saw those explosions. He readjusted his mike and spoke to the fire direction center.

"Looks as if we hit the jackpot. Enemy supplies and ammunition dug in deep. Let's dig them out."

The change of fuse timing further complemented the carnage already inflicted on Black Face. The shells that struck the mountain caused small puffs of dirt above ground. Then a dull rumble could be heard from deep within the damp earth as the mountain shuddered and trembled like an active volcano.

Delayed-action-fused shells penetrated deep into the ground before exploding to destroy enemy bunkers. Shrapnel, fire, and concussion wreaked havoc with the enemy's hidden supplies and transformed his underground haven into a safe forever.

"God damn, Captain, who the hell called for artillery on Black Face?" Bitterly I took off my green beret and threw it defiantly at a pile of sandbags.

My team chief, Captain Blound, shook his head.

"Beats me, Sergeant. It's a good thing that neither you or I did, for we're in enough trouble with Group as it is."

The knowledge we of the Special Forces A-Camp had about the target caused us to question the unnecessary vengeful shelling that lasted till dawn. First light showed the fury that had been turned loose on that mountain. The red cross panel could be detected among piles of blood smeared bandages. Aerial photographs taken of the impact area and the supporting documents quickly received a "Secret" stamp.

A few days prior to that fire mission, Captain Blound had made an attempt to express what knowledge he had pertaining to the enemy on Black Face, but was cut short by our colonel."What do you know about enemy activity inside that mountain? You have not run a patrol into the area for months."

After the fire mission, we wished that we had enough rank to say, "See, we told you so."

Fifteen torturous jungle miles southward from that mountain, so soon to become famous, lay the U.S. Army Special Forces (Airborne) A-Camp 106. A radius of 17 miles surrounding the camp was designated our Area of Operations (AO).

Near the camp, on the side of a slope, leaned the scattered longhouses and stilted huts of a hamlet we had named Ba Cat. The primitive structures which housed the people served only their most basic needs. The hamlet had been hastily built for the once nomadic mountain Rhe Tribe.

They were part of an incredibly small and primitive people whom the French called Montagnards. Our U.S. Army Special Forces (Airborne) (SF), also known as Green Berets, called them "Yards".

Special Forces operating in South Vietnam were organized into many specialized eleven-man A-Teams, a few B-Teams that were tactical commands, one C-Team that was responsible for logistical support, and a Group Headquarters with over-all control of SF missions.

Who really controlled SF in Vietnam was for a long time a $64 question, and a question many refrained from asking.

It was often whispered, "They're the military arm of the CIA," and another time a high-ranking officer cursed, "We have built an army within our Army, and they think that they can do as they damn well please."

Captain David M. Blound, the SF A-Team leader, and I, Master Sergeant Tony Blondell, the team sergeant, were ordered to report to the Group Commander at Nha Trang. Problems had developed between us and our counterparts, the eleven South Vietnamese Special Forces men.

We stepped out of the helicopter onto the concrete pad while the chopper's blades slowed and finally stopped. A hum of vehicular traffic reached our ears as we came to the road which ran close to the airstrip.

"Wow, sergeant. What a smell! To me it smells like garbage, unwashed bodies, and open sewers. You'd think that the wind from the South China Sea would carry it away".

"You're spoiled, Captain. Too long away from the real world. Nha Trang is like any French town serving a farm community. Not too interested in organization. They smell better after a good rain, though."

Most of the houses were plain, square, whitewashed buildings that received additions as the owners prospered. Each time a room was added to an original structure, no one cared if the new addition went next to or above the initial structure. If it happened to encroach on a neighbor's property it was inconsequential, for the neighbor also added rooms in a haphazard manner as the years went by.

It was not uncommon to see that two houses had attached themselves at the second or third floor. As to the reason for the slaphappy attitude of French construction methods, one remembers their ephemeral status in Vietnam that was initiated by the Dien Bien Phu debacle. Many of the buildings were leased by the United States, and it became a constant source of amusement to find yourself lost inside your own home. An invited guest might leave your living room to go to what served as a toilet, never to be seen again. When the guest tried to find his way back to the living room, he might become a guest in another house or find himself out in the street without knowledge of how to get back to you.

The same carefree effort was extended toward utilities. Dirty streets and open drainage ditches separated some houses. The drainage ditches conveniently carried away whatever came out of the houses, but only when it rained.

When you looked up into the usually clear blue sky, it seemed that tons of cooked spaghetti had rained down onto the poles and the houses. Each person that wanted electrical power added his own wires, connected the wires, and hoped for the best. When it rained, sparks would fly from pole to pole. They sometimes made the ground tingle.

Close by, in stark contrast to the city, was the organized power of the U.S. Army on the move along the north-south highway, a highway that stretched for many miles along the flat coastal strip of South Vietnam. Some of the world's most beautiful, soft, white sandy beaches paralleled the road.

A warm feeling came over me as we began to walk among young American soldiers. They were truly dedicated professionals, serving the call of our nation with vigor and pride. I felt a closeness to all of them that. As for myself, I had to believe in something. I certainly believed in my United States.

"We're not alone in this mess, Captain," I muttered.

"What's that?" asked my captain.

"Nothing really, Sir, just thinking out aloud. I'm flabbergasted by all this massive movement of our regular Army."

"Yeah, one hell of a lot of power here. You think maybe you and I got ourselves locked into the wrong war out there in our mountains?"

"First chance, I'm gonna ask just to make sure that we two are not in worse trouble than we are supposed to be in," I answered somewhat bitterly.

"I don't expect Group to hang us, but I have a strong feeling they're real pissed off at us. Maybe if we play it down a little, kind of keep a low profile, we'll only get the firing squad. More dignified that way."

The captain did not sound happy with what we could expect at Group.

"I am sorry for the trouble I caused you because of that damn radio message," I said.

I honestly felt sorry for a mistake I had made back at our camp. I had foolishly sent a radio message directly to our group commander asking him to remove a South Vietnamese Army officer before I killed him.

"Don't worry, Sergeant. I'll...you and I, we'll weather this one like we've weathered many others in the past."

Some U.S. Marines were going by on a truck. "Captain, maybe Group will use Marines for the firing squad. Those bastards are all too busy with news and film releases to have learned to shoot straight."

The captain smiled and said, "That's a thought."

A shiny jeep with "5th Special Forces (Airborne)" written on its bumpers slowly pulled up to the curb. "Taxi for Group, Sir," the young SF sergeant said, while giving the captain a smart salute and me a friendly nod. Watching the captain return the salute, I couldn't resist a joking remark.

"You're doing okay, Captain. You still remember how to return a salute."

"Yeah, feels good to know that we have soldiers in our Army who salute officers. Soon as we get back to camp I want you to teach our men how, if you know. Maybe you can find out how, while we're getting ourselves chewed out here at Group."

He pretended to be confident but we were both apprehensive about what to expect when we got before the group commander.

A column of tanks, with a few armored personnel carriers among them, clattered loudly in clouds of dust over the chewed-up dirt road. They seemed to be in one hell of a hurry to get at something to shoot at. We had to wait for the last tank to get by before our driver could gingerly move forward without running over pedestrians and the thousands of mopeds.

"How about this jeep? Pretty, isn't it?" I said, thinking about stealing it.

The captain smiled. Then he looked over his shoulder and shook his finger at me, "Not this one, you don't."

We were in need of a replacement jeep. The quickest and surest way to get one was to steal it, and then sweet-talk a helicopter pilot into airlifting it to the camp. The latter was usually effectively expedited with a bottle of scotch.

Zigzagging slowly with controlled precision, the driver avoided traffic and obstacles on the way to Group Headquarters.

"A little different jeep ride from what we're used to," the captain said, good-humoredly.

"Yes, Sir," We were thinking about the way our men treated our dilapidated ex-U.S. Marine jeep.

At 5th SF Group Headquarters we were taken to the staff briefing room, where a number of officers were expecting us. Among those present were our group commander and our immediate B-Team commander, Lieutenant Colonel Becket.

Colonel Becket was small of stature. This was especially noticeable since most Special Forces men were physically well-developed and tended to be large men. His red hair and fair complexion indicated that he would be susceptible to sunshine and outdoor living.

The colonel must have suffered more than his share of bullying from stronger boys during his school days, and therefore found it necessary to be always on the defensive. I wouldn't have cared how he chose to live except that I was the one who met with his displeasure most of the time. Perhaps I reminded him of some bully of bygone years.

Colonel Becket was also known to those under him as "Colonel Booby Trap", a nickname he certainly earned. He had a habit of disregarding that sound military axiom: "You can delegate authority but you cannot delegate responsibility." Colonel Booby Trap firmly believed in blaming someone else for any snafu regardless of the consequences to the innocent. Most of the men under him considered it safer to defuse a booby-trapped mine than to be singled out by him for personal attention.

"Captain Blound?" inquired a lieutenant in a formal manner.

"Yes, I'm Captain Blound," answered my captain.

"The colonel will see you now, Sir," said the lieutenant and held open the briefing room door.

I was left standing in the hallway that separated the many offices making up a SF Group Headquarters. Signs on the doors along the polished hallway identified the function of each.

I saw many eight-by-eleven glossy photographs of SF men killed in action. The pictures were neatly displayed, row upon row, on the buff-colored walls of the hallway. Images of my departed friends stared at me from their graves.

The photos showed proud, smiling, healthy young men and boys — "America's Best" — who ended their precious lives thousands of miles from their loved ones. I just shook my head, and to the nearest one, a 20-year-old whom I had known well, I whispered softly, "You'll soon have to make room for my picture along this wall. And Babe, wait for me up there." The term "Babe" was often used among SF soldiers. It emphasized the camaraderie among men who were rigorously trained and motivated for the sole purpose of defending the freedom and interests of the United States of America. "Liberate the Oppressed" was our motto.

As I continued to glance along the photo-studded walls, my eyes rested on the picture of a black SF sergeant. He was killed the very first week that he reported to my A-Camp. His brother, whom I had known for many years was also in SF. Slowly, I walked over to the picture.

"Jim Morsby, I hope you're in the right place, Babe. Your brother, Tom, and I often speak about you. He is a good one, that brother of yours. Right kind of guy to have around when things get tough.

"He named his second oldest boy after you. I was there when the boy was born. Also Babe, you'd be proud of Tom if you could hear him tap out Morse code. The fastest radioman in SF."

My mind flashed to the Tom Morsby I had known when I was first sergeant of a rifle company in Fort Benning, Georgia, shortly after the Korean war. Tom was a corporal in my company. I smiled when I remembered the morning when I called the powerfully-built corporal into my orderly room for disciplinary action.

Tom had knocked on the orderly room door and entered.

"You sent for me, Sergeant?" he asked.

He knew why he was sent for but acted as if he had just come from confession in church.

"Yeah, I sent for you," I had said sternly. "You know why they send us newly-commissioned second lieutenants?"

Tom merely shook his head as if he did not know a thing about lieutenants or anything else. He was good at acting dumber than he really was. And that was saying a lot.

"I'll tell you, since you seem as dumb as you look. They send them to us so we can teach them how to lead dummies like you into combat. You pull another one of your smartass stunts on a second lieutenant and I'll take one stripe off you and you'll be cleaning grease traps for a month. Now get out of here while you still have your two corporal's stripes."

When the door closed behind him, the company commander asked, "What gives with Morsby this time? What did he do?"

"It's kind of funny, Sir. Lieutenant Crocker told me to give Morsby a three-day pass. I didn't ask why, but just gave him the pass. Later I heard that he had told the lieutenant that his wife was going to have a baby. So far so good, but when he was asked by the lieutenant on his return if it was a boy or girl, he answered that he didn't know, since it took nine months."

The company commander laughed.

"Good lesson for the lieutenant. And by the way, Sergeant, you may see Morsby again. He has volunteered for that special unit the Army is activating in Fort Bragg. The one you'll also be transferred to soon. I think they will be called Special Forces. All of you will be airborne and ranger-trained."

"Then, Captain, we'd better make him a sergeant. He can use the extra money with that fast-growing family of his. I met his wife, Maggie, when I gave him a ride home one day. She'll keep him straight."

I never regretted having promoted Tom to sergeant before he started Special Forces training.

For about 30 minutes I reminisced as I slowly walked from picture to picture on the two walls of the polished hallway. "What is the price of freedom?" I softly asked myself.

While I was waiting in the hallway, I took it for granted that my captain was being reprimanded, and that my reprimand would follow. I was wrong.

The problem that my captain and I thought we had was of little concern to the command. It did, however, border on a real problem the command faced in the form of a mission it was given by Eighth Army Headquarters. That mission read in part, "Launch a diversionary attack on the enemy position located in GS 1015." Within this grid square was the mountain named Black Face. The Montagnard unit at Ba Cat was chosen for the mission.

The officers in the briefing room merely wanted to find out to what extent the problem that we had had at our camp would affect the mission.

At the time, unbeknown to us, there was an operation on the way that included the 23rd South Vietnamese Infantry Division. This division had launched or was in the process of launching an attack deep into Laos against North Vietnamese installations, and Ba Cat's Yards were to cause a diversionary headache for the enemy at the same time.

That particular operation of the Army of the Republic of Vietnam (ARVN) 23rd Infantry was kept under security. The U.S. Army did not like the operation, thinking that it might turn into a disgraceful catastrophe. It did.

The ARVN 23rd was kicked out of Laos in disarray, soundly defeated, leaving weapons, ammunition, and just about everything else scattered around as a present for the enemy. The soldiers fled for their lives back into South Vietnam.

"Sergeant Blondell," called the lieutenant. "Report to the colonel at the head of the table," he ordered while holding the briefing room door open.

At the head of the table I reported to Group Commander, Colonel Richard Paegel.

"Sir, Master Sergeant Blondell reporting to the Colonel as directed, Sir."

The exemplary military manner in which I reported to the colonel gave the true ring of a tough infantry sergeant.

"Relax, Sergeant, and pour yourself a cup," said the colonel with a friendly smile. He pointed to a coffeepot on the table. "Sergeant, it's nice to see you again. Last time was in Fort Bragg. How have you been doing?" The room was uncomfortably quiet for me. I could feel all the officers' eyes on me.

"Fine, Sir, until now." I faked a smile.

My nervousness was not lost on the colonel. Like the great leader of men that he was, he did something to dispel it.

"You and your captain have been doing an excellent job out there in your A-Camp, and I commend you two for it."

"Thank you, Sir." I looked at my captain. He seemed relaxed, so I thought that perhaps we were going to ride it out after all.

The windows of the briefing room rattled ever so softly. A B-52 strike was taking place more than 30 miles away. If it had been closer it would have shaken loose the overhead tiles. At that particular time I would have welcomed those tiles scattering over the shiny table.

A gesture from the group commander to the chief of staff, and the chief of staff took over. "Sergeant, as to the matter of the South Vietnamese Army Captain Van Trang, nothing indicates that either you or Captain Blound acted improperly."

He shuffled some papers in front of him and acted as if he did not like to say the following, "Perhaps a little more diligence on your part... but then we were not there to fully grasp the situation as it developed."

Silence ensued for a few awkward moments before the chief of staff continued, "The damage seems not complete, and I understand that the Montagnards at Ba Cat remain an effective fighting force. I believe we can still turn the camp over to the Army of the Republic of Vietnam as scheduled."

All eyes focused on me. My palms began sweating. "Here it comes," I thought.

Colonel Paegel said, "Captain Blound will not be going back with you to the camp. You will return alone, with Colonel Becket following a day later. Some matters will first have to be settled with the ARVN B-Team commander in reference to Captain Van Trang."

The colonel picked up a message form from among the papers in front of him.

"Finally, we can get this over with," I thought.

"Did you send this message, Sergeant?" He did not seem as perturbed as I had expected him to be.

"Yes, Sir,"

"Explain it to me."

Before I could answer, Captain Blound spoke up. "Sir, excuse me for interrupting, but I feel strongly about being totally responsible for all and any messages that are sent out of our A-Camp."

"Yes, of course, and that is how it should be; however, I want to hear what the sergeant has to say about it. The wording of the decoded message is rather strong, especially the part I quote, 'Get Van Trang out of here before someone kills him,' unquote."

Colonel Booby Trap leaned toward me, "Well, Sergeant?" he challenged with hostility showing in his face. At the best of times, he had difficulty not showing his dislike for me. On this occasion, he had court-martial charges on his mind.

"I just felt at that time that someone might do Van Trang in for insulting our captain."

I was thinking fast. Someone had changed the wording of the message to save me real trouble. I was sure that Booby Trap knew that the message had read, "before I kill him," and had been changed to, "before someone kills him." Somewhere along the route, a friend of mine had realized what damage the message would do.

"Were you that someone?" asked Booby Trap. "It sounds like your personal threat since you sent the message." The group commander interrupted, "No, I do not see it that way. The sergeant would not threaten to kill an officer or for that matter, anyone." He smiled and continued, "The only killing he would do is the enemy, and then he would not speak about it, but simply do it, as he has done quite a few times."

It was clear to those at the table that the matter was to be dropped. Colonel Paegel looked me over, wanting to see what impression his next words would have on me. I felt that the colonel took note of my physical appearance. He must have been impressed with the vibrant health and strength I evinced when I was needed.

"Sergeant, how do you feel about Captain Van Trang now?"

"Sir, I do not like the man. He is very difficult to work with, but I can handle it. For the four weeks that he has been with us, my captain has taken the brunt, and surely I would let my captain down if I could not carry on where he left off. I also understand, Sir, that our A-Team will have to stay at the camp."

"Yes, Sergeant. Well put. I am not going to have this matter die or have it swept under the rug, but these things take time, and in the interim our hard-earned gains in your area must not fall back into enemy hands, and of course, the final handing-over of the A-Camp to the ARVN must take place as per schedule."

"Yes, Sir, I understand." I felt good, knowing that I was still needed at the camp.

"I take it you are a fair manager of chaos, so just do your best. You are a well-trained and exceptionally strong infantry sergeant. Hang on to that camp for us, Sergeant."

With those words Colonel Paegel dispelled my fears. Finally free of apprehensions, I asked, "Sir, may I speak?"

"By all means, Sergeant, whatever is on your mind." The colonel settled himself comfortably back into his chair.

"Sir, what happened out there in our camp was very nasty. Captain Van Trang insulted my captain before the enlisted men, and if Captain Blound had not immediately ordered all of us into our bunker..." I shook my head. "Colonel, Sir, you would not have been happy with the way things would surely have turned out. Our captain saved the day for all of us."

I noted just the slightest blush on the captain's face. I knew him to be a modest person.

"Also, Sir, it was when we enlisted men were in our bunker, that I sent the coded message directly to you, Sir. Captain Blound would not have approved the wording of that message, neither would he have approved me skipping the chain of command by going directly to you, Sir, if he were in the bunker with us."

I looked at Booby Trap to see how he took that "skipping the chain of command" part. It stood out blatantly that I did not trust him to do right by us, and therefore went directly to our group commander. The look Booby Trap gave me carried the promise:

"You just wait...you...you...I'll make you pay for that!"

Colonel Paegel nodded his head in agreement with me. He looked at the captain.

"Your sergeant is not the only one thankful for the way you handled that tricky situation. I'll not forget it, Captain."

The colonel addressed me again, "Thank you, also, Sergeant, for keeping your cool. Understand that I shall follow up on this matter with higher authorities. Relax here at Group. Colonel Becket will see you later."

As I pushed my chair back to stand up, Colonel Paegel motioned me to sit down again. "Sergeant," he said smilingly. "You know about the menagerie we keep on the island of Quang Tri? Well, we need a large boa constrictor or a python. If you find one, as a favor to me, see what you can do to get it to us. We have just about everything else there to show our young troopers what they can expect out in the jungle. So far it has been a good orientation for the new arrivals, but we have no large snake."

Everyone except Booby Trap smiled.

"Yes, Sir. We do see them from time to time. I'll radio back next time we find one."

The colonel nodded, and I was dismissed.

I stood up, saluted the colonel, made a smart military about face, and walked out of the briefing room with the same number of stripes I went in with. Once outside I silently gave thanks to whomever changed the wording of that message. An American soldier does not threaten to kill an officer with impunity, whether it be one of his own or an allied officer.

I knew that I would not find out who had covered for me. It was the way we infantry soldiers did things for each other.

As I had anticipated, I received a seemingly well-rehearsed tongue-lashing from Booby Trap.

"Sergeant," He said to me while he seemed to fight for self-control. "You have tried my patience once again. Apparently, you chose to disregard the most basic behavior expected of a master sergeant. Do not, yes, do not for a minute believe that you are going to get away one more time with disobeying standard operating procedures."

I could tell that he strongly objected to the message by-passing him and winding up in Group Headquarters before he could get his own story straight, so as to blame me and my captain for everything that took place.He suspected that there was a wording change in the message that had cheated him out of being able to have court-martial charges filed against me.

Colonel Booby Trap's final orders to me were for me to return to the camp the next day, and he told me that he would see me in a day or two with orders for a combat patrol.

"The patrol order will call for considerable strength, so see to your ammunition supply. And again, Sergeant, I warn you, I don't want trouble in that camp again. You just keep a low profile for now. I have four other camps to worry about."

He added as if he just thought of something new, "That is, if you ever in your life learned how to keep a low profile."

There was no humor in any of his words. It was obvious to me that he would have relieved me if he had not been ordered to leave me as the A-Team sergeant by our group commander.

I spent an afternoon and an evening and then an entire night safely tucked within the folds of our 5th SF Headquarters plus a Mike Force and what seemed to be the entire U.S. Regular Army.

The Mike Force was a well-trained and motivated indigenous infantry unit with mobile capability. They were kept on alert to be immediately inserted wherever needed.

I felt like a baby in the loving arms of a tender, caring mother. But since things were seldom static for me, I soon started to feel like that unfortunate soul who saw a light at the end of his tunnel, only to find it was a locomotive barreling his way. Colonel Booby Trap always did that to me.

My thoughts were simple and uncomplicated, and under the circumstances seemed quite normal to me. All I had to do was relax with a few drinks, go to bed, get on a helicopter in the morning, go back to our A-Camp, and shoot that damn ARVN captain. End of problem.

I was unhappy with the knowledge that my young captain would not be going back with me. He was a good team chief, always pleasant, and ready to smooth things over when one of our men got into trouble, which was often. Green Berets do not tiptoe through life. I hoped another such captain would soon take his place, not relishing the thought of having to deal with Van Trang without the buffer a U.S. Army captain could provide.

We had over 500 combat-trained Yards under arms. We were also saddled with having to care for almost 1,000 non-combatant family members of our Yards. Caring for the families was the duty of the eleven ARVN SF A-Team, our counterpart, under the command of Captain Van Trang. But since we, the U.S. SF, controlled all logistics and indirect support fire, in reality we governed matters and were stuck with the families. We were blamed when things went wrong but received none of the glory and satisfaction that should go with the successful accomplishment of the mission. We were ready to turn the camp over to the ARVNs, with our "Mission Accomplished" stamp on some vague document. After that, the South Vietnamese government would pick up the cost of operating the camp. A conservative estimate of that cost was $5,000 per day. It was not a mystery as to why the ARVN gave us their secret weapon, Captain Van Trang, to scuttle the turnover of the camp.

If we failed in our mission, then God help us. It was difficult to control 500-plus trained and well-armed wild Yards in their element. They existed in high mountains that were partially hidden by almost impenetrable, triple-canopy jungle growth. Little did I dream that I was going to give Booby Trap the appropriate wording for his report on that matter. I also did not imagine that soon I was to get into so much trouble that many would want me dead.

That night I stayed alone in a hut which had been set aside for A-Team sergeants. Throughout the night, I could hear the distant violent thunder of artillery harassing fire. I could hear rumbles and earth-shaking sounds of a B-52 strike, 30 or 40 miles away.

Elimination flares popped overhead to spread their eerie lights across the outer defenses, where miles of barbed wire entanglements cast weird moving shadows as the flares drifted down. My mind went to the thought of murder. Murder it was going to be, no matter what justification I gave it. Neither the North Vietnamese nor the Vietcong presented so great a threat to our mission as did that Captain Van Trang.

After all, I rationalized that as the Army had taught me, the mission came first. Thirty years of combat training, leadership training, thousands of hours of weapons and tactics — all designed to accomplish the mission. I could not condemn myself or hold myself accountable for the strange twist of fate which demanded that the U.S. soldier lie, cheat, steal, and even murder to accomplish the mission.

Alone in my dark hut, I pondered over the many years that I had walked in harm's way: in World War II, the beaches of Normandy, in Korea, the frozen mountains north of the 38th parallel. In Vietnam.

No, I said to myself firmly. I was not going to let Vietnam give me an excuse to consider the adoption of some phony, service-connected syndrome designed to qualify me for a free ride through life.

I had mastered a simple technique for maintaining reasonable sanity. When I was afraid, which was often, I sought solace behind a comfortable, gray mental veil that took years of living in harm's way to perfect. That comfortable veil and my well-developed subconscious mind complemented each other. This behavior, I believed, suited a coward like me.

Through the years I had learned a few other things. I had learned not to dream the impossible dream, nor to expect a mountain to obey me. Like Mohammed, I would go to the mountain, if that mountain refused to come to me. Quietly I lay on my bunk staring up at the ceiling, while overhead the electric fan sounded like a distant helicopter. I couldn't sleep. I decided to send the room maid for one of those ladies of the night that were always on standby for the men who came to group headquarters from A-Camps.

"Mama-san!"

She was expecting my call, and shuffled to me.

"You be want big one, small one, fat one, all no be problem. Me be take good care, Sargy. Me be gets young one. Boo coo be young."

"Okay, I no be want big one. I be want little one be young." I did not have to say "little."

All the women that the Mama-san served up to us were small and the finest for miles around. That was the reason she retained the job of keeping us happy and also keeping the enemy happy by supplying it with information on SF soldiers to be used if ever we fell into their hands.

I didn't have long to wait. My door slowly opened and in slipped a lovely, tiny, young girl. First I received the usual shy giggle, the coy look, and the sideways shuffle, as if she were a virgin who had slipped away from a nearby convent and could not quite come to grips with what she knew was going to happen.

Often these girls were the slaves of some powerful crime syndicate operated under ARVN protection. They dared not tell us that they were forced into prostitution under threat of death.

I opened my arms. She did not hesitate to snuggle up to me. I had the feeling that she was seeking safety in my arms, and perhaps she was, but she sought it from the wrong man and at the wrong time.

I had been stuck for months at my A-Camp and she was one lovely, soft, yielding girl of at least 16. We had a strict law against the Mama-san bringing in girls that were younger than 16. No one delved into the significance of 16, nor were birth certificates ever produced.

Within the first few seconds you could usually tell if the girl was newly-launched into service by her performance. When you were through with her and told her to scat, if she begged you not to complain about her performance to the Mama-san, she had been forced into prostitution. A bad remark about her from a customer and she or her parents might be beaten up or simply disappear.

War has a tendency to bring out the worst in man. Add the word "civil" before "war," and God and the angels had better look the other way.

The girl was not a virgin. Virgins were only supplied on demand. For me to have delved into her problems would have been a useless exercise, and the prevalent attitude of SF toward women in general precluded getting emotionally involved with them.

During our early training in SF all of us became so brainwashed with our motto, "Liberate the Oppressed", that we had but a single aim in life. Nothing else mattered, not your wife, girlfriend, family members, or worldly possessions. We were welded to each other. We had to fight as a team.

A Green Beret had to be the best that the United States Army could put in the field. The demands placed on us were all-consuming. We lived for our mission and with each other to such an extent that some of us became like programmed men — programmed to win the hearts and minds of oppressed humans anywhere in the world, and to help them free themselves by the use of firearms.

We had to overcome many stumbling blocks. We did not burden ourselves with the niceties of conventional behavior.

Once, when we tried to be nice and followed orders to the letter, the Bay of Pigs fiasco developed. We learned that our concept was sound, but we had to be on guard against those who gave us the mission, and then told us how to accomplish that mission.

Chapter 2

The Yards

The next morning I was choppered back to our A-Camp. No commissioned officer accompanied me. I could hardly have expected the command to subject yet another officer to the abuse which Van Trang was sure to continue handing out.

As we circled over the camp, waiting for the all-clear signal for a landing, I marveled at the sight. The camp clashed with the mountainous jungle surrounding it, rejecting its presence in the only way it could: it was silent, sinister, and hostile, as if waiting to win the area back from us.

Our camp was next to the hamlet named Ba Cat. The camp and the hamlet were the only two man-made scars visible from the air in brazen contrast to the otherwise natural surroundings.

Along the western fringes of South Vietnam's central highlands, the mountains, lush with tropical vegetation, merged with the blue sky so that it was difficult to see where the mountain ridges ended and the heavens began. They slumbered, content and unspoiled, with beauty more lovely than any other place on earth. When the days drew to a close and the shadows progressed into darkness, that same beautiful area became a deadly, sinister habitat.

Eastward, the mountains gave way to gently rolling hills. The thick, multi-canopy flora of the mountains was replaced by strands of tall palm trees that towered above the blend of banana, guava, papaya, mango, bamboo and other tropical plants.

Still further eastward, where you could smell the salt air of the South China Sea, the terrain flattened out and signs of habitation became evident. Scattered villages and hamlets straddled clear mountain streams. Cultivated rice paddies and vegetable gardens hugged the many dusty roads and footpaths. The roads and paths seemed to shun the countless white-painted sepulchers between bomb and shell craters.

On Thanksgiving Day morning, I sat deep in meditation on the bank of one of the minor tributaries of the San River, a short distance from its headwaters, high up among the nearby mountains. I watched the playful ripples in the clear water where it danced across and around smoothly worn pebbles and specks of shining mica.

On military topographical maps, this gentle stream was depicted as a river where it approached the San River to the southwest; however, where it slipped peacefully through the folds of the high mountains, it was but a lovely, spring-fed stream, enhancing a flawless landscape. All around, nature had painted a silent masterpiece and framed it in serenity.

Often during those dangerous and troublesome days, I would wander off by myself to sit by the water's edge, there to feel unburdened and untainted. There, too, I could cloak my mind with nostalgia, to enjoy for a brief spell a closeness to permanence, in my otherwise wrecked and unreal world; a world I had helped to pollute with the unsavory smell of death.

When I looked at the densely vegetated mountains around me, I was aware that their beauty was superficial. In reality, they were putrid, steaming, insect-infested, hostile, and enemy-contested.

With each combat patrol I commanded to seek out the enemy in that wild entangled maze, I became more and more convinced that some vindictive demon and not God had created our U.S. Army Green Beret world. It was a world where physical and mental endurance were the only requisites. A bonus came if one had little brain and a lot of brawn.

Early in the United States' involvement with South Vietnam, I was one of the A-Team members of the 5th U.S. Army Special Forces (Airborne) who jumped into the Quang Tri province. We made contact with some Montagnards. With the help of interpreters we found among former French Foreign Legionnaires, we immediately set about winning their hearts and minds.

It was easy. A few pounds of table salt was usually all that was needed. For centuries, the mountain tribes had been under threat of death, by being denied access to the coastal regions where salt was available. Even the French, well into modern times, questioned the human status of a Montagnard. There was a time in history when they were considered wild game and were hunted as such.

The overall operational plan to which we were committed was sound. On the drawing board it looked good. It was the callous and blatant disregard for human values in favor of monetary gain by our counterparts (each of us had one member of the Army of the Republic of Vietnam as a counterpart) that sometimes turned our well-meant efforts into criminal negligence.

We were saddled with an additional problem while we trained and motivated our Montagnards so that they would fight for us. It was the deep-seated, tactless arrogance of the Vietnamese in their dealings with the Yards.

Green Berets do not admit to failure and conveniently give up. When things get too tough for others, it is just right for us. Consequently we stuck to the mission and swore that we would never give in.

Considering what was to happen to our Montagnard Rhe Tribe as the result of our involvement with them, it would have been better had we been less determined to accomplish our mission.

Initially all our efforts were directed towards training the Montagnards in the use of our weapons. We had to give that a priority for we were inside areas controlled by Viet Cong and North Vietnamese regulars. At the onset of the program we had the support of the individual South Vietnamese soldiers, for they too realized the dangerous situation we faced in our hastily built A-Camps.

It was only after we had to some extent pacified the area with our growing strength that the animosity between the Vietnamese and our Yards started to manifest itself. We became hampered by the very same people for whom we American soldiers bled and died to save from Communism. As for me, my years in Vietnam were mostly wrapped in a 17-mile radius piece of jungle-covered, mountainous real estate, at the center of which, grotesquely in contrast to the natural surroundings, stood our SF A-Camp.

Snugly squeezed between misty peaks, the camp occupied the only flat ground for miles around. The total level area, mostly made by our Army's Combat Engineers, was about the size of four football fields laid side by side. A lovely clear mountain stream formed a horseshoe pattern between the mountains and our camp.

When I looked towards the camp, mixed emotions slowly robbed me of the temporary tranquility the stream had afforded me. Much too vividly, it stirred memories of all the blood which had been spilled to hold onto that camp and surroundings.

Outlined against the maze of barbed wire entanglement which encircled the entire camp, were the bold black and white letters of a sign which read: "A-106, U.S. Army 5th Special Forces (Airborne)". Below this a cocky Green Beret had painted in bigger letters: "Try us again you Commie Bastards". The words were indicative of the camp's team spirit and morale.

Two times during the course of one year our camp had been overrun by the North Vietnamese Army (NVA). Each time we had completely destroyed the camp and whatever enemy had managed to penetrate into its interior. Each time the enemy paid dearly. Within the well-fortified camp dwelled approximately 550 combat-trained mercenaries (our Yards) under the control of a few Regular Army volunteers. This combat force was roughly broken down into three rifle companies and a headquarters section that consisted of an ever-changing number of men.

The headquarters section was made up of eleven U.S. soldiers (Green Berets) their eleven counterpart ARVN soldiers, a varying number of cooks, ammunition bearers, and medical personnel. Last but far from being the least in importance were my scouts. They were indispensable, and I relied on them heavily. It was because of them that I lived while better men than I died.

The scouts, usually 14 in number, were not subject to the same military discipline we subjected our combat command to. They wore no uniform but remained in their native attire that was only a skin loincloth. Their weapon was the homemade but deadly crossbow. This indigenous weapon was as much a part of a male Montagnard's life as was his daily need to eat.

The crossbow was made of hickory wood about one-half inch thick. At the center it was two inches wide, tapering to one-half inch wide at each end. The total length of the bow was two and a half feet, bent to about two feet. The two ends were then strung with catgut towards each other until the desired tension was reached.

From the center of the bow extended a flat piece of wood about one-half inch thick by two inches wide, a kind of stock. The catgut string fitted into a slot at the rear of the arrow. The arrow and string would be pulled back until caught into a notch in the stock.

The string always remained strung when our Yards are out on patrol. Their arrow tips were well soaked in human excrement, and with a flip of the Yard's thumb the arrow would be released to fly at a terrific speed for about twenty meters. Each arrow weighed less than a wooden pencil, but could penetrate quarter-inch plywood at close range.

A 150-foot-wide belt of barbed wire entanglement surrounded our camp. Within the barbed wire we had planted thousands of anti-personnel and anti-tank mines. All but the virulent Claymores were invisible to the eye. The Claymores we staked and cemented in place so that enemy sappers could not turn their lethal killing power around, and aim them at us.

Close to the Claymores and only partially buried in the ground were 55-gallon drums of homemade napalm. These consisted of a lethal concoction of sixty percent used engine oil and 15 percent liquid soap topped up with battery acid. Inside the drums were Thermit grenades wired for remote detonation. One exploding drum cleared the enemy for a radius of 40 feet. For many feet beyond that, it could make a religious believer out of many a hardheaded communist soldier. Those who were killed by the initial blast were the lucky ones.

Then there were those damn, overfed, noisy, geese. We started with 50, but it was not long before only 40 were roaming through the minefield. Their slight weight could not set off an anti-personnel mine, but we had to make eating a goose a hanging offence to keep the count at 40.

I often wanted to open up with a machine gun on the geese because of the terrible noise they made whenever they were disturbed or just wanted to antagonize us. They acted as if they had learned that they were the property of the U.S. Army, and thus were not worried about being cooked for food.

Our young American soldiers often took the geese's behavior personally, as a direct attack on their nerves. They would gladly have braved the minefield just to get at a goose's neck.

The geese were the most skittish at night. They would wake the entire camp for the slightest of reasons. Their status as property of the United States Government was the only thing that saved them from being shot by an insomniac. They made it impossible for enemy sappers to cut their way through our mine field without setting off our geese alarm, for each time the geese made a noise at night, we fired illumination flares over our outer defenses.

The Army's purchasing agent for the geese must have been strange. He apparently did not know the difference between ducks and geese, so we received some of each and all the geese were male geese. I found that out when I noticed the backs of the ducks. At first I thought that the ducks had lost their back feathers due to a defective diet, until I saw the hilarious antics of a big horny goose trying to rape a small duck.

On the inner edge of the barbed wire enclosure we had strung a wire mesh standoff fence, that would cause incoming enemy SA-7, Strelas, and other rockets to explode prematurely, thus minimizing their penetration power.

Away from the standoff fence we had many sandbag re-enforced defensive firing positions. These firing positions were connected by tunnels to well-stocked ammunition bunkers and also to the cool, damp bunkers where we lived in harmony with the rats.

We had also erected four 25-foot wooden towers from which we controlled our defenses. At night these towers stood out like three-legged giants, staring down on us in diabolic silence.

Within 500 yards from the main entrance of the camp lay the hamlet. It consisted of a primitive conglomerate of some 30 plywood or bamboo-laced longhouses and other huts built two feet off the ground on stilts and covered with corrugated iron or thatched grass roofing.

At first glance, it appeared as if some plan had been followed in the construction and layout of the hamlet, and then abandoned with malice, to leave but a few huts in line with each other. It was easy to see where we, the U.S. Army personnel, had lost interest in the hamlet's construction.

The thousand-odd humans residing in the hamlet were mostly family members of the Yards who fought for us. There were a few stragglers from other tribes, who were also unceremoniously herded together so that we could more effectively gauge the results of our expertise in winning hearts and minds. With most, it was a simple matter of giving them rice, salt, and meat. With others, the bayonet was more productive.

By retaining these people directly under our control, and confining them to a small piece of ground, we could effectively deny the Viet Cong (VC) and the NVA the use of our Area of Operations (AO) to move war material from China and North Vietnam through neutral Laos and Cambodia to the population centers of South Vietnam.

The very nature of guerrilla warfare, which was the only type of warfare the enemy could use against us, demanded that troops receive logistical support from the local people. We simply took those local people away. For every human we removed from enemy control, one Vietcong and/or North Vietnamese went hungry.

To our stateside expert planners, all was simple. To them all people acted the same. Perhaps the planners fed their data into a computer and then pushed buttons to have that computer spit out the right answer. One expert that we had to cope with was our then Secretary of Defense — a veritable computer brain with little common sense.

Each eleven-man A-team was assigned an AO with a radius of 17 miles. This particular distance was chosen to make sure that we operated always within the range of our U.S. Army artillery.

We recruited all the able-bodied Montagnard men, trained them, and with them we controlled our AO. Our first mission was to clear our AO of all human beings and move them to an area directly under our control. After that we killed or captured anyone moving within our AO.

Up to that stage of our operation all seemed logical. Unfortunately, our strategical planners in Washington did not understand the dense mountainous jungle that stretched for many miles in all directions from our camp. In that jungle were well-trained and well-motivated North Vietnamese soldiers, who could wait in safe areas outside South Vietnam to strike at any time they chose.

A weekly air re-supply was established, either by winged aircraft parachuting the supplies down, or by helicopters that sometimes landed in a clearing outside the camp.

Usually, two steers and six pigs, plus rice, potatoes, and whatever else our C-Team decided we needed, were scheduled as our weekly supply. Weapons and ammunition were supplied on call and received instant attention by our people. Many hundreds of pallets of ammunition were always sitting on airstrips throughout South Vietnam ready to be airlifted to A-Camps.

Next, we brought in consumer goods for the Yards to buy with the ten dollars worth of piasters per month that we paid them to fight with us. As an added incentive we also offered a reward of ten dollars worth of piasters for each kill, but we demanded proof, for they soon learned how to lie to us.

We did what we had to do and seldom received criticism until one sad, memorable morning when a U.S. Army quartermaster major screwed things up for us. This major had a good thing going for himself on the side.

A very beautiful Dutch woman, about 30 years of age, was a remarkably successful free-lance reporter. There might have been some question about her expertise as a reporter; however, there was no doubt about her ability to get guarded and classified information. She mostly bought her stories with her body.

One bright morning that major flew illegally with this woman into our A-Camp, and landed the helicopter right next to a small combat patrol that was returning from a night's raid. Six communist heads were swinging from the belts of the Yards. We knew that they were communists' heads because our Yards told us that they were.

That sexy Dutch woman must have creamed herself thinking she had pictures and a story. Then my captain and I busted her camera and damn near shot her and the major.

The major was forced to become a civilian. The woman had to be bought off with a flight over North Vietnam in a U.S. Air Force fighter-bomber in return for her promise not to write the story about the swinging communist heads. She must have received other favors, for I saw her a couple of times after that incident. She was still in the company of high-ranking U.S. officers, and peddling her inexhaustible wares for stories.

Once, when she caught sight of me in at Group Headquarters, she gave me a come-and-get-it look. She seemed to have forgiven me for having busted her expensive camera and treated her roughly that morning at our camp. She would have loved to get a few stories from me, and I was ready to give her some real bang-up lies, but a full colonel had a firm grip on her at the time.

Often I wandered among the people of the hamlet. The feelings of discontent and downright unhappiness, evinced by many of those unfortunate human creatures, were pitiful to see. There was no way for us to make them understand the necessity of being cooped up instead of being able to roam freely.

What they did learn early in their new way of life was that if they left the hamlet, even innocently in search of healing herbs, death and destruction would suddenly rain down on them. Our artillery and air support were always standing ready to engage any human movement we detected within our AO. Some sophisticated electronic heat detectors assisted us greatly in our mission.

I made some effort to make the Yards understand the why of it all. Perhaps not the way the Department of the Army thought of doing it, but I tried.

A few of them had gathered around me when I spoke about the communist threat they were facing. It started when one woman asked, "What be comnis?"

I thought for a while, then said slowly and in a way I hoped they could understand, "We, you, me, all people hamlet gots this many (I held up four fingers) way of life. One, you be gots two cow water buffalo. Chief, he be take one, he no be pay you. You be gets boo coo pissed off chief. Chief he be gets more boo coo pissed off you, he be kick you all over hamlet."

I could tell by the looks they exchanged with each other, and the few Montagnard cuss words they muttered that they did not much care for that chief, but they wanted me to continue.

"Other way. You be gots two cow water buffalo. You be take care buffalo but chief he be milk your buffalo, then be make you pay for milk. You no pay, chief he be gets so boo coo pissed off you, he be burn down your hootch."

That chief caused stronger cuss words to be heard from them, but again they soon became quiet. They were sure that there were worse chiefs still to come.

"Other way. You be gots two cow water buffalo, chief he be take you two buffalo. He no be pay you for buffalo. Chief he be milk buffalo then he be throw milk away. You be gets pissed off chief, you be tell chief him boo coo sad chief. Chief him be shoot you. That be comnis."

At this they all became more excited. Half of them could no longer remain seated. Other Yards, women, old men, and children, had by that time gathered around us, having been drawn to us by the commotion around the fire. Soon all became quiet so that they could hear more about hamlet chiefs.

"Other way" I continued, "you be gots two cow water buffalo. Chief be give you use his bull buffalo. You be sit back see what happen."

I waited for them to stop screaming with laughter and rolling in the dust.

"You like one?" I held up one finger. All laughingly shook their heads." You like two?" I held up two fingers. More laughter. "You like three?" Some laughed but also a few motioned the cutting of the chief's throat. I held up four fingers. "You like? It be Sargy hamlet chief."

More laughter followed and looks of proud understanding. I knew the word would finally get out as to why we shoot people roaming through the jungle. It all had to do with water buffalos, and stupid hamlet chiefs.

A subject I effectively learned to tiptoe away from was one that all the women of the hamlet had agreed on. They had agreed that it was time I took a young Montagnard girl for my wife. They had one picked out, and on a number of occasions had this girl sit around the fire with us as we settled hamlet problems that concerned the camp.

All Montagnards are small regardless of age, but looking at that little girl, I could not help but think that she was no more than ten years old. Pretty, yes, but a child and a Montagnard.

For one of us to have given in to such an arrangement was unthinkable, even if it met with the blessing of all the hamlet's women. For obvious reasons, one did not mess with their women, not if one wanted to live.

Some nights, either my captain or I would join the old women of the hamlet at their social fireplace, particularly when we needed to enlist their aid to solve a problem. In their matriarchal society, the older women of the tribe carried the burden of leadership. I had seen that in practice, even though many people claim that their society is a patriarchal society.

One by one, they would say a few words. Trivial things to my mind, but the kindness and caring they expressed to each other could teach our western world much.

Usually, while I waited for my time to express an opinion or broach the subject which brought me to their fire, I kept my eyes on the flapping flames around the burning logs, so as to give all of them an opportunity to marvel at the differences in our appearances. They were dark of skin, with dainty features and black eyes that seem to express kindness and a certain sadness. I often wondered at that sadness. Perhaps we were the cause.

Once, when it became my turn to speak, I carefully approached a ticklish subject. It concerned their swapping different colored pills that our medical corpsman had dispensed. Somehow it had developed within the hamlet that the value of pills was directly related to their color.

The pills that were routinely dispensed for headaches, plain white aspirins, had less value to the recipient than those dispensed for diarrhea, which were blue. The value of other colored pills also fluctuated with availability.

I turned my attention to the oldest woman in the fireside circle. "Ma ma, me not be boo coo happy hamlet people." I knew that I had their attention for extra betel nuts and coco leaves were passed around. It was a sure sign that they needed additional fortification before hearing the bad news.

"Sargy be speak, we be listen," said the old woman.

"Doc he be say he be boo coo pissed off hamlet people be swap pills. Two be white pills not be same-same one be blue pill. White be go head, blue be go stomach.

"Others too. No be swap one be red for three be brown. Doc him be say, him make all pill same-same color one moon after plywood, you no be stop the swapping."

The plywood. Yes, that darn plywood incident. I had once sent a message to Colonel Booby Trap requesting one sheet of half-inch plywood to be used as a map board when I briefed the patrol leaders.

A screw-up along the line caused Booby Trap to give the order for two pallets of one-eighth-inch sheets of plywood to be airlifted to our camp.

The helicopter had the plywood in a sling 40 feet below it when it came over our camp. Most unfortunately, just at the wrong moment, three enemy incoming rockets exploded where the chopper wanted to land.

The pilot jerked his helicopter up and away out of danger. The sling broke and released 80 thin sheets of plywood into its down-blast.

The 80 sheets became separated, scattering in all directions over the hamlet and the camp. Some sailed as far as five miles into the jungle. Our Yards screamed with laughter, rolling in the dirt in childish merriment, at the unexpected entertainment. Some had to duck for cover as dozens of sheets shot like projectiles into the ground inside the camp.

Since the Yards knew of no AD or BC eras, they readily adopted "before the plywood" as BP and "after the plywood" as AP, although not in the presence of our commanding officer, Lieutenant Colonel Becket, aka Booby Trap.

One time, a friend of mine, a Captain Brown, Group Chaplain, came to visit us at our A-Camp and was exposed to the results of the plywood incident. He thought it hilarious. Later in the presence of a number of officers with Booby Trap also listening, he related what he had learned pertaining to the plywood. I believe he said something like this:

"Some dummy sent Sergeant Blondell two pallets of plywood to take the place of the date Christ was born." Booby Trap blamed me as the person who put the chaplain up to carrying that story back to Group.

The day following my admonition to the hamlet's women in reference to the pills, my medical corpsman stormed into my bunker very much upset. "Tony, what did you tell the women about pills? There is a run on my clinic as if it were a bank. Dozens of women demanding that I make good the values of the pills before I change the pills' colors."

It took me a few minutes to calm Doc down. The young sergeant was an excellent medic but perhaps a little too conscientious in the performance of his duties out there in our strange world.

Doc and I were from two different worlds. His was one of love and kindness in a home where money, politics, and social power among family and friends could cast a protective blanket around him.

My family kicked me out at an early age because there was just not enough food to feed the eleven children that were already cluttering up our small apartment; more were on the way.

I became street-wise at the age of ten and could lick boys much older than I was, and I had to, so that I could control a gang in poorly lit back-streets. Like wild and dangerous animals, we had to seek out a means of survival during the stark depression years, or die of hunger like so many who were born with less aggressive genes.

The life of an immigrant family during those terrible years was harsh, especially in the big cities. Factories were shut down, and money was scarce. A good war could have given the economy a boost, but, alas, we did not have one then, so the people starved. In 1938, when I was 17, a judge gave me two options: join the Army or go to jail. There were so many minor charges against me at the time that the first option sounded good.

When the police van dropped me off inside a military compound, the uniformed soldiers looked me over from head to toe. Immediately I realized, that without help from somewhere, I could not lick that bunch, so I joined them instead.

Quickly, I fell into the strict Army life. It was the first time that I had had three wholesome meals prepared for me each day and a clean bed to sleep in at night. The rigors of infantry training I took in stride, having been blessed with excellent health, endurance, and more strength that the average man.

The dark clouds of war had started to spread. We were told that we would enter the war in Europe. The build-up of our armed forces had started. I made rank fast to sergeant first class and then to master sergeant and that was as far as I could go.

I had no formal education to speak of, but what I had learned fending for myself in the dark streets of Philadelphia, and in keeping a gang together, somehow paid off for me in the Army. I did not recognize this at first. Later, I often marveled at the willingness with which men chose to follow me and accept my leadership without question.

I became so involved with the Army that I took everything the Army did as being good. Even to believe that if the Army wanted me to get married they would have issued me a wife. This did not happen so I stayed happily married only to the Army.

I had promised to honor and obey the Army until death do us part, etc. That promise I wanted to keep, and this was the reason that I found myself ready to do in that ARVN Captain Van Trang. I was not going to sit back and let that damn ARVN captain rub the nose of my Army into the dirt.

From the day that I returned to the camp I was the ranking U.S. Army soldier in the camp. Consequently, that obnoxious ARVN captain, Van Trang, was my counterpart. He did not like that development.

He was agitated by my inferior rank, and because I, an enlisted man instead of a U.S. Army captain, controlled all requests for food, ammunition, and other logistical supplies for the camp and for the people of the hamlet. It became an additional spark flying around an already explosive situation.

This situation should have been previously evaluated by the command; however, it was only much later, with too many dead and mutilated bodies spread over the battlefield, that a shameful number of Monday morning quarterbacks crawled out from behind their paper-littered desks looking for someone to blame.

I was sitting on top of our bunker when my medic, Sergeant Terry Waldon, joined me. He sat beside me, stretched out his long legs, let his back rest against a sandbag, and gazed up into the blue sky. In his strong New England accent he said, more to himself than to me, "How much do you think we can get for the camp if we sell it to the VC and NVA?"

"With or without Van Trang?" I asked.

"He goes with it." Doc did not hesitate to say that.

"Then it goes for peanuts," I smiled at the pleasant thought of Van Trang in the hands of the VC or NVA. A picture flashed through my mind of Van Trang tied to a burning stake and our enemy throwing bamboo darts into his eyes.

We were silent for a moment. Troubling thoughts probably occupied his mind as they did mine. The world around us had become unnaturally quiet. The constant and usual distant rumble of artillery fire and air strikes had stopped momentarily. The sounds of war had become so much part of our lives, that their sudden absence seemed unnatural.

"You know we have trouble, eh?" I said more to myself than to Doc.

"Yeah, we have trouble. Like always we have trouble. We two, we've been together 18 months now, and can you remember a time that we did not have trouble?"

"This time it is different. The VC and the NVA we know how to deal with, but Van Trang?" I said bitterly. Then I came out, reluctantly, with what was really on my mind.

"I am going to do the bastard in."

Doc looked at me as if he did not fully understand what I had said.

"I did not hear that, Tony. Let us do what we can to keep this camp until Group turns it over to the ARVN. Surely even Booby Trap must know what is going on here."

The way Doc said that, it was obvious that he did not want to hear about my killing Van Trang. I did not blame him. His moral values were built on a firmer foundation than were mine, and therefore had suffered less deterioration through the years.

There was much I did not understand about Doc. He was a great asset to the A-Team, not only because of his medical expertise, but also because he became some kind of a role model to the younger team members.

It was during his senior year at Harvard College, well on the way toward making his parents' dream for him come true, that he had an automobile accident which caused the death of the girl he loved dearly. Even though the law exonerated him of all responsibilities, he believed that it was his father's money and political influence that achieved this.

He joined the Army, where he continued in his chosen field of medicine. This was especially possible within the SF where a medical corpsman is assigned to a surgeon for on-the-job training, sometimes for longer than a year. Doc's feeling of guilt was real. He lived with it every moment of his life. He did not lie to himself, but relived that fleeting last terrible moment prior to the accident. His mother just pined away when her only child joined the Army, She said, "This is the end of life." Then she closed her lips. She never spoke again, not even to her husband, until on her deathbed, when with her last breath, she asked, "Where is my son?"

It was too late then. Terry was far away at that time, fighting for his life behind the last remaining strands of barbed wire entanglement surrounding a SF A-Camp.

Terry, or Doc as he was called by all, was a good medic for my team. He knew his job well and performed all duties assigned to him in a pleasant and professional manner. But he caused me uneasiness at times.

None of the protective insensitivity innate to the doctors under whom he studied had rubbed off onto him. He was dedicated to saving all from suffering and took the loss of life too seriously for a front line medic.

Perhaps if he had walked over dead bodies the way I had in Korea, he might have learned not to love his fellow man as much. After all, the professional soldier in the infantry is a fool if he allows himself to become emotionally involved with anyone, especially with those in his unit.

It was this quirk in his character that often caused me to jump down his throat. Some things that I did, which he objected to on humanitarian grounds, made him censure me. I did not take his criticism kindly and, because of that, we were often at odds with each other.

On a number of occasions he told me that he was duty bound to report an action of mine to the command, unless I could justify what I did within reason.

"You do what you think necessary, and I'll do what I think necessary. So make your damn report, but you'd better first do as I order you to do."

He did report some of my actions after having told me about them; however, not once did the command as much as mention the things that Doc reported. Of course the command knew that everything Doc reported had to come first through me and the team leader, the captain, before our radio operator was authorized to transmit it.

A helicopter skimmed a few feet over the top of the nearest mountains surrounding our camp. Then it powered directly downward to a flat area adjacent to our camp and disappeared in a cloud of dust. Lieutenant Colonel Booby Trap had arrived.

The erratic performance of the helicopter was indicative of the pilots' viewpoint of the approach to our camp. They had long since became gun-shy when near our camp. Booby Trap's helicopter by that time sported at least five patched-up bullet holes.

Enemy snipers in the dense jungle foliage around our camp were not easy to find, but I could not get Booby Trap to believe that. He believed that it was I who had a contract out on him. A time came when I regretted not having one.

We seldom saluted our officers in the field. It was a carryover from other wars where a salute could pinpoint an important target to an enemy sniper. Because of that remote but intriguing possibility, I gave Booby Trap a smart salute in greeting.

"You are looking fine, Sergeant," he said in too friendly a manner.

"He must have some bad news for me," I thought.

The colonel pointed to four plain wooden coffins being unloaded from the helicopter,

"The one with the darkest wood..."

The coffin he identified for me was for the Stay Behind operation. When it became evident that, with the corruption of the South Vietnamese government and their armed forces, we were mired in a losing situation, we had launched an intelligence operation with the code name Stay Behind. It consisted of the clandestine positioning of war material that could later be used by dissidents. Just another nail we hoped would be driven into a communist coffin. Even if it was of dubious value, it was inexpensive and did offer certain possibilities.

The first action under that operation took place when a Yard died of wounds at our Yard hospital that was operated by our SF C-Team. Instead of the body being encased in the wooden coffin, we placed in the coffin an anodized aluminum tank which contained M-16 rifles, ammunition, anti-personnel and anti-tank mines, 60-millimeter mortars with their high explosive shells, and a few other items.

Swiss francs, American dollars and propaganda leaflets were also added. The entire cache was specifically intended to make it dangerous for some future communists to sleep safely at night. To insure the caches' longevity, items were vacuum-packed and cosmoline was used as a rust-reventive covering.

I was ordered to draw a sketch and also make a map overlay of the exact location where the cache was buried. Permanent reference points were used to insure that no problems later surfaced when a Stay Behind operation was activated. My finished document was sealed and handed to Booby Trap to be forwarded to the CIA.

"Sir," I addressed the colonel. "Those dummies at our C-Team are again making the coffins too heavy, and also they should sprinkle some body fluid in the coffin to make it stink like the others."

"Good point, Sergeant. I'll see to it. Now, how about you and Captain Van Trang?"

"Thus far okay, Sir. I did what you ordered me to do. Keep a low profile."

"That is good," he said sternly. "I do not want any more problems from this camp. Then he took out his little black book. "Take down these coordinates." As a standard procedure, he gave me sets of grid coordinates which were to be used in the event U.S. personnel had to be extricated in an emergency while they were out on patrol.

"I am going to give Captain Van Trang orders to run a combat patrol up Black Face." He looked me in the eyes expecting me to say something, but I knew I had better not. I was puzzled by the mission, and wondered why Black Face.

He was not going to let me get away with remaining silent.

"Something on your mind, Sergeant? Let's hear it."

"Van Trang is not going to lead a combat patrol that close to the Laotian border where we believe the 5th NVA Infantry Division has moved to, Sir. As soon as you leave, he'll have his brother in Saigon vacate your order, Sir."

I saw immediately that my words did not sit well with him. Once more he must have regretted having asked me a question to which he already knew the answer.

"Then you take the patrol out, and you will be on Black Face as I order. Do you understand, Sergeant? Come to think of it, with or without Van Trang, I order you to go on that patrol and make it at least of company strength. Is that clear to you, Sergeant?"

"Yes, Sir."

At least I had the last word to soothe the rebuff I had just then received. I was not finished, though. There were other items to clear up with him.

We had walked some distance from the helicopter. From the center of the camp I saw our ex-marine corps jeep, overflowing with men, careening crazily along the zigzag path through the barbed wire opening toward us.

"Sir, before you call Van Trang, there are still some things I need to speak with you about." He didn't like what I said, but could not very well refuse to listen to me.

"Go ahead, Sergeant, but make it short. I have to speak with Captain Van Trang."

"Sir, we are going to be fired on by heavy artillery from Laos as soon as we get close to Black Face. It will be like when we attacked Nui Coto."

Nui Coto was a mountain in the upper Mekong Valley where we had received 155mm artillery rounds that had been fired from Cambodia. We lost 200 of our Yards without being authorized to return the fire. Our Secretary of Defense refused to believe that there were North Vietnamese Regular Army Units operating against us from inside "neutral" Cambodia.

"So what do you want me to do about it? I did not start this war." I could see that he was losing patience with me, but I had to clear up a few other items with him. After all, he was my commanding officer. Without his orders to me I had earlier decided to be on that patrol. What Van Trang decided to do did not matter, since I was going to kill him.

"If they do, Sir, may I go after the guns?" I asked, even though I knew what his answer would be.

"That is something you will — hell, no. You do not go after the guns." His face had turned redder than it usually was. He did not care for that question. He knew that he could be held accountable for his answer.

"Anything else on your mind, Sergeant?" He hated to ask me that.

Then he thought that he'd better cover himself better.

"Sergeant, I'm going to forget that you asked me to go after the guns in Laos. I also order you to forget that you asked me. Do you understand me? We did not discuss the guns in Laos. Is that clear, Sergeant?"

"Yes, Sir," was all I could say to that. "Just one more item, Sir." I did not want to, but I had to bring up another thing.

"Go ahead, Sergeant, but be brief. I can't keep Captain Van Trang waiting any longer."

"Sir, he is still selling some rice and C-rations to the VC. And the weapons that disappeared from our camp, I found out that he sold them to some NVA unit in Cambodia. The Yard that deserted last month and came back to us was his courier."

I felt like biting my tongue for having made the mistake of talking to Booby Trap about that incident. For a moment, I had forgotten that he knew nothing about it.

There was a mystery involved as to what had happened to that Yard after we captured him. We had a secure stockade, located within the camp, large enough to incarcerate four people at a time. When we brought the deserter into the camp, Van Trang insisted that he should personally handle the matter. I saw nothing wrong with that, until the next day when the prisoner was found dead in the cell. He showed horrible scars and bruises where he had been beaten.

Later that same day, one of my camp's informers told me that he saw Van Trang and two of his sergeants beat the man to death with their pistol butts. What a fool I had been to have believed Van Trang when he told us that he was going to send the man to an ARVN headquarters for trial.

Both my captain and I had decided at the time that it was an ARVN affair, and also that to report the situation to Booby Trap would merely complicate matters unnecessarily. We felt this way especially after Van Trang had shown us a radio message that we understood he had received from his headquarters on the matter. The message in part read, "Subject is an internal affair of the Army of the Republic of Vietnam." Then it went on to say that they, the ARVN, would conduct the necessary investigations pertaining to the deserter and his accidental death.

Booby Trap looked at me for a long time without saying a thing. I did not flinch but it took some doing for me to keep looking him in the eyes. Reluctantly, he asked, "What deserter, and why was I not informed earlier, and what happened to him? These are all questions you'd better think about, Sergeant, when next you talk about enemy guns firing from out of Laos. You see, we'd both better forget some things. Understand, Sergeant?"

"Yes, Sir," I responded immediately and automatically since I certainly had had much practice using those two short words. I had also had much practice at being stubborn, so I persevered. "Sir, about the weapons and rations?"

"I told you before, Sergeant. I made a formal report to the ARVN CID about the matter. One CID captain told me that they were not about to come out here and arrest him. They do not care for incoming enemy rockets, nor do they care to run afoul of Van Trang because he is married to the Finance Minister's daughter. So forget it. Do you understand? Just carry out my orders."

It looked as if with every passing minute that Booby Trap was with me, he was getting more and more unhappy with me, so I wanted to help him a little.

"Sir, would you consider my request for a transfer? Maybe another master sergeant could work better..."

He interrupted me. I knew I had pushed him as far as I was going to.

"No! You stay here. If I wanted you out of here I would not wait for you to ask for a transfer." Then he motioned for Van Trang to join us. "You stay here while I give him the patrol warning order."

Then with apparent friendliness toward Van Trang, he shook his hand, saying, "Pardon me for keeping you waiting, Captain. I had to reprimand the sergeant. You know how it is."

"The bastard," I thought. The two of them seemed to enjoy a secret understanding of the difficulties of controlling enlisted men like me.

Lieutenant Colonel Becket continued in a mode of confidence with Van Trang.

"Your B-Team commander sends his compliments and apologies for not being able to come personally to give the impending patrol order."

I suspected that he, too, did not like incoming enemy rockets.

Colonel Becket then gave Van Trang the mission and the warning order for the patrol. I was surprised that Van Trang just stood there and listened without interrupting with objections. When the colonel had finished, Van Trang spoke up casually, making it a statement, not a request.

"You send helicopters for patrol."

Booby Trap shook his head. "I shall not authorize helicopter transportation for this mission. It is too close to the Laotian border."

I was surprised at Van Trang thinking about helicopters for the patrol. With possible enemy anti-aircraft artillery close to our objective, it could become a major invasion of Laos to suppress ground fires.

"Then I no go patrol. Job for U.S. sergeant."

Van Trang reached for a cigarette.

Booby Trap had his work cut out for him.

"Please excuse me, Sir. I see they are handling the coffins wrong." I did not consider it right that he should have to eat crow in front of an enlisted man. "I need to check on it. May I be dismissed?"

I wished that some expert enemy sniper might be looking down on us from the nearby hill, so I gave both of them a smart salute and walked off, with my ears straining, hoping to hear the sound of rifle shots.

A large number of women had gathered around the three coffins. They were confused as to which coffin belonged to whom. Damn, I muttered to myself, those dummies at Da Nang have again not marked the coffins. I took charge. "This one, he be Mo Duc Gia, this one, he be Doc Tu," I lied.

Then I approached the Stay Behind coffin. "This one he be that Bru we be gots last patrol." With that they were all happy. Smiles of approvals replaced the earlier discontentment. With what sounded like happy chattering among themselves, their small bare feet stirred little puffs of dust along that well-traveled path leading from the helicopter pad to their graveyard. I often pondered the unfairness of fate when I saw who had paid the price for whose freedom.

From time to time a soft chuckle came from the slowly moving funeral procession. To them a burial was not a morbid affair. It was as if they understood that the one in the coffin was finally receiving his reward of a reunion with ancestors.

The six Yards who carried the weapon cache were staggering with the overweight coffin. I had to stop the procession before they dropped the thing. If the casing were to break and spill the weapons out among the funeral procession, I would get a good chance to find out just how effective a liar I was. The test would have come when I explained how one dead member of the Bru tribe had been suddenly transformed into a bunch of weapons instead of enjoying himself with his ancestors.

Aloud I said, "Boo coo be sand this coffin, we be stop."

One pallbearer answered. "Yes be Sargy, boo coo be sand." He was glad for the rest. We always used a few inches of sand under the body to absorb the body fluids, lest the stuff dripped through the cracks in the coffin's wood and messed up the helicopter floor.

I then walked over to where Dock Tu's widow was basking in her moment of glory, she being the next of kin to one of the dead. I put my arm around her as a sympathetic gesture, and with as much reverence as I could muster, lied.

"Dock Tu him be say me one time before plywood that him be built hootch there." I pointed at a lovely spot for a hut.

"He be fight like hell comnis. He be good damn Yard. I be see hootch be built you."

This was yet another project for my SF troopers, but it was worth it. The Yards on the Stay Behind coffin had a breather.

While I was with the funeral procession, I was joined by Captain Mock. He was one of our Montagnard company commanders. He and I had been together a few years and had developed a close friendship. Like all the Yards he was small of statue, dark skinned, and somewhat daintily built, but he nevertheless gave off an image of strength and determination, qualities he certainly possessed.

"Sargy Tony," he said softly to me. I knew he wanted to tell me something in confidence. He and I walked a little distance away from the coffins.

"Yes, Captain, what's on your mind?" I asked.

"De ARVN SF, dey again be take one young Yard girl into dey bunker for to rape. Six Viets be fuck her, she be tell me," Mock said sadly. He felt helpless and unable to do anything about it. That type of thing had happened before.

I realized that if I approached Captain Van Trang and his men about it, I could very easily invite a shootout with them. Their arrogant manners would not let them even admit that they would touch a Yard woman and they would take it as an insult if I accused them of raping one.

"Mock, old buddy, I don't know how to handle it. Is the girl hurt much?"

"Yes be Sargy, she be much hurt. Now she no be gets husband. All fambly be say she be dirty now."

"Okay, Captain. Let me think about it. Somehow you and me will put a stop to it. We cannot let those bastards keep on raping your girls."

I felt as if my hands were tied behind my back. It was useless for me to seek help from our commander, Colonel Becket. That bastard thought only of his own welfare, and if I told him about the situation, he would probably blame me somehow.

After the burial I did not immediately return to the camp. I sauntered slowly down to the stream where I could gather my thoughts and also kill time until Booby Trap could finish his business in the camp. I knew that he would send a runner for me should my presence again be needed.

"Black Face Mountain," I thought. "Why that mountain?" My military mind had analyzed the situation and come up with a disturbing thought.

Could it be that we were to be the bait that would lure the enemy's 5th NVA Division out of Laos to where we could destroy it with our superior firepower? I quickly discarded that thought as nonsense, because I found it difficult to believe that the U.S. Army would deliberately plan the sacrifice of a company of Yards.

From NVA prisoners that we had interrogated we had learned that the 5th NVA Infantry was a unit of well-trained fanatics. Each soldier had a tattoo under the arm that read, "Born in the north — die in the south." They were radicals who slaughtered women and children with as much satisfaction as another soldier would get out of successfully defending a position against superior forces. I did not respect them as I could most enemy soldiers. To me they were bloodthirsty animals, and to be treated as such.

I saw the helicopter lift off and fly down towards the stream where I stood, and then, with all power given to the blades, it shot upward over the nearby mountain. Out of our lives went Booby Trap. I could not be sure but that I saw him smile and wave to me as they flew by. He could afford to smile at me.

When I approached the camp, I received a pleasant surprise. There in the bright sunlight stood a six-foot-one, powerfully built man, as black as the ace of spades, and an old-time buddy of mine. He was grinning from ear to ear.

"Tom, you bastard, good to see you, Babe." We hugged each other with great joy.

This was the Tom Morsby I had known at Fort Benning, when I had saved his corporal's stripes for him. When he joined me at Ba Cat, he had the rank of sergeant first class.

He and I had pulled duty together at a number of A-Camps and also for a memorable four-month period along the Vinh Tay Canal, a canal that separates Cambodia and South Vietnam between the Mekong River and the Gulf of Siam. There among the floating rice fields of the Mekong River Valley, during one very long and terrible night, I had saved Tom's life.

During the dry season, the water level in the Vinh Tay Canal dropped so low that our navy could no longer effectively control the areas along both sides of the canal. Visibility from navy boats would be blocked by the high banks, so it became an army problem to stop enemy movement from across the border of Cambodia into Vietnam.

Tom and I were ordered, with two platoons of Montagnards, to man a strategic stretch of the canal's bank during nighttimes. There we had learned just how long a night could really be. During those nights we dared not move nor make a sound. The enemy knew that we were somewhere around there, but had to pinpoint us before they would open fire on us, and then try to cross the canal.

There was a large North Vietnamese combat force dug in on top of a mountain called Nui Coto on the Vietnamese side of the canal. The enemy units located in Cambodia infiltrated across the canal regularly to stay in contact with their comrades on Nui Coto.

The enemy created the perfect environment for a soldier to drop his smoking habit. Tom and I became born-again non-smokers, and I recommend such a setting for anyone who wants to quit smoking, but finds it too difficult to do so. All we had to do was light a cigarette to immediately be entertained by fireworks.

Once the firing started it became a madhouse, with tracers flying in all directions, and neither they nor we dared to cease firing and let the other side pin you down. There were no places to go, no holes to creep into, nothing to hide behind, and if you were hit you rolled into the water and drowned.

One night during a firefight, Tom was hit by a large piece of shrapnel from an enemy artillery air burst. The piece of steel did not penetrate his flak jacket but knocked him out cold and tumbled him head first into the four-foot-deep rice water.

Luckily a few illumination flares exploded just then overhead, and I saw Tom's body break through the floating rice and disappear from sight. I jumped in after him and immediately lifted his head above water.

Within a few minutes the firing stopped, but I knew that things were not right. There were enemy soldiers all over the area that we had earlier controlled. My Yards had been overrun and those still alive were being bayoneted.

For the rest of the night I held Tom's head above the water. The piece of shrapnel had partly paralyzed the lower portion of his body and his legs could not support him. We had to remain still for fear of being discovered. Close to daylight I heard the Navy's riverboats return. Tom was badly shaken, but I knew he was going to live.

Our Yards did not much care for duty along the canal. In the mornings which followed each of our firefights, they usually saw the bodies of their comrades floating in the water on both sides of the bank, being eaten by fishes.

We used to scoop up the mangled pieces of bodies the best we could and stuff them into the black body-bags for proper burial, but it did little to console our Yards.

The Navy river patrol boats which transported us each late afternoon used to jam their bows into the muddy banks of the canal and wait there for daylight when they would take us back to Chau Doc. When a firefight developed between us and the enemy, which happened on an average of three times per week, those heavily armed boats could not help us. Each time they would kick their powerful engines over and, at maximum speed, clear away from the flying bullets.

It was a question as to who did the most damage to the Vietnamese's morale, we or the Navy's river boats as their wakes swamped the many houses along the banks of the canal during their frantic dash for safety. Our mission was to win hearts and minds, but the Navy lost hearts and minds faster with their river patrol boats than we could win them.

It was at Chau Doc, a lovely city, half of which floats or precariously balances itself on stilts, where I saw Tom last. One evening the two of us were having dinner in a popular restaurant frequented by a transportation unit stationed nearby. Tom had left me to go to the toilet when six black soldiers came into the restaurant. One of them just walked up to me and told me to get out because I was a honkey and they did not eat with honkeys.

That one I hit beside the head with a bottle and laid him out cold, but his buddies piled into me with fists flying. I managed to kick another one in the balls, but soon was getting the worst of it and would have found myself swimming in the sewer-like water over which the restaurant was built had Tom not showed up when he did.

Between us, we made believers of the four that were still on their feet. When it was over, I had to laugh when Tom emptied all their pockets of cash, kicked them one by one out of the restaurant, and he and I sat down to enjoy the evening with their money. That was until I wanted to order a fish dinner.

"Babe, you sure you want a fish dinner?" Tom had asked.

"Yeah, why not? They have some great fish in this restaurant. Big ones too. You order fish and you get more than a pound. Well spiced and fresh fish, too."

"Man, you better not go see where dey gets de fish. But you will when you go to de shithouse. It's over de water and dey net dem when a customer want fish. I sees ten big ones ever time I look down de hole."

I had steak than night and marveled at the many fish dinners the other customers ordered as we enjoyed our night.

It was also in Chau Doc that Tom almost got himself kicked out of the Army and narrowly missed having to spend the rest of his life in the federal prison at Leavenworth.

Tom was involved with a brothel that had a beautiful and cooperative staff. Our U.S. Navy personnel, of which there were enough along the river to keep Tom's business flourishing, had no complaints. One item did not sit too well with Tom, though. Being a respectably married man with four young boys to support, he wanted things to be run in a proper moral vein.

The women had children and often brought their young kids, some of them girls of under ten years of age, to their work place. To Tom it was disgraceful to have these children exposed to that kind of thing so early in their lives.

Each Wednesday he had his women examined by a local doctor to protect the future of his business. During those scheduled examinations an old woman was contracted to take care of the children. One such Wednesday an explosion rocked the brothel and killed the old woman and all the children.

Investigations conducted by the U.S. Army and the local police concluded that the VC had planted the bomb. Some suspicions were, however, cast in Tom's direction when the Army dug a little deeper into the matter and found that he had another building ready for business that same day, and also that Chau Doc's police were personal friends of Tom and obstructed our Army's investigations.

Tom was transferred and it became unlikely that he would ever be promoted or be left alone to open any kind of business while he was still in the Army. To me, he was a friend.

"Honkey, it's good to be here with you. It's been a long time, man. I heard you gots trouble, so I aks Booby Trap to come hep you." He took a deep breath, stretched his muscular frame and continued.

"De air is good, man, just what de doctor order for dis nigger. I's gonna love it back heah." Tom had not lost his habit of talking too much.

"Yeah, but you're in for a shock, Babe." I said. "And I don't think you asked Booby Trap for this camp. He joined the KKK since you were here last and you are the first nigger of his quota."

I looked him over again. "Man, you look more like Joe Louis each time I see you, only blacker."

"Yeah, you say dat before. Maybe my Mom she step out some, fo my dad he was a light nigger."

We both laughed. Tom turned to me with a frown on his face.

"What dis trouble you talk about, Babe? We always have trouble, VC, NVA so what? We shoot em, and no more trouble."

"This is ARVN Captain Trouble. I'll fill you in as we go along. For now I have a patrol warning order to tend to. By the way, you get ready, too. You and Doc will be going with me on this one."

Tom shrugged it off as if it were of no particular consequence.

"Say, Babe," Tom said while we were slowly walking along the zigzag path through the perimeter defense. "You still have dat college boy, Terry Waldon, as your medic?"

"Yeah, he is still the best on the market. He'll be glad to see you, even if the two of you get on each other's nerves. Like me, Tom, he knows that you are a great man to have around when things go wrong. And believe me, things are going to go wrong on this patrol."

Tom stopped me and held me at arms length. "Man, what give wit you? Dis is not like you. ARVN Captain, we buy him off. A few dollars and he eats out of our hands. De patrol — so what? You and me, we can handle it."

"Not this ARVN. This one isn't going to come back from the patrol. I'll see to it,"

I said, and we resumed our walk back to our bunker.

"Dat bad, eh? Okay, you say so. No problem. We do him in."

"Not you Tom, just me. I want the bastard to look me in the eyes when I blow him away."

My mind switched to the patrol. It was a simple mental process to formulate a patrol plan. I had kept myself abreast of intelligence matters pertaining to our AO. The terrain I knew, and the enemy situation came updated over our radio every four hours.

As to the friendly situation, I knew which artillery batteries were in range to support us and also what close air support I could call on. It was Booby Trap's responsibility to alert the units that might be called on to give us close-in fire support. The rest was taken care of by the extensive training and experience I had.

By the time Tom and I entered our SF bunker, where Van Trang was sitting comfortably on an ammo crate, I was ready to speak with him about the patrol. Initially it was necessary for the two of us to review what current intelligence we had on the enemy situation.

We had to decide on the strength of our patrol, to include what weapons we would be needing. After that I would go through the five-paragraph field order for a patrol. The latter was designed by the Army so that a field order would follow in logical and comprehensive steps.

First was the situation of the enemy and friendly forces, followed by the mission, that was stated in a few short, direct words. In our case it was: Occupy Black Face. The third paragraph spelled out the operation. It was the way we were going to do the job. It usually went into considerable detail. After that came the information on units alerted to support us, and lastly the command and signal. The latter pertained mostly to where the leaders were to be during the operation and what special signals were to be used over the air so as not to have the enemy interfere with things.

As I proceeded with the review of the tactical situation, I was surprised to find Van Trang attentive. I fully expected him to be his usual arrogant and obnoxious self, especially because of the refusal for transport helicopters.

While he listened, he even gave a few agreeable nods and when I finished, he said, much to my surprise, "Excellent, Sergeant. Now we can get Mock in here and give him the orders."

I knew that he was hiding something from me, but what it was I hesitated to speculate on at the time. Van Trang was indeed a strange individual, with little or no regard for the feelings of others.

Some of his arrogance was expressed by his chain-smoking habit. This in itself would indicate nothing if it was not that he was essentially a non-smoker. He used his smoking as a status symbol and a means of humiliating someone.

From the time that he took the cigarette out of his pocket until he took the first puff, the handling of the cigarette, the matches, and the pack itself were all ritual-like deliberate movements that seldom varied. During the ritual he would create a silence that discomforted whomever he was with.

Each action was accompanied by facial smirks. I supposed the smirks were intended to convey his superiority over all, and how gracefully he suffered himself to have dealings with them.

One incident was a glaring example of just what stupidity Van Trang was capable of, and which had almost made me pull a gun on him. While the camp was enjoying a welcome lull from enemy activity, with our Yards just lazing around, Van Trang called them all to listen to a story.

"I have finally discovered the origin of you Montagnards," he said, then reached inside his pocket for his pack of cigarettes, but did not take it out. He had an air of superiority plainly written on his face. That should have been a signal to me to stop him, but I did not, so he continued.

"Many, many years back, a king lived in these mountains. He had a very beautiful daughter. Oh, she was so beautiful that everyone loved her. She was very kind to all the people. She used to play with the children and help all the old people. Yes, everybody loved her.

"One day she got lost in the jungle. The poor, lovely little girl was lost all alone in the cold and dangerous jungle. Van Trang stopped. An agonizing silence started his first slow move of the cigarette along the chain of his ritual. Tears were beginning to show in some Yards' eyes.

He took the first puff on his cigarette and continued. "The king then promised his daughter in marriage and all of his mountain kingdom to whoever found his daughter. All the young men searched far and wide for her but still could not find that beautiful little girl."

He stopped again while more tears could be seen as the Yards suffered in silent suspense to hear the conclusion of the story, which they hoped would have a happy ending. This time Van Trang took three puffs before he continued.

"One day, a dog found the girl and brought her back to the hamlet, and the king, being a man of his word, gave his daughter in marriage to that dog. And you Montagnards are the offspring of that marriage."

No one laughed. An electrified silence spread like a promise of death among our Yards. The entire camp had become a volatile mixture which just one wrong move could have set off. I acted fast.

"Extra meat and time off for the company that gets the least gigs in weapon inspection ten minutes from now," I hollered out to my nearest interpreter. The interpreter in turn relayed my words, loudly and clearly, to the Yards.

My action served to dampen the glowing cinders a little but many stares of hatred were directed towards Van Trang. Slowly, and reluctantly, the Yards walked toward their bunkers to get ready for my inspection.

Van Trang and I were inside our U.S. SF bunker that was located near the center of our camp. I had finished with all the preliminaries that were necessary prior to briefing the four platoon leaders. It was something that our Montagnard Captain Mock was supposed to have done under the direct supervision of Van Trang.

"You seem to agree with all that I have laid out for the patrol, Captain," I said while hoping that he would put out the cigarette that had already polluted the bunker.

"Yes, I agree with your plan."

"Do you want me to give it to Captain Mock, or would you rather do it?"

"No, it is your plan. You give it."

Too pat I thought, the bastard is up to something.

Captain Mock, one of our three Montagnard company commanders, was waiting outside the bunker for us to call him. He had earlier received the warning order and had readied his company, plus one extra platoon from another company, to move out at my command.

We had promoted him from the rank and file for his outstanding performances in many shoot-outs with the enemy. To an amazing degree he possessed all the desired qualities to command a 200-man rifle company. He was ruthless to the point of excess when it came to enforcing discipline, but tireless in his efforts to ensure that his men received what was promised them, which was in itself a real problem while Van Trang was near.

Captain Mock's physical appearance was typical Rhe Tribe. He was five feet two inches tall, and darker of complexion than the average Vietnamese. Like most Yards, he had hands, feet and facial features which seemed almost childlike, including the upturned nose one often sees in children.

On the average, a Yard weighed around 100 pounds, but nothing in their makeup could be interpreted as weakness. They were tough mountain and jungle fighters, and possessed that one indispensable quality necessary in an effective infantry soldier: lack of imagination as to what could happen to them in a given danger.

Mock lacked imagination to a greater degree than most. It was, perhaps, what made him the most daring man in the command. He was utterly incapable of predicting harm to himself or to the men under him. Finally, his total loyalty to me was what I valued most in him.

Before I called for Captain Mock, I wanted to hear from the two U.S. SF men that were to go with me on the patrol: Tom and Doc.

"What do the two of you think? Let me get some feedback from you. You especially, Tom. I know that Booby Trap sent you to me for an important reason, so don't bullshit me about having asked for this camp. It is common knowledge that you are the best radio operator in SF. I received a message a while ago ordering me to take you with me. First damn time I was ever told who the hell to take with me on a patrol." Things were crowding me and I was getting short-tempered.

Tom said, "Man, tings is kind of strange, but why worry. We handle everyting as we always does. Shoot it." He smiled, and I was satisfied that I could expect nothing further from Tom.

Doc just shrugged his shoulders. "Nothing from me. I'm with you all the way as usual, Tony. Let's just get the patrol over with."

I turned to Van Trang. He said, "Me, I don't care, VC, NVA, all same me. Fifth NVA fire heavy guns, we get air strike."

"No way." I looked him over carefully to see how he took that.

"Okay, you say no way. All same me," he gave me a smirk which he perhaps intended to be a smile.

"Tom, will you please get Captain Mock in here."

Tom stuck his head into the ventilation duct and in a loud voice hollered, "Mock, you and de lieutenants, you birds get your asses down heah on de double."

"I could have done that. And don't talk to Captain Mock and his platoon leaders like that." I had to cool myself off. I was getting too uptight.

"Okay, Boss-man," Tom said amiably.

With Captain Mock and the four platoon leaders around us, I spread a U.S. Army 1:50,000 map out so that all could see it. I placed my pencil in the center of the brown contour line that gave the highest elevation of Black Face.

"This is our mission: occupy Black Face and await further orders."

I skipped fast through the rest of the five-paragraph field order and ended with the command and signal. The latter was mostly of concern to Van Trang, Mock, and me. It was necessary for the three of us to know where in the column we would be and which signals we would use for indirect fire control.

"Captain Mock, the extra rifle platoon that we have from C Company will stay directly under the control of Captain Van Trang. You are not to commit that platoon except through the captain. Is that okay with you, Captain?" I asked Van Trang.

"Oh, yes, Sergeant. You control the reserve platoon." He took out a cigarette and started his ritual, in full anticipation of my next question.

"What do you mean, I control the reserve platoon? You are in charge of this mission."

A maddening silence ensued while he continued with his cigarette ritual. The first puff of smoke he blew directly and fully into my face. I jumped up and drove Tom back against some ammo boxes that were stacked in a corner.

"No, no, Tom!" I held him momentarily. His eyes were burning with hatred. His dagger was out, but I held his hand and he slowly relaxed.

"Not now," I whispered to Tom. Then I turned to Van Trang, who was smiling with obvious contentment. He did not see the full significance of Tom's behavior. He knew, however, that we all saw him blow the smoke in my face intentionally. He was especially content that Mock saw it. He had served his ego effectively.

Quickly, I changed the electrified atmosphere in the bunker. "Captain Mock, please release your four platoon leaders so they can brief their squad leaders and get ready to move out as soon as darkness settles in. The time now: 1400 hours. We move at 1900 hours. And also, Captain, please get the scouts out ASAP."

Prior to launching an operation, it was wise to have the surrounding terrain combed for possible enemy reconnaissance elements. Failure to take such a precaution could place us at a distinct disadvantage. Weapon designation and strength were directly related to success or disaster.

Seven reconnaissance elements, our scouts, who worked in two-man teams, slipped out of our camp and disappeared into the mountainous undergrowth. They were totally naked but for the deer-skin loincloth which each wore. For weapons, they had their indigenous crossbows, with one of the tiny reed arrows strung and ready to fire.

Across their backs were tied a few more arrows. Each arrow was well soaked in human excrement. A wound sustained from one of those thin innocent looking reed arrows was fatal unless immediately tended to by a well-prepared medical person.

Each team also carried a PRC-6, which was a U.S. Army infantry squad radio for communications between squads and with the command. Their transmissions were monitored by all the platoon leaders, Captain Mock, and me. Tom, too, could receive their traffic, but he was usually too busy with his own transceivers, which were our umbilical cord to the power of the U.S. armed forces.

Chapter 3

Raining Livestock

I stood alone outside our bunker. A short distance below, I saw the jungle growth spread like a thick green carpet. The hot sun's rays danced around and over the clear waters of the nearby creek, and cast strange shimmering shadows against the creek's banks.

I looked up. There, outlined against the blue sky, the peak of Black Face stared down on me. During the day it was less than sinister, but when darkness set in, and the moon glowed aloof against a black sky, Black Face was hostile, formidable, and evil.

Many of our Yards were afraid of the mountain. They believed that a very large snake used to live halfway up the mountain until the VC killed it. Since then, the bad spirit of the snake had wondered around at night looking for revenge.

Alone and above ground, I paced back and forth as I often did when I wanted to think clearly. I calculated the composition of the patrol: four rifle platoons of 48 men each. Each platoon carried two M-60 machine guns, one 60mm mortar, two 3.5-inch rocket launchers, 42 M-16 rifles, and an unknown number of .45-caliber pistols.

Then we had our silent killers, the crossbows. Not only our scouts carried them, some Yards even slept with their crossbows. To them this was just as normal as sleeping with their wives or their machetes.

With the headquarters section, which included the 14 scouts, the ammo bearers, medics, and others, the total manpower of the patrol came to about 250. Each platoon leader had the prerogative of taking whomever they chose with them, as long as they did not disturb the integrity of the eleven-man rifle squads.

The rifle squads trained together, and we demanded that they should fight together. Because of that practice, I usually did not receive a true count. I expected the count to be plus or minus about ten.

When operating against the enemy with a rifle company, the company commander's main control effort was centered around his three rifle platoon leaders and his heavy weapons platoon leader, and for him to count his men would have been a wasted exercise.

I was ready for the patrol, and also for Van Trang. One of my camp's informers had reported to me that Van Trang had transmitted a message to the Palace Guard Headquarters in Saigon, informing them that the U.S. Army had shelled an enemy hospital and wanted to shift the blame onto the ARVN. This, he radioed, would happen if he obeyed the order to run a patrol to that destroyed hospital.

His request to have the order vacated received immediate approval, and a new order came to him from a higher headquarters that read, in part, "You are forthwith relieved of your command. Additional orders will follow."

I had the information transmitted to Booby Trap. His reply came back almost instantaneously, and read, "Carry out your mission. Secure objective no later than..."

I had 72 hours in which to secure my objective. Again, a nasty puzzle had been injected by Booby Trap. "Why the hell the time schedule?" I asked myself as I started toward Van Trang's bunker.

"Hi, Babe!" Tom hollered to me as he stuck his head out of the communications bunker.

"Helicopter with your cows and pigs just took off from Tra Bong, heading dis way. Pilot wants to know about de ceiling."

I looked up at the sky, which but a little while earlier had been clear. Since then, a black cloud had drifted over to blanket o ur camp. To make things worse for the approaching helicopter, the cloud had completely covered one of our nearest outposts. The Yards who manned that outpost were skittish enough to fire on anything their limited imagination could not instantaneously grasp.

That helicopter will not land, I thought.

Quickly I entered the radio bunker, took the mike from Tom and transmitted, "Blue Bird Niner, Tiger Zero Six. Over."

"Tiger Zero Six, Blue Bird Niner, over," came the immediate response from the helicopter pilot.

"Blue Bird Niner, cloud cover over your destination. I need the meat. Come on down. Outposts notified of your approach. Over."

"Blue Bird Niner, no chance. I don't trust your Yards. Buy your meat somewhere else. Out."

"The S.O.B.," I thought. But I did not give up. "Blue Bird Niner, Tiger Zero Six. Over."

"Blue Bird Niner. Over."

"Tiger Zero Six. Stay high and drop the meat over the camp. That is unless you're lost, Hansel, and co-pilot, Gretel. Over."

There was a silence. Then I could hear the distant sound of the helicopter. "Tiger Zero Six, Blue Bird Niner. Okay, wise guy. Look out below. Here go two scared cows and six screaming pigs. Sweep up your minced meat. Blue Bird Niner. Out."

By this time all the U.S. Special Forces troopers were finding the radio transmission hilarious. In their minds was the thought of how Van Trang was going to react to that novel and unconventional development. The weekly meat delivery was a regular source of illegal income for him. Some of the meat he sold to the hamlet. He often accused us of being "cheap Americans" when we did not deliver the meat because of cloud cover over the camp or enemy action.

"Van Trang is gonna swallow his cigarette over dis," said Tom, as we all cautiously peeked out from our bunker. I was silently praying that the meat did not hit any of our Yards who were loitering around in the open.

It came with one hell of a splash: eight bulky silhouettes suddenly appeared through the clouds and hit the earth with such speed and noise that it stirred the entire camp into action. Montagnards poured out of their bunkers to see what had happened. To them, carnage was funny and they soon filled the air with laughter when they saw what had happened. Animal blood, meat, and bones were strewn throughout the camp.

Captain Van Trang was furious. He did not even take the time to light a cigarette before he pointed a threatening finger at me. The color had drained from his face. A fleeting thought crossed my mind that perhaps the man was somewhat deranged.

He screamed at me, "You...you...I see you get court-martial for dis...you Yank bastard!"

I stopped him with both arms raised, palms open toward him, as if I wanted to surrender to him.

"Watch it, Captain! Wait till we are alone, before you say anything more," I warned him.

The entire camp had become unnaturally silent. I sensed disaster in the air.

Van Trang did not heed my warning. "I no wait no damn American bastard tell me what I do."

Either he did not care, or he forgot, that he was confronting professional American infantry men and that there was no American commissioned officer to hold them back. So he made the last mistake of his life. He dropped his right hand down to his side arm.

Many things happened all at once. Out of the corner of my eye, I saw an ARVN sergeant slam a round into the chamber of his M-16 rifle. I dived down to the ground, and landed rolling toward some sandbags, firing as fast as I could pull the trigger of my .45 pistol. Every round I fired hit that ARVN sergeant.

I saw a knife flash past me and caught a glimpse of Van Trang pitching forward. At the same time, rifle bullets peppered the ground around me as another ARVN soldier fired his rifle at full automatic at me.

Within that cacophony of sound I clearly heard, "Kill Viets! Kill Viets!" Dozens of rifles had opened fire about the same time that I did. Later we could not determine how many bullets hit the two ARVN soldiers who were out in the open. They were both completely blown apart before they hit the ground. Both of their bodies had some resemblance to the carcasses of the cows and the pigs that had been dropped. Many 30-round clips were emptied into them.

Before I could stop the firing, I saw Van Trang with blood pouring out of his mouth. He jerked curiously, with both arms outstretched, trying to crawl in two directions at the same time.

I bent over him, to see if it was necessary for me to finish him off, when Tom pushed me aside and pulled his dagger out of Van Trang's neck. Van Trang then stopped his antics with one more kick, stiffened one last time, and died. "Cease fire! Cease fire!" I ordered loud enough for my voice to carry through the entire camp. The firing subsided, but not before a few hand grenades exploded inside the ARVN bunker killing the rest of them.

"Captain Mock," I called. He came to me on the double, jerked to attention in front of me, and gave me a smart salute in full view of the Yards.

"What leadership!" I thought. He wanted the camp's complement to understand that I was to be respected.

We had to act fast to restore command and control. "Captain Mock," I addressed him formally. "Thank our Yards for saving my life." A shadow of a smile crossed his face. He understood.

He made a smart about-face and gave the order, "Attention!" The command came to attention. "New Camp Commander he be say you be safe him life. He be boo coo happy you damn Yards." (I seldom failed to find comical the Yards' pidgin English and the French word "beaucoup" which they pronounced, "boo coo".)

Some Yards, those who understood, rejoiced with happy screams. Mock then repeated what he had said in their own language. That time they all released their pent-up emotions. Once more, discipline was relaxed and replaced by jubilant howls that traveled deep into the surrounding jungle.

The scouts who were out screening our surrounding area, came in on their radios and asked about the noise that was going on in the camp. Some of them must have been at least a mile from us at that time and still they could hear the commotion within the camp. To our Yards, what had just happened was the dawn of a new and better era — a sweet life without the constant fear and disharmony, which Van Trang and his men had created.

Doc came to me and reported the casualties. "They are all dead. The eleven ARVN SF. Inside their bunker everything is totally destroyed. Radios, records etc."

"Thank you, Doc. Have someone else make out the official casualty report and have it transmitted to Booby Trap. You get ready for the patrol. We leave in 20 minutes," I ordered. Many things flashed through my mind. The killing of the ARVN soldiers was going to freak out Booby Trap for sure. I almost broke out with a nervous laugh when I remembered Booby Trap's orders to me. "You keep a low profile...I don't want more trouble ..."

I felt like slapping my own face to get back to reality.

My men gathered around me, evincing solidarity in support of whatever was to follow. They were all professionals and capable of handling whatever fate had in store for us. There was defiance clearly written on some of their faces, especially Tom's. He was the first to speak.

"Tony, Babe, we finally won de ARVN's hearts and minds. Only, it ain't gonna do much good, man, de sad shape dey is in."

I waved a pointing finger in front of all my men. "Who was it that explained our present situation to Tom? For once he got things straight.

"Sergeant Summers, you are the ranking man when we leave. Get another combat patrol out to the south and east of us. The usual mission: search and destroy. I want this camp further weakened."

I turned to Tom's assistant. "Message to Booby Trap: Control of camp presently in question — Stop — Recommend MIKE Force alerted for possible interdiction — Stop ? Situation report to follow in three zero minutes — Stop — End of message."

I waited for the sergeant to finish taking down the message in his notebook before I continued with my orders to him.

"In that 30 minutes, do not acknowledge any of Booby Trap's messages. Take your time to analyze the situation carefully: what strength remains in the camp, the attitude of the Yards, and the approximate strength of the two patrols.

"Be careful not to make recommendations to him, unless he requests it, and even then take care. The bastard will hold you accountable should things deteriorate further after I leave."

I looked at Tom. "Damn you, Tom. What are you still standing around for? Get ready for the patrol. We leave in a few minutes."

"Okay, Boss. I is gone." With that he disappeared into his communications bunker.

I left the men to themselves and went into my bunker to make the final preparations for the patrol. I looked over my alert field equipment. Everything was always in readiness to move out on a moment's notice. It lay in the corner of my sleeping area, all items carefully packed and ready for me. It consisted of the basic load of ammo for my M-16 rifle, water canteens, first-aid package to include a blood plasma can strapped to the cross-strap of my load-bearing harness, the all important extra socks and underwear, plus some other equally necessary items.

I stripped naked and used the remaining water from my jerry can to give myself a thorough wash-down. I put on clean underwear, dressed in field clothing, and was ready.

I called for Captain Mock. He showed up fully dressed and ready to move out. I noticed that he, too, had a few extra grenades hanging from his pistol belt.

"Mock, old buddy, we're in deep shit."

"Yes be, Sargy. Me know. Viets no be like we be kill Van Trang. He be boo coo fambly Saigon."

"Yes, I know," I answered bitterly. "Especially because of that brother of his in the Palace Guard, who is not only a full colonel but also married to..." I stopped. Mock did not follow me. I had to repeat what I said, but in Yard English.

"Yes be. Van Trang him broder he be boo coo pissed off you, Mock, my good buddy. Me, I be tell he one Yard Captain Mock him boo coo bad Yard. Him be kill the good Van Trang. That full colonel he be come here personally do you in."

All I got from Mock was a toothless, shit-eating grin. He seemed to have enjoyed my speech and was quite content to let me joke about the killing of Van Trang.

I opened a bottle of Scotch and poured us both a generous shot. Mock drank his down in one gulp. Then he said, as if he did not have a care in the world. "No trouble, you, me. We be go patrol." He smiled. "We be go Laos, we be kick ass, NVA division. NVA he be gets boo coo pissed off Sargy, me. We run like hell. NVA he be try catch we. We be hide jungle. NVA be find Sout Viets. Kick ass Sout Viets. Sout Viets be gets hand too boo coo full he be forget Yards kill Van Trang. No can go Ba Cat."

"You'd better have another drink, old buddy. Then maybe you be tell me how we be gets 250 men hide in jungle and how we be gets disengage NVA division. Fifth NVA Division, no like run from fight. We be fuck around Laos, we be gets wipe out."

"Much be good drink. We be take whisky wit?"

"Okay, but you carry it." Mock stuck the bottle into his combat pack. I wondered what Fort Benning would say about us taking a bottle of Scotch out on a patrol with us. It was just not done in the U.S. Army.

I slipped into my fully hooked-up load-bearing harness. It felt heavy. Two hundred and fifty rounds basic load for my M-16 rifle, about 20 extra rounds for my .45 caliber pistol, plus the grenades and other items brought the total weight to about 60 pounds.

While Mock stood waiting until I finished dressing, I adjusted that one hand grenade which we always carried strapped close to where we took our heart to be. He approached me.

"I be do dis, Sargy."

He bent the safety pin of the grenade so that it would slide out easily. I did the same to his. In that war, where only stark hatred existed between ourselves and the enemy, the worst fear we all had was to fall into enemy hands alive. Death by torture would have been the best we could have expected from them. Too often even that was denied us. The last grenade gave us assurance against such an eventuality. Also it catered to the strange personal desire most of us had acquired through the years of fighting against communists.

"Take as many of the bastards with you as you can, when you go." The dream was to wait, when capture became imminent, until your enemy came close to you, then pull the pin. After that, who knew, maybe it would be a matter of interest to learn who went with whom to heaven or who went with whom to hell.

Chapter 4

Out of the
Mouths of Babes

Darkness descended on the camp, leaving the surrounding mountains to stand out like towering sentinels against a clear, starry sky. The camp was deathly quiet, while many small figures disappeared into the damp, black undergrowth of the triple-canopy jungle. More than 250 well-armed, determined men were swallowed up by the darkness, drawn as if by a magnet to close with and destroy the enemy.

The moss-covered ground rose steeply upward along the 13 miles toward the summit of Black Face. We started our ascent in wedge formation. Three platoons, slow, silent, and with a methodical rhythm, cut tunnels through the thorny vines, bamboo thickets, orchid, rattan, pitcher, and other plants. Deeper and deeper we worked our way into the rich flora, where only scant sunlight penetrated.

It was a teeming world, hostile to man. It was the world of the cobra and pit vipers with their long, poisonous, movable fangs. There were boa constrictors and pythons, both arboreal and terrestrial, which reached lengths of 30 feet. It was a world where fungi, molds, and leeches could grow in and on a man's skin. Blood-sucking leeches and ticks stuck their needle-sharp suckers so deep that unless burned off, they would break off and bring secondary infection. Anywhere clothes clung tightly to our skin, these thirsty insects would fasten, then gorge themselves on our blood.

Scorpions and spiders, hairy and smooth, were in abundance. Their poison was potent enough to incapacitate a soldier.

At times the night was illuminated by inch-long fireflies. There were many fruit bats, also known as flying foxes, that would fly blindly into your face, leaving fine itchy hair and fleece smears on your sweat-covered skin.

Every leaf, every branch, every square foot of rotten deadfall that covered the earth, was damp. It effectively muffled sounds so that a herd of stampeding elephants would not awaken a sleeping baby, that is, if it were not for the many different noises made by the wild jungle creatures when disturbed.

Ahead of me and on both flanks were men with machetes cutting tunnels through the mass of vegetation, moving ever closer and closer to our objective. I estimated that we were moving at a rate of one-quarter mile per hour. At some places where Agent Orange had been used, our progress speeded up. I was a hardened advocate in favor of the use of Agent Orange over the entire Vietnam, North and South. How easily we could then have smashed the North Vietnamese and VC's will to fight. Their main defense against the firepower of the United States Army was to hide. Any time we found them, we killed them.

There were some tunnels and trails made by humans and animals through the thick layer of saplings and seedlings close to the ground. To use them was dangerous due to punji sticks, booby traps and ambushes.

Throughout the night I felt Tom's strong presence, although I could not see him. During the many years that we had been together, a solid friendship had developed between us. I was aware that part of that friendship came about because of our similarities in physical strength and endurance, which were well above those of the average man in the SF.

Once I overheard Tom tell another team member, "That honkey, he is a good one to swim de river wit. He is almost as good a nigger as I is." A compliment like that, coming from a man like Tom, I liked.

Tom was raised in a small town in Alabama where the black man had to tiptoe through life. I do not believe that he had ever felt comfortable in the company of a white man until he and I became friends. He knew that I respected him for the man he was.

Ahead of me was the 2nd Platoon and a connecting file. Behind me came the 4th Platoon with Doc and his seven-man medical section. Then came Tom with the rest of my headquarters. Scattered among us were some ammo bearers and runners. On each flank was a platoon. The diamond formation, even though difficult to control in that type of terrain, was the best formation to guard against a surprise attack.

As we moved through the undergrowth, frightened monkeys, leopards, lizards, tarsiers, gibbons, and even an occasional tiger made more noise than did the entire patrol.

One hour before daylight, I gave the order for the first halt. Every man sank down where he was, and nestled himself into the damp leaves. With closed eyes we listened to the wild life around us.

I had just sat down when I detected the first expected movement near me. One of my bodyguards would usually come close to me as soon as we halted.

"Sargy, Sargy," softly whispered a Yard. It was one that I had known for too long a time to consider him as just another expendable body. I had unsuccessfully tried not to get myself emotionally involved with him. Tom called him "Tony's Shadow."

He came close. "Me be damn scout Ding. Me be go back kill VC he be follow."

"No Ding, you be stay me. I be know maybe two maybe three VC be follow." I knew that the Fifth NVA Division would have some scouts out to report on our movements, but they could do nothing with the information at that time. First they would have had to slip past us and then head for the Laotian border with the information. That they could not do, at least not until we had stopped and it was daylight.

Every man in the patrol, through prior training, knew his exact position and kept that position under threat of death. Anyone not where he was supposed to be was instantly shot at. Since we were roughly heading in the same direction as the enemy scouts would have to go, those enemy scouts had a real problem to solve.

At daylight, I planned to have my scouts ambush them. I chose the time of 0700 hours. I whispered to Mock.

"Radio all platoon leaders. Zero seven hundred hours all halt and no noise. We want to trap VC scouts."

Nothing more needed to be said. We went into an operation that we had practiced many times during training. I hoped that Ding would take a prisoner from whom I could get valuable information on enemy positions in Laos and perhaps on Black Face Mountain.

When all movement ceased, the unnatural jungle sounds, the ones we caused, faded away. The sounds all around us settled down. The monkeys we had disturbed became quieter. More noticeable was the absence of the terrible screech made by the monkey-eating eagles.

Ding moved close to me. I felt his cold, damp body as he pushed against me. Two more small bodies, also cold and damp, moved tightly against me. Even though they had a strong desire to protect me, their main reason for being close to me was the cold.

Montagnards suffered when it was cold, and we were high enough up the mountain to feel the chilly damp air. It was a choice of our scouts not to wear jungle fatigues. Dressed only in loincloths, they could move with ease to search out the enemy.

After a 30-minute break we resumed our upward move. Where Agent Orange had been kind to us, we saw the twinkle of friendly stars overhead.

If it were not for the enemy scouts that we planned to locate, those clear areas would have made safer places to rest and also to consolidate the unit. But, since it would have made it too easy for our quarry to slip past us, we hurried on to the next undestroyed terrain where we waited to tend to the enemy scouts.

Slowly, some daylight started to filter through the overhead leaves. All around me I began to discern the huddled forms of our Yards. They were quietly resting in a tunnel through the brush that the 2nd Platoon had cut for us.

Ding and two other scouts were cuddled up next to me fast asleep. I did not move. I wanted them to sleep undisturbed. At times my heart ached for those little mountain men. They had a stone-age acceptance of life and death. No imagination, happy unto the day, and ever ready to be led, without knowing if it was beneficial or not.

Often I had to exercise that well-cultivated ability of all professional combat soldiers to place a blank mental wall between what was agreeable and what was not, when dealing with our Yards.

With the dim daylight, some measure of friendliness replaced the dark hostility of the undergrowth. Colorful butterflies and moths fluttered through the rich flora. Giant grass-family bamboo thickets reached hundreds of feet upward through the herbaceous plants to the top of the highest trees, where they could soak up some sunrays.

What little intelligence we received about the area prior to commitment of our SF, we gained in fragments from foreign soldiers and an occasional missionary.

Not far from where I sat quietly in meditation, I saw the long nose of a proboscis monkey. It was a living caricature of man. He twisted his head in jerking motions with a puzzled expression on his face. It was obvious to me that he could not believe the strange sight we presented to him. A few times the monkey almost fell out of the tree because he had become so excited that he forgot to hang on to a branch.

I could not resist the temptation to have a little sport with our Yards.

"Wake up, wake up," I whispered.

From Yard to Yard traveled the signal that it was close to 0700 hours and to remain absolutely quiet and in place. I pointed at the curious monkey who had fallen complete victim to his own curiosity by coming to within a few feet from me.

"Captain Van Trang's brother," I whispered to a Yards near me. I had no sooner said it, than I fully regretted it.

All who heard me burst into loud laughter, which spread to the flanks, up ahead and to the rear of the column. The monkey almost killed himself flying into the brush to get away from us. Before I lost sight of the monkey I saw him run into a tree trunk, bounce off the tree trunk, and disappear into the underbrush.

Tom just shook his head and said, "I don't know what you told dem, man, but I don't believe it's happenin'."

Doc had also moved close to me. He too shook his head.

"Any man in his right mind would never believe that an infantry master sergeant in the U.S. Army would pull such a dumb stunt as you just did."

"Don't worry, you two, the enemy won't believe it. Even I can't believe what I did." Then in a loud voice I hollered.

"Shut up, you damn dumb Yards, before I cut lose with my rifle on all of you."

It was another dumb statement. They were by then in too humorous a mood to settle down immediately. Everywhere I looked I encountered smiling faces, many of them showing their toothless red gums in a grin. They looked at me as would a child to a caring and loved parent. It took a few more minutes before the patrol was settled into silence.

"Ding, you be know that small young Bru? He we be take last patrol?" I asked.

"Yes, be, Sargy. He be boo coo dumb Yard. All time he be slow. Me be think he be boo coo lazy."

"Okay, okay. Just listen. I want you take him with you. You two go after VC scouts. He be want no front teeth."

Ding smiled and pointed his index finger proudly at his mouth. "Okay, Sargy," he nodded his head enthusiastically, and silently disappeared toward the rear of the column.

"Bet you 50 dat Ding come back in 30 minutes wit blood all over him and his bayonet," said Tom.

"No bet. I know Ding too well. That small Bru, Mo Duc, may slow him down, though."

That little Mo had some time earlier asked me to give him a chance to lose his front teeth.

A strong belief had taken root among the Yards. They came to believe that if they killed an enemy soldier, cutting his heart out and eating it would insure immunity to enemy bullets. More important yet, it would serve to escalate them out of adolescence into manhood.

As to the missing front teeth, well, there were some unanswered questions about that. The questions, however, did not detract from its significance. During the rigorous and dangerous ranger training, Yards were required to rappel out of helicopters. The helicopter's landing struts protruded some three feet below and outward from the chopper's floor.

It was necessary and wise to jump backwards and well clear of those struts before you checked your fall. Failure to do so would cause you to be jerked unceremoniously inward, to smash your face hard against the aluminum strut and leave your teeth scattered on the ground below.

Among the Yards the absence of front teeth was proof that the man had gone through Ranger training, which set him in a social status well above that of the average Yard, that is, one with front teeth.

Since not all Yards could go through ranger training, and not all of those that did go through lost their front teeth, a new way was found to mark their badge of courage: simply smash them out yourself. There was also the ancient Rhe custom of filing off or breaking off front teeth in puberty rites.

Approximately an hour after Ding left me, a radio message reached me telling me that Ding had taken care of the enemy scouts. We then resumed our movement forward, and started to make better progress. By noon, I estimated that we had covered ten miles, and were only three miles from our objective. We had entered a draw between two mountains where heavy rains had washed away much of the deadfall and the going had become easier. Our avenue of approach was parallel to the Laotian border only two miles to the west of us.

Tom came close to me. "Someting's not right, man. I is picking up transmissions which are garbled but of strong signal and in Vietnamese language."

"Can you raise headquarters?" I asked.

"Yes, five by five." Five by five was a U.S. Army radio term for loud and clear.

"Then ask them to get cross bearings on the transmissions."

"Will do," Tom answered, and immediately started to beat so fast a tattoo on his transmitter key that his dots and dashes seemed to run together.

Within a few minutes Tom came back to me and handed me a leaf from his message book on which he had scribbled the answer from Booby Trap.

"Babe, we're getting VIP treatment. Never got dis fast answered before. Make me tink de brass is standing by to see what you're doin."

"Maybe they're just bored." I paid no attention to what Tom said. I had caught sight of Ding and the incredibly small Mo coming toward us. I was disappointed. He did not bring a prisoner.

The message from Booby Trap read: "Intel on enemy short wave transmissions will follow ASAP — Stop — Unconfirmed weak transmitter reported close proximity your position — End of message."

I halted the patrol and motioned Captain Mock to me. "Captain, have the men eat. We stop for one hour. Get all the scouts to us. We need to brief them, but let them eat first. No fires."

"Okay, Sargy." Over his PRC-6 radio, he gave the orders to his platoon leaders.

Ding and Mo stood in front of me with wide grins spread all over their dirty faces. They acted like two children who had, for the first time, washed the dishes for their mother without breaking a single dish. Just by the look of all the blood on them I knew what had happened, but did not want to spoil their moment of glory.

"Okay, you two, tell Sargy what be happen."

Mo held up a messy piece of pulpy flesh for me to see. Ding pointed to it and said smiling, "We be gets Nort Viets. Dis many we be kill." He held up two fingers. "One he be run like hell. Mo him bayonet in back. Mo him be boo coo lazy no be catch. Mo, he be..."

"Okay, okay, Ding." I had to stop him. He always talked too much. But nothing I could say could wipe off the proud, happy looks on both their faces.

Without saying a word Mo took a big, tearing bite out of what looked to me like human liver. Ding told the onlookers that it was indeed liver and that Mo was too dumb to know the difference between liver and heart.

"Mo him boo coo dumb damn Yard. Him no cut heart him be cut liver," Ding informed me. He was, after all, an authority on the matter.

A reverent attention settled over all those around us. Mo picked up a rock the size of my fist and proceeded to smash his own gums, lips and teeth into an unrecognizable mess.

With each sickening blow that Mo delivered to himself, the head-quarters section around me hummed softly in unison, "*Ba giau, ba giau.*" It was explained to me that "*ba giau*" had to do with some spirit that was friendly to brave warriors.

I was the first to congratulate him by shaking his hand. Small pieces of liver stuck to my hand but I did not wipe them off. The Yards around us all praised him in their own way.

Another 12-year old Montagnard of the Bru Tribe had graduated into full manhood, and to my everlasting lamentation, I inherited the dumbest Yard in all of Vietnam, Mo Duc.

"Ding you be tell this Bru he be go back you for scouting."

Ding just shook his head at me. "Mo him be say him be stay Sargy now." He made it sound like a flat statement that I was supposed to obey.

"Damn, you two dumb Yards, get the hell away from me and back to scouting." I had taken my map out and was studying it, but when neither Ding or Mo moved as I had ordered, I stood up ready to throw both of them into the brush.

"No, no, Sargy, we be stay Sargy now. VC, NVA be near. Mo him be say him too be Sargy Yard," Ding said, but he nevertheless backed away a little, not being sure what I would do.

That's all I need, I thought. I did not want another Ding to follow me around acting as my personal servant and bodyguard.

Tom came to me. I could tell by the look on his face that we had trouble.

"Look at dis, Tony." He handed me a message and continued, "One radio, Group says, has a very powerful transmitter like is organic to a division communications center. De odder is of weaker output like dat of a recon unit."

On the message form, Tom had recorded the coordinates of Group's intercepted enemy transmissions. After consulting my map, I said, "Look at this, Tom. One is inside Laos, two miles west of Black Face and the other is just about where I place ourselves to be."

"Yeah, we is gonna get it, Tony. My guess is de two transmitters are interested in dis patrol."

Doc had joined us with his train of medical helpers. "What is new, you two?" He asked.

"We seem to have gotten the attention of the NVA across in Laos. Don't know what their intentions are, but I think we are going to find out soon," I informed Doc.

Then Doc saw Mo. "Oh, no. Not another one," he said in disgust while he reached for his medical kit. Mo wanted to run.

"Catch him, someone," I hollered. Ding grabbed him and held him for Doc to administer first aid to his lips and gums.

Captain Mock came close to me. "Scouts be say Black Face clear all enmeny. Much, much shell hole on mountain. All tree they be cut small pieces. Black ash burn all over. Me be think all VC hostipal no more."

"Thank you, Captain. Group radio say NVA close to us with radio. Have all patrol still. Same operation: 'Close Search.' Then have all scouts look for NVA radio."

"Okay, Sargy." He transmitted the order to his platoon leaders.

I realized that the NVA soldier who operated the radio was in close proximity to us. However, at that time I could not be sure exactly where we were. Our area was covered with dense vegetation, which restricted visibility to a few yards.

I was just about to direct my attention back to Ding and Mo when from overhead came a terrible rumble, like the sound of a runaway locomotive, as heavy shells from Laos swirled through the air above us.

The earth shook as the shells exploded. They were well off target. I estimated about a mile away, and to the east of us. I also immediately established that they were firing from coordinates given to them by their forward observer. That was why they fired the battery volley instead of one white phosphorus shell to zero in on us, and after that direct the guns.

Two things were apparent: first, they did not know exactly where we were, and second, the bastards that reported us did not really know where they themselves were. Thus they were unable to direct effective fires on us.

A third item flashed through my mind which I knew I had better consider very carefully, and for our sake, I had better come up with the right answer ? Why were they interested in us, and to what extent? Once we cleared the undergrowth and made the final assault on Black Face, we would become sitting ducks for any enemy artillery forward observer to direct effective fire.

Group's shelling of the mountain and the enemy shells that just then flew over our heads made me think that the enemy was not going to let me occupy that mountain without a fight. That thought was also supported by Booby Trap's orders: "Make it at least a company-size patrol." He had not been honest with me.

Something was missing. If the patrol had been composed of American soldiers, instead of "expendable" Yards, a comprehensive friendly situation report would have been incorporated in the patrol order. If the patrol action was part of a bigger operation, then that information should have been provided us. It had not been, and I blundered on.

Another battery volley of 155mm shells rumbled overhead. That time their impact shook me up. They were too close. Pieces of timber and rocks, blown up by the explosions, clattered through the trees nearby. I still waited. I was undecided as to what to do.

The third volley consisted of airbursts. Stupid, I thought. Air bursts, in that type of terrain, could accomplish absolutely nothing. The radio pulses of the variable fuses on the projectiles would bounce off the tops of the trees and cause the shells to explode harmlessly in the air. It did, however, serve to make up my mind. The enemy acted too determined; they were expending valuable ammunition in a wasteful manner.

"Captain Mock," I called. He was close by. "Swing lead platoon to 270 degrees. Inform all platoons of new direction of march."

Two interpreters were close by. As usual Mock would glance at one of them if he did not understand me readily. He quickly read my mind at that time for he too wanted to destroy those guns.

Within minutes after I gave the order for the new direction of march, Doc and Tom were next to me. Tom seemed happy with the new development. "Tony, Babe, wine, women and gold. Good thing, too. Let's get dem bastards at de guns, before dey catch us out in de open."

"You're nuts, both of you. Group will hang you, Tony," said Doc. I could tell that his objections to going into Laos were serious, but I paid no attention to them.

"Doc, we have to shut those guns up. If we don't, the minute they find us out in the open, they'll slaughter us as they did on Nui Coto."

"I understand that, Tony, but which will be worse? Take the pounding on Black Face and some of us come out of it alive, or hit those guns and the 5th NVA wipe us out completely. Should you walk out of it, and that is most unlikely, Group will send you to Leavenworth prison for life."

"That's a chance I'm prepared to take, Doc. We go after the guns." I said in such a final tone that Doc just walked off shaking his head.

Tom could not resist further antagonizing Doc. "You ever tought about joinin de girl scouts? Take up bird watchin, college boy?" Doc ignored him.

Another volley roared through the air above us. That time their shells exploded so far away from us that it seemed to me, momentarily, that they were not firing at us.

I took out my map of the area. The plans for the attack on the guns were quickly formulated in my mind. I waved to Captain Mock to come to me.

"Captain Mock, please halt the patrol in two hours. Get all our scouts to close in on me immediately. When we stop, have the platoon leaders also close in on me." One of our interpreters mumbled to Mock and he reached for his PRC-6 radio.

"Tom," I called. "See what you can do with your buddy in the 38th Artillery. We may need him soon. And give this message to Booby Trap."

I had written a message down for Tom to transmit: "Receiving 155mm fire — Stop — Request Counter Fire info on enemy battery location — Stop — Info may facilitate us finding enemy forward observers — End of message."

I had to word the message carefully so as not to alert Booby Trap of my plans. Our Army had the capability of pinpointing enemy indirect fire weapons just about as soon as they fired. That was the information I wanted.

The U.S. 38th Artillery was one of the units that was in range to give us indirect fire support. Sergeants in cahoots with sergeants in Fire Direction Center could, with impunity, pass embellished data to their guns, and thus lay fire on a restricted target.

A quick analysis of our situation indicated that the enemy was aware that a large force was heading toward Black Face. Their knowledge of our objective was deduced from the shelling of the mountain a few days earlier, and also, they must have received ground reconnaissance reports on our general direction of march.

Another piece of intelligence that I considered of significance was the fact that the enemy acted as if secure in the knowledge that the U.S. would not authorize a ground attack or an attack of any kind into Laos at that time.

"You bastards," I thought. "My men and I are considered expendable, so normal rules do not apply to us."

The higher we climbed, the thinner the vegetation became. The vines, bamboo, and mosses gave way to grass and areas where trees could grow free of clinging vines. Finally, just before we halted, spots of sunshine began to break through the overhead branches.

The earth had started to show bare spots where smooth black slate stones lay loosely on the ground. A clear spring trickled out of a rocky crevice where one side of the mountain lay exposed to us. Animal sitings and also visibility increased.

Group, perhaps on purpose, failed to forward to me the necessary information from a counter fire unit as to the exact location of the enemy guns. But it did not discourage me. I had my fourteen scouts and was confident that they would find those guns.

"Ding, you and interpreters listen carefully. This I want. You find where NVA big gun be located. Me, I think this direction." I pointed to an azimuth of 300 degrees. "Maybe six miles. I want prisoner. Woman, child, anyone that know about where guns. Okay, you scat."

Just a few mumbles from the interpreters and all the scouts, with broad smiles and toothless gums shown to me, took off like hunting dogs on the scent of a rabbit. They quickly disappeared in the direction I took the Laotian border to be.

"Tom, get the word out. Radio silence. Do not acknowledge friendly traffic. With luck Group will not find out what we're up to."

"Okay, boss." Tom sounded cheerful.

After the enemy had wasted four battery volleys, it became evident to me that they had lost us. Our new direction of march must have confused them.

The progress we had made during the two hours since I gave Mock the last order was as good as could have been expected. I estimated that we could hold up until the scouts came back with a report. I thought that the most likely place for the guns to be was near a village or hamlet that was marked on my map but was not given a name.

The village had water. It was along one of the many Ho Chi Min Trails, and in an area flat enough to move heavy weapons. The area my headquarters was bivouacked in was at the beginning of a deep, open, slate-covered creek bottom. Up ahead, the 2nd Platoon reported that the creek widened considerably and looked as if it would continue into Laos near where I guessed the enemy artillery battery was. First I had to wait for our scouts to report.

The prearranged signal for radio silence had gone out to all the platoons. I did not even want to use the infantry squad radios while we were that close to the enemy. Their oscillations could be picked up by the enemy and maybe pinpoint the direction from where they came. With success dependant on surprise, I dared not take chances. If I lost that advantage, all would be over for us.

As I sat down, a grinning Yard slipped through the brush toward me from the direction of the 3rd platoon. His wide toothless grin told me that he was happy about something.

He gave me a wild fruit, not unlike a pomegranate in size and looks. To him it was a great moment, giving me what he obviously considered a great prize, until Mo jumped on him and took the fruit away from him.

"What the hell..." was all I could say. Mo took a small bite with his bleeding mouth out of the fruit, smiled and then gave me the rest. The three of us sat down together. I could not but feel that Mo was taking charge in the absence of Ding, and that the Yard who brought the fruit was allowed to sit with us only as long as Mo suffered him to do so.

"Twelve year old and already cocky. I'm going to have trouble with this one," I thought.

"I'm going to straighten you out, Mo," I said knowing full well that he could not understand me. He just grinned, showing off the awful mess he had made of his mouth and gums. He was basking in added importance by sharing the fruit with me on an already eventful day for him.

"Doc, can you do something more for Mo. He looks a sad mess."

"You dumb Yard," was all Doc said. He took some salve that he tenderly rubbed over Mo's lips and gums.

I did not identify the fruit. Most of the area's plant food was known to me: taro, breadfruit, yams, arrowroot, cassava, edible berries and nuts. All these were in abundance where we were, but no pomegranate-like fruit such as we then ate.

After eating the fruit, I took a bite out of a long-range patrol ration (LURP). It was a large, sausage-like, concentrated mixture of vegetables and meat with vitamins added, which some anti-war activist must have invented. I washed it down with water.

As usual with me, I had to fight my desire to drink more water. It had always been difficult for me to abide by water discipline. I perspired freely, which could have been the reason for my excessive thirst. Often I thought of asking my fellow Green Berets if they too craved water as much as I did, but fear of being considered weak stopped me from doing so.

Mock touched my arm to draw my attention to something not far from us. He pointed to a dark spot about ten yards from us and a few feet off the ground in a tree. It seemed as if I was the only person that did not spot whatever it was. All the Yards around me were excitedly babbling among themselves with their attention directed toward where Mock pointed.

"Tamarara," he said. "Big snake."

Only then did I see it: first the outline and then the full monstrous body of a giant snake became visible. I was surprised that I had not seen it sooner. It did not at all blend with the foliage. Slowly the snake, which I immediately identified as a python, circled the tree trunk toward the ground. It gave no indication that it was the center of attraction for the Yards.

"Yards kill with crossbow. Okay Sargy?" asked Mock.

"Okay," I answered, "no rifle, only crossbow."

Half the python was still in the tree when a Yard's arrow flew through the air and with deadly accuracy shot clear through the snake's head right between the eyes. The arrow disappeared through the other side of the snake.

"Damn," I said aloud. I had forgotten Colonel Paegel's request for a live boa. It was too late. The snake was dying. I had to jump backward even though I was well away from the thing. With lightning speed the huge snake had formed into a tight coil, then shot straight out, scaring the hell out of all of us.

Its huge body was as thick as a child's waist and almost 30 feet long. It swished through the thickets with terrible force. The Yards were exulted, laughing loudly with obvious glee at the dying antics of the python.

About 20 of them quickly discarded their load-bearing harnesses and rifles. Armed with only bayonets, they moved in closer to the very alive and berserk snake.

I did not believe that they would jump the snake, but that was what they did. They acted in unison without signals or commands. Each jumped on a part of the snake nearest to him, desperately hanging on to the slashing and twisting body. It seemed to me that if each Yard had a piece of rope and a stick they could conceivably have immobilized the snake by tying the sticks to its body. I filed that information away in my mind.

Then the carnage began. Pieces of snake flew, as they cut the python into chunks and threw the chunks to their fellow soldiers. Many Yards cheered them on. One of the Yards was wrapped in double coils, but before the unfortunate snake could tighten the coils, the battle was over. Such a spectacle one could expect to see but once in a lifetime, but of course I was not clairvoyant, so I called Mock to me.

"Captain, next time we see a boa or a python, no be kill. Yards be tell me I take charge." Mock looked at me as if I had lost my mind, thinking that I wanted to kill the next one all by myself. But he still nodded his understanding.

"And Captain Mock, please quiet them down before we get the entire 5th NVA Division down on us," I said, feeling like a bystander instead of the person responsible for their conduct.

Mock gave me one of his rare smiles. "Men be like VC and NVA now be come dis way for to go Ba Cat. Snake spirit no be like. All same VC be kill snake Black Face."

"So we are even now," I thought. Both we and the VC had killed a snake on Black Face. But Mock's interpretation of the situation would not stand much scrutiny.

Aloud I said, "That is well and good, but still tell Yards be shut up. We combat patrol, not be pikke nick." It took a few more minutes before things settled down. The morale of our Yards was noticeably elevated.

"Man, you is getting worse. Your patrol is run exactly de opposite from what Fort Benning Infantry Center teach," Tom said, while pushing a smiling Yard away from him. "Don't you give me no snake. I just had dinner."

The Yard looked hurt but stuck the piece he had offered Tom into his own mouth. A sickening greenish fluid dripped down his chin but he seemed to enjoy the fresh meat.

I took the piece that was offered me by Mo. If I had been stationed in Germany, I would have justified my eating it by saying that protocol demanded it. There in the hostile mountains of Vietnam, among dangerous primitive humans, the word protocol had an empty ring.

The Yards considered me one of them, an important part of them, a part that had to be taken care of for their sake as much as for mine. I liked it that way, for I still retained some hope of seeing my beloved United States again.

It was a simple matter of never setting yourself up as different from them. Captain Van Trang was perhaps a too-vivid example of that. I had found it productive to pretend to like the same things they did.

What the hell, I thought. "Eating a raw piece of snake won't kill me." I had to add aloud, while Tom almost lost his dinner.

"This is good, Tom. Just like lobster."

That did it. Tom lost his long-range patrol ration.

I had to see to another important matter, the readied graves. "Captain Mock, please have the graves dug over there, fifteen of them." I showed him my ten fingers, then five more and pointed to a little mound a few yards away.

"Get it done before darkness. Better Yards see we care."

Prior to going into action against the enemy we usually dug some graves. The Yards then understood that they would be treated with respect prior to meeting up with their departed ancestors.

"Yes be, Sargy. Me tink dis many be too much," He showed fifteen fingers. "Dis many be nough," he held up five fingers. I merely shrugged my shoulders in agreement.

I watched the grave-digging detail lay out five ponchos on which they placed the top layer of grass on one side and the earth they had dug up on the other side. Later that grass would be replaced over the graves to hide all signs of the excavation. The excess earth would be scattered away from the graves.

This was an extra precautionary exercise to preclude the enemy's discovering the graves while the bodies could still be used for propaganda purposes. The NVA and the VC would mutilate the bodies and show them to their people. This was supposed to prepare their soldiers psychologically to face us.

They believed that to drag a live prisoner through their area would have more rewarding effects on their minds, but prisoners were not easy to get. It was those very barbaric practices of theirs that made it so. Our people went to great lengths not to be taken prisoner by the VC and NVA. We Green Berets made sure that our Yards were aware of what to expect if they fell into enemy hands.

First two, then four more of our scouts returned. They all reported having seen the guns. I could pinpoint the position of the enemy artillery battery. We were six miles away with easy terrain to cross to get to them. I estimated our march to an assault position to take no more than four hours.

The sun threw its last rays through the branches to reflect numerous bright colors. Not a sound could be heard from the more than 250 men. They had all been briefed on the coming attack on the 5th NVA Division's artillery, with detailed emphasis placed on the danger of losing the element of surprise.

The necessary warning had to be repeated before it finally penetrated their limited understanding of the necessity for stealth as we crossed the six miles toward the guns. They were told not to expect indirect fire support, and lastly that we had a mission to accomplish after hitting the guns.

At the last light, Ding and another scout came to me. Between them they had a woman prisoner. The first thing Ding did was to give me the white-and-black-checkered scarf all women VC members wore with pride to identify themselves.

She looked about 18 years old and was of dainty proportions and very scared. She had reason to be scared. She had probably participated in, or at least knew about, the horrible atrocities that those same frail women performed on Green Berets that fell into their hands. I was sure that she expected the worst, and I was not going to disappoint her.

"Interpreter!" I called. Three of them came immediately. The interrogation was of great importance to me, so I did not want misunderstandings.

I took my bayonet and approached her. She tried to back away but two Yards held her fast. I placed my bayonet under her belt, and with a quick upward slash cut her belt. Most of her upper garment fell open to expose two small firm breasts. I moved my bayonet downward and slit her trousers open and let them fall to the ground. She was then deprived of hope, modesty, and perhaps more likely to give me the answers I direly needed.

"First, Ding, you be tell me how you catch and where you catch."

"I be catch hamlet. She be carry food fo guns," Ding answered.

I addressed one of my interpreters. "Find out if she has been to the guns with the food many times."

"Yes, Sergeant Tony, she says she carries the food two times each day."

"Find out from all the scouts if they were seen by anyone across the border."

"They say they do not know where border is, but none of them say that they were sighted by anyone. One scout say he came very close to the guns and saw most of the gun crews were just lazing around not expecting any danger."

"Ask the prisoner if all the guns are dug into holes. Tell her if she lies but one time, I'll let all the Yards have her."

"She say all the guns are in holes. Four of them." She was shaking and all color had drained from her face. "

"Ask her where the infantry soldiers are."

Her voice had gone so soft that the interpreter had to slap her in the face to make her speak louder.

"They are 2,000 yards from the hamlet."

The interpreter who was asking her the questions ran his fingers into her hair and pulled her head backward and showed her his bayonet, pretending to slit her throat.

"Ask her what guards are at the guns during the night."

She had to be held up. Her legs would not support her.

"She does not know. She says no one is allowed to go near the guns at night."

"Ask her where the tanks and armored personnel carriers are."

"She says, the armored personnel carriers are very far away from the hamlet, near the big lake. She does not know about tanks."

"Last question, any supplies stockpiled near the hamlet."

"She does not know."

I called Ding close to me and whispered to him. "Take her, Ding. Do what you want with her, you and the scouts or any one else for all I care. When you're finished, do her in."

Darkness engulfed us. Only fireflies, mosquitoes, moths, and an occasional screeching monkey disturbed the darkness. My Yards instinctively blended with nature in body and mind, each and every one of them, not unlike resting gazelles in a field where the tiger stalks.

They rested as long as the surrounding jungle also rested in harmony. The instant that harmony was disturbed, little black eyes would stab into the darkness, nostrils sniffing the air and ears straining. Little heads gave quick jerks from side to side, like birds in the wild. When they had established the direction from which the danger came, they would relax and fondle their weapons.

Tom and Doc sat next to me. We were comfortably nestled in a damp layer of dead leaves and moss. Our backs were supported by thick vines. We, too, took in every sound that penetrated the darkness; however, unlike our Yards, we were disturbed more often by a new sound or the abrupt silence of another. Civilization had so blunted our senses that they had to be supplemented with reason.

We were not tired or sleepy. The movement from our camp had tapped very little of our reserve endurance.

Tom was the first to speak. "Tony, I've been thinking dat dis will be my last patrol."

"Go to hell, Tom." Each time Tom called me by name instead of Babe, which so many SF troopers use, I felt apprehensive.

"Honest, man, I have a bad feelin about dis mission."

"If you insist on talking crap, then go ahead. Only bad feeling I have about this patrol is what you're throwing at me now."

"Take it easy, Babe, tink about it. Monts ago Group ordered us up Nui Coto. De NVA shelled de hell out of us from Cambode, man. Just as if de whole ting was planned to give our side a reason to go into Cambode. Dat time dey had strange-acting helicopter just hovering overhead watching tings. Maybe dey was foreign news people gettin evidence dat de enemy is usin Cambode."

"Damn, Tom, you talk a lot of shit. And we did not go into Cambodia."

"Yeah, not yet we didn't, but just wait till de rainin season let up. Yeah man, why wouldn't Group order us up Black Face and let de same ting happen deah? Den de newspapers have a ball blamin de commies for using Laos. Same dey did in Cambode."

"Everyone already knows that they are using Laos." I wished Tom would go to sleep and let me think about the attack on the guns.

"Yeah, man, dey know. But if'n dem foreign news people could be shown de actual shellin, like dey were at Nui Coto, den..." He left the obvious unsaid.

We were silent for a long time. Doc spoke for the first time on the subject.

"I heard what you said, Tom. The part about you thinking that you may not walk away from this one. Well, Tom, you scare me too. It is not like you to get skittish and dream up things like that.

"As to the rest, I think you are way out in left field. Our Army does not do things that way. So let us get some sleep."

"Tony, you and Doc," he sounded very serious and we both noticed the sadness that had crept into his voice. "Like I said, I feel I aint gonna walk away from dis one. If I don't, I want you two to promise me dat you will go see my family and tell my boys I wasn't afraid. Just a little lie like dat will go a long way wit dem boys of mine. Dey tink I's a real hero."

We did not answer him for a long time. Then I said. "Tom, we promise to do it, but, partner, don't talk like that. I don't know you this way. In the past we laughed at this type of thing. What's got into you?"

"Oh, forget it Tony. You answered me. Now we can take a sip of dat bottle Mock hid in his combat pack."

"Captain Mock," I called. He was squatting on a log eating a patrol ration. "Come join us. We be see how much bottle you be drink."

He gave me one of his seldom used smiles and took the bottle out of his combat pack and handed it to me. As soon as the bottle was passed around, each of us took a healthy swig. The whisky warmed my brain so that life became just a little nicer.

I touched Tom on his shoulder. "Say, nigger buddy, you sure you can handle that radio after those two heavy slugs you took?"

"Man, dis nigger can tap out a coded message with his toes, blind drunk, faster dan Group can copy," said Tom. His mood had improved.

"That's better," I said. "No more talk about getting killed."

"You know, Tony Babe, de last time I was home, I was just in time for de birth of my fourth son. Kind of lucky too, since I was gone for two whole years. Healthy son, too."

"You should be ashamed of yourself, joking like that, Tom." Doc said, reaching for the bottle.

"Why ashamed? and why joking? I gots mahself anoder healty son. Dat's good, eh college boy?"

"Oh, let it be, Doc. Main thing is we have Tom on our side. He is the best man to have with us on any patrol." Doc and Mock nodded their agreement on that.

Mock spoke up. I could tell the drink had loosened his tongue. "Sargy Tom, he be like Sargy Tony, boo coo be strong. No be need rifle. One time be hit VC wid fiss, VC be fly, blood be spash..." He conveyed what else was on his mind by a hiccup.

"Back to de patrol, Tony" Tom whispered to me, "just no good, man, to lie to maself. If I don't make it, please tell me you will also tell my boys some good tings about me. Tell dem I took a lot of gooks with me when I went."

"Okay Tom, I'll tell them, but buddy, don't talk like that any more. You and me, we've gone through much and we're still around. Besides you make me nervous. Let's finish this bottle."

I was fully alert. Step by step I went through a mental exercise of what I had planned: what actions I could take in many eventualities, some of which were encountering enemy armor, running into strong infantry units, walking into enemy anti-personnel mines, and encountering various man-made or natural obstacles prior to making contact with the enemy.

Once satisfied that I was mentally prepared for most contingencies, I slowly relaxed. Even though I had brought myself some measure of relief through that exercise, I was aware that I would remain the victim of my impulsiveness.

Although I reflected on what I would do in certain circumstances, in the past most of my actions had been spontaneous. Everything that I did under pressure was the direct result of military training. We, the U.S. infantry soldiers, are the best-trained soldiers in the world. We react instantaneously, thus making fewer mistakes. A poorly-trained soldier must either first reason things out or blunder headlong into disaster.

I was aware that intelligence is developed by danger, as in the fox; by want, as in the criminal; and by training, as in the infantry soldier. Combine want, danger, and training, I silently reasoned with myself, and things should fall into place at dawn the next day when we attacked the gun positions. I also knew that I was going to have problems disengaging from the enemy.

Doc moved closer to me. "I heard what Tom said in reference to the set-up for the news media. Some surprise that he would think that one out."

"You too, Doc? Do you now think that maybe, just maybe, we are being set up to be slaughtered?" I asked.

"Yes and no, Tony. It is not easy for me to believe that our people would deliberately set us up as sitting ducks for the NVA to pound, the way they did on Nui Coto. As far as drawing them out, yes, that, maybe.

"The big brass are as bloodthirsty as you are, Tony, when it comes to fighting the commies. They can't send combat forces openly into Laos, but they would give much to catch that 5th NVA Division on this side of the border."

"You know something, Doc," I said. It had dawned on me that our mission might make sense. "The proximity of Black Face to one of the main arteries of the Ho Chi Min Trail ? that is the key. The NVA and the VC will not let us occupy Black Face. We are going to draw part of that division out for sure." That thought made me feel better.

Doc shook his head. "I don't know, Tony. You going into Laos may not be what this operation calls for. Group is going to hang you for it. You want to reconsider, Tony?"

"No, Doc. We're going after those guns. I may give the order to pull back if we lose the element of surprise. Control of the patrol will be easier when we clear out of this undergrowth. We are going to get the guns and still occupy Black Face in good time."

Nothing further was said. We settled down to rest. With the first rustling noise I heard, I automatically lifted my arms. A small body slipped up against me.

"Mo, damn you," I thought. He was supposed to be out with the rest of the scouts. I had inherited another Ding.

A moment later Ding also moved up against me. I did not know how long we huddled together, maybe an hour, when I heard soft footsteps approaching us. I became wide awake and pushed the two Yards away from me. Four half-naked scouts came close. I heard Mock, who was a few yards from me, exchange soft whispers with them.

In front of me, Ding and Mo had taken up positions with their rifles at the ready. Their little black eyes strained to peer through the darkness.

Mock's voice came to me. "Scouts be come from guns again. Dis time they be catch nodder prisner. Him be NVA solder from village Attopue. He be gets good info NVA guns."

It was soon established that our scouts had not compromised the element of surprise. We were fortunate in that respect. In addition, we got some very useful information from the new prisoner, who was a non-commissioned officer in the 5th NVA Division Artillery.

The four 155mm guns were dug into firing positions, large ammunition stockpiles were located close to each gun, and two guards were all that stayed on duty during the night. The prisoner was not on duty when captured, he was walking toward their latrine when he was captured.

No land mines were implanted anywhere near the guns. A hamlet, housing about 500 dependents and support personnel of a military police unit, was located one mile west of the guns.

The prisoner did not know where their tanks were but did see armored personnel carriers (APCs) close by a few days earlier. Finally, a very large number of infantry troops were still moving northward from Cambodia.

"You did a wonderful job interrogating him, Mock old buddy." I slapped him on the shoulder. I was elated with the additional information, and immediately scribbled most of it down in the standard format in which field combat information was transmitted to our Group Headquarters.

Most important was the information that the 5th NVA was still in the process of moving out of Cambodia. My report was lengthy, since our scouts and the other prisoners also gave combat information.

"Any more you be want be know I make prisner be speak?"

"No, Captain, that is all, and thank you."

Mock stuck his bayonet deep into the POW's back with the point of the bayonet angled upward. The prisoner died before Mock pulled out his blood-smeared bayonet.

When I completed the report, I took another few minutes to review what I had written. I had gained a wealth of Combat Information from our scouts and the POWs. I wanted the report to be as correct as possible. When I was satisfied with it, I handed it to Tom, who encoded it immediately and transmitted it to Group.

"Let's move," I ordered. "Get the word to the men that the guns are the same ones that fired on us at Nui Coto. Rifle platoons take no prisoners. Show no mercy. Just remember Nui Coto."

Mock touched me on the shoulder. "Now we be make Yards fight like hell."

"Keep them quiet until we clear the creek bed, then, after the line is formed, I'll signal the attack. It will be at 0500 as we covered during the briefing last night."

I ordered Ding. "I be want two prisoners from guns. You be tell scouts they be kill guards then get away from line of fire of platoons."

How they were going to accomplish that neat trick, I did not want to think about. What I did think about was that there were safer ways for them to make a living.

Point security, and connecting file from the lead platoon ran swiftly past me. Each man had his bayonet fixed. All fatigue, cold, hunger, and other discomforts had completely disappeared. A wonderful, exhilarating feeling shot like adrenalin through the ranks in anticipation of positive action against an enemy they viewed with defiance and burning hatred. To them all Vietnamese were Van Trangs and worse.

We climbed higher until finally the slate creek bed petered out into a relatively flat plateau. There the ground was dry, and short grass and thorn bushes covered the land. Isolated trees, of the same type that were covered with moss further down into the dense growth, stood scattered everywhere. The air was sweet and clean, unlike the musty jungle smell.

I looked toward the east, where a red glow was fast spreading to announce another day.

"The last for many," I thought, "perhaps even my own."

A soft breeze rustled the grass around me. How acute a man's senses become while he walks in harm's way. I noticed things like a wet blade of grass, a twinkling star, and a clod of earth crushed under foot. I heard all the sounds that were part of my surroundings.

Signals went through the ranks that the enemy was in sight. Little Montagnard bodies crouched forward as they shifted silently and laterally into the skirmish formation. The 2nd and 3rd Platoons were abreast, and the 1st Platoon held slightly in back of them to take care of all mop-ups, as the two leading platoons carried out the assault on the hamlet and the guns.

The 4th Platoon, in reserve, remained in the diamond formation to provide security around my headquarters. Our ammo bearers, Doc's helpers, and the rest of the support personnel followed in column formation behind me. My 60mm mortars were set up to fire.

I peeled the green tape back from my wristwatch. It was 0440 hours. Mock touched my arm and whispered in my ear.

"Scout they be kill two guards on gun. All NVA be sleep inside holes."

The Yards had killed the guards with those lethal crossbows. When shot through the neck, the victim died without a sound.

All movement had ceased. We were ready for the attack on the hamlet, the enemy's artillery, and the sleeping gun crews. Not a sound or movement came from the enemy to indicate that it was alerted. My men lay flat on the ground, tense and waiting for my order to move in closer. Twenty minutes to wait. I needed more daylight and could afford the delay, for even if the enemy were alerted during that twenty minutes, they could not save themselves now.

Mock and I trooped the line. We went from man to man, whispered a word here and there. I noted with pride the obvious affection those little mountain people had for me, but with a heavy heart I noticed the innocence with which they accepted what lay ahead. How we had changed them! Never again would they be satisfied to roam freely though the mountains.

That early dawn awoke a new and strange sensation within me. I felt the first pangs of guilt because of what I was doing. I have made killers out of primitive people, motivated and directed them to kill. That I could maneuver such a powerful combat force undetected to the assault position made me think that some evil, yes, some terrible evil power is succoring me. Surely, a kind and just God would not have suffered me and my expertise to survive till now.

The proximity of the hamlet to the guns, which made it necessary to destroy it as well pricked my conscience. It was of little consolation to know that a Military Police unit was in the hamlet and made it a legal tactical target. I refused to dwell on the knowledge that there were also women and children there.

I asked myself, Who the hell am I to play God?

Be that as it may, the feeling of guilt had flashed through my mind. I quickly defended myself by saying, they initiated the inhuman set of rules under which we fight. Damn, I cursed myself. I was well aware that such an excuse fell under the same category as that of the murderer who said his father had molested him 30 years before, therefore he should not be held accountable for his actions.

There were 500-or-so humans in those grass-thatched, flimsily-built shacks, and they were sound asleep, unaware that but a few hundred yards through the darkness waited savage guerrilla fighters. These fighters had but one purpose: to kill with high-powered automatic rifles that would send their lead projectiles for approximately 400 yards, three to four feet above the ground, the killing zone.

What a slaughter it's going to be, I mused, and I, yes, I alone, had the power to stop it from happening. I suppressed the stupid sentimental thoughts. I was in my element and programmed to instill that last ounce of motivation in my men.

Most of the men that I had with me were veterans of many battles. The bitterest battle was the one we had fought on the mountain of Nui Coto. It was a strange mountain formation that seemed to have grown like a living thing from the flat, floating rice fields of the Mekong River Delta Area. On that infamous mountain, under fire of NVA guns which were emplaced in the safe haven of Cambodia, we had had to abandon two hundred dead and mangled bodies.

As I went along the line I whispered to man after man. "Guns from Nui Coto... guns from Nui Coto..." In return I received many silent toothless smiles and dirty little fingers pointing to their bayonets. Bayonets were going to do the work that day.

I looked at my watch again. We had five minutes to wait. The morning's dim twilight had almost disappeared, outlining the gun parapets against the morning haze.

The hamlet too had started to come into view through the early morning mist. I even saw an old woman shuffling slowly toward a nearby creek with an empty bucket on her head. It was probably the last chore of her life.

Mock and I took our position in the center from where we could best control the action. Six runners hugged the ground around us. Tom, too, came a little closer to me in case things went wrong and we would have to inform Group of our whereabouts.

During those final fleeting moments I again experienced that vivid awareness of my surroundings. The earth beneath my feet, the nearby mountains which had slowly become visible through the fast retreating night sky, the crisp, cool, clean morning air, all became very real. And, as if for the first time, I felt a closeness to it all.

Chapter 5

Nui Coto Kill!

A t 0500 hours my military mind took over. I waved the 2nd and 3rd Platoons forward. The 1st Platoon quickly took up position where it could support the center of the line. Behind came the reserve platoon. Silently they advanced: 300 yards, still no sound from the enemy; 200 yards, and still all quiet. After 100 yards my nerves were taut.

This can't be. All too easy, I thought.

In our rear, our 60mm mortars sounded like an old typewriter as they fired the dozen rounds, as ordered, into the hamlet. More than 200 charging Yards uttered blood-curdling screams as they stormed into the hamlet.

"Nui Coto kill! Nui Coto kill!" could be heard above the rifle fire. Other Yards swept the gun position clear of crews. I saw one gun, the furthest from us, level its barrel at our charging Yards, but they were too late. That alert gun crew died from rifle fire instead of the bayonet.

Sustained fire from M-60 machine guns and M-16 rifles intermingled like steel sickles, and mowed down all in their path. Within the parapets, the enemy had been cleared from the guns. Many half-clad enemy soldiers lay dead and dying between where they slept and their guns.

Others were desperately trying to put up a fight while fleeing, only to fall victim, first to bullets, then to bayonets.

As enemy resistance ceased near the guns, Mock led the main body into the hamlet. The 4th Platoon had the mission of destroying the supplies. They found large stacks of rice, dried meat, and clothing stored underground. Soon billows of smoke rose into the sky.

Near the hamlet, my men ran into light resistance. I paid little attention to it. Tom and I, aided by a dozen ammo bearers, were hastily at work on the destruction of the guns. Tom lashed two concussion grenades onto the outside sliding mechanism of one breechblock. He tied the pins together, pulled them out, and slammed the breech half-shut.

The grenades caused enough damage to the finely machined surfaces of the breech to render it temporarily useless. Tom completed the destruction of that gun by firing a 3.5 rocket round which penetrated the barrel near the breech.

On one gun I used a Thermit grenade to see what damage it would do to the breech's sliding surfaces. When I pulled the pin on that grenade I heard Tom scream.

"Get dat god damn Yard away from de gun muzzle!"

I made a flying tackle on Mo, and rolled with him on the ground just as a piece of steel flew out of the gun muzzle. He had his head stuck into the tube, being fascinated by the gun's shiny lands and grooves.

"What are you doing here you...you!" I picked him up and he almost flew into the air because I used my strength and did not expect him to be that light in weight.

"You're supposed to be with Ding in the hamlet." I pointed at the gun muzzle. "You no be look inside...oh, what the hell." I let it go. He did not understand me and I had things to do. He stood there looking at me with that famous Montagnard shit-eating grin spread all over his dirty face and battered lips. If he had had a tail, he would have wagged it.

Ding came back and jumped into the parapet where I was.

"Ding, you tell this damn Yard that I am not his father, and also, that he is a scout and is supposed to be with you and not following me around," I said while helping Tom to tie some C-2 charges to a gun carriage.

"Me be tell Mo, but him be plenty dumb. He be say he be stay Sargy all time, VC, NVA no be kill Sargy." Ding had his own version of a shit-eating grin spread generously over his face.

"You gots anodder one, Babe. May as well get used to him. If you don't like de looks of him you can always stuff him in your back pocket. He's small enough," Tom said, while he backed off to blow a gun carriage.

"Hey, Tom," I hollered out to him. "Do you know these guns are American made? They're 155s. We lost some of them in December 1950, to the Chinese in Korea."

"Yeah, what you want me to do? Take em back to de States? You afraid Uncle Sam is gonna make you pay for em? You're nuts, Babe. Let's bust 'em up and not tell Uncle Sam."

Tom was enjoying himself. His secondary specialty was demolition expert.

Our ammo bearers reported that we had no more plastic explosive charges left. We had to use the 3.5-inch rocket launcher ammo. We inserted this backwards into the gun barrel, partly shut the breech, and applied the electrical spark to the projectile. The shape charge of the rocket cone blew the breech to scrap. It was capable of penetrating eleven inches of armor.

"Damn, Tom, where did you learn that one?"

He just smiled while we both looked in wonder at what had happened to the rear end of that gun.

"That one is gonna go for scrap for sure," I said. The blast had blown the breech clear off the gun.

It was not easy, but we managed to damage all four guns before Mock and some Yards filtered back to us. One 3.5-inch round was fired into a pile of ammo. It completed the demolition of the enemy's 155mm battery.

When the enemy's small-arms fire subsided, I watched the hideous carnage sweep like a nightmare through that hamlet. Men, young and old, women, and children fell to bayonets. Our Yards stabbed and slashed indiscriminately while simultaneously demolishing the hamlet's structures.

The screams of women and children were almost drowned out by the crazed piercing cries of "Nui Coto kill! Kill...Nui Coto kill! Kill..." A veritable holocaust ensued while God looked the other way, and the new day lingered in shame before it fully illuminated man's inhumanity to man.

I caught a glimpse of two uniformed NVA officers being taken prisoner by my scouts. Earlier I did not believe that they would be able to get prisoners, and I was pleasantly surprised to see that they did. Group would be glad to get the information those two officers could provide. Mock would make them talk.

I signaled for Captain Mock to consolidate the command for a retreat back toward Black Face. He signaled his orders via PRC-6.

It took ten minutes before the men responded by closing in on their platoon leaders. A characteristic wildness, closely akin to the world wherein they lived, had surfaced once more. When they were turned loose to kill Vietnamese all their pent up hatred for those people would burst forth and be vented in an all-consuming vengeance.

Everywhere I looked I saw wild, darting, glazed black eyes searching for signs of Vietnamese life. It mattered little to them whether it was a child, woman, Vietcong, or a Vietnamese soldier.

Many of the Yards had returned to their hamlets to discover their women and children had been put to the bayonet, but not until the Vietcong had tired of the sport of rape and torture.

I caught a glimpse of Tom receiving items from our Yards. I had thought for some time that Tom might get gold, diamonds, and perhaps money when we destroyed an enemy stronghold. Since his actions were not detrimental to our mission I took the least line of resistance: I did nothing about it.

The 4th Platoon rallied on me and as planned, threw up a defensive line close to the edge of the plateau. It was close to the beginning of the downward slope from whence we came. Their orders were to hold against any enemy counterattack, so as to give the main body a chance to withdraw.

"Tom, you stay with Mock. He is going to move on to Black Face as soon as possible. He should not have trouble since the enemy will expect us to retreat directly back to our camp."

"Okay, Boss. I hear you good," Tom answered at once. His pockets seemed bulgy to me. He saw me noticing it and edged away.

"See you on Black Face or maybe sooner." As an after thought I mentioned to Tom, "I expect the enemy to come at us with armored personnel carriers to where the ridge is. I am going to assume that they are stupid enough to expect us not to leave a rear guard this close to them."

Tom nodded, and pointed to a procession of Yards who had five half-clad prisoners among them. Four were Europeans and one a Vietnamese. I caught a glimpse in the sun of long, blond hair swinging in the wind as the prisoners were forced at bayonet point to run.

"Damn, what de hell have dey der?" Tom shouted irritably.

I saw a woman, skimpily dressed, three white men, and one Vietnamese in underwear being rushed along at bayonet point. All had ropes around their necks and were unceremoniously herded toward Tom and me.

I became very upset about the Yards having disobeyed my orders of "no prisoners." Taking prisoners was the job of my scouts and then only on my orders.

We were not engaged in conventional warfare with conventionally trained soldiers. We were fighting terrain, weather, and an enemy about as unpredictable and nasty as rattlesnakes. The poison of hatred had affected those nebulous rules of engagement to such an extent that some of our American soldiers were also affected.

I did not want to take prisoners for the simple reason that they became a burden. They had to be guarded day and night. If I wanted to get them into a safe stockade I had to risk the lives of American helicopter crews. Then a problem arose when some foreign Red Cross person believed the lies they often told about our mistreating them.

Sometimes the prisoners would lie about our conducting military operations inside Laos, Cambodia and North Vietnam. Also that we destroyed villages full of women and children. There were enough damaging lies for the hostile press to wallow in without me giving them more.

I almost opened fire on the new prisoners and the Yards who were escorting them. Later I came to regret not having done so. When they came close to me I gave Tom an order.

"Get them down into the brush to where we bivouacked last."

Tom looked at me as if he was not going to obey me.

"Why not just shoot de bastards? Dey're commies."

"Tom!" I said.

He understood that he had better not argue. Reluctantly he walked off with the prisoners.

I remember looking at the motley procession. The woman's perfectly formed body was partly exposed through her nightgown. She frantically stumbled over rocks and brush with the Yards' bayonets but inches away from her lovely low-slung ass.

The sun came out from behind a cloud where it had hidden in shame. It came over my shoulder, which was advantageous to me. Enemy soldiers would go into the sun to get to us, and since the rays were still at a low angle, they could blind them somewhat. At least that was what I was hoping for.

My 4th Platoon was in place. They had occupied the usual L-shape formation that was best for ambushing a column. All was ready for the enemy. To my right, well camouflaged, were six 3.5-inch rocket launchers. We waited while Mock moved the patrol further away.

"The white woman?" I asked myself. I surmised that she was a Russian or perhaps French. Some Russians were military advisors to the NVA, but I did not believe it was that. The Russian advisors seldom came close to where we used ground combat units.

She was more likely French. Many Frenchman were sympathetic to the VC and NVA. Some of us that were fighting in Vietnam believed that they would have us fail in Southeast Asia as they had at Dien Bien Phu, where the Vietnamese deflated de Gaulle's Napoleonic aspirations.

"To hell with the extra prisoners," was my final thought on the matter. Captain Mock would take care of them, and if he did not, I would give the order.

"No, not an order," I thought. I was a mere advisor to Captain Mock. It was he who was in charge, and thus responsible.

Next to me stood Mo.

"You be one dead Yard if you don't get back. Oh, hell. You don't understand a damn thing I'm saying."

He looked at me with a large, terrible smile. His lips were so swollen I wondered if he could eat.

"Come here," I waved him to me. Slowly he came toward me, appearing ready to sprint away. I took out my first-aid kit and dabbed zinc and starch powder on his lips. An interpreter told him not to remove the powder. For my efforts I received a toothless smile.

Outlined against the sun's rays I saw a cloud of dust as a number of armored personnel carriers (APCs) came toward us.

"The enemy is coming!" I hollered at the men. "Rocket launchers, only fire when I say so."

They had been briefed on exactly how to engage the APCs.

On they came at maximum speed. I counted two ahead of the dust cloud. Another two were behind them. Four APCs, with eleven men each. We were going to have our hands full.

"Machine gunner, when I give the order to fire, spray your fire high to silence their mounted machine guns and also let your bullets ricochet off the armor plates. You riflemen, hold your fire until they dismount. Then go for the killing at full automatic."

As fast as I talked the interpreters relayed what I said.

I had the platoon leader go down the line to control the rocket launcher crews. They were my best bet for success and I wanted all to hold their fire until I gave the order. The armor plating on the APCs could stop a rifle bullet and shrapnel.

The shape charge of the 3.5-inch rocket projectile would explode against a steel hull of a tank or an APC, and drive a cobalt bolt through eleven inches of steel. The bolt would ricochet throughout the inside to destroy just about everything in there.

Behind me lay 100 yards of open terrain, then a steep downgrade with heavy foliage where I could lose the enemy. I had to destroy the oncoming enemy before I dared to move. If I failed, that 100 yards would become a gauntlet.

I knew how the ambush was going to turn out. They could not see us, and I reasoned that they would believe we had retreated to the creek bottom. They would blunder right into us, giving my 3.5-inch rocket launchers point-blank ranges. Just as well, because they were too inaccurate at distances over 300 yards.

They were regulars, trained NVA murderers, so I screamed with the Yards when the first rocket slammed into the leading APC. The round hit the fuel tank and incinerated all inside.

Exuberance took hold of the platoon and I too joined them in screaming "Nui Coto! kill...Nui Coto kill! Kill," as I sprayed my M-16 rounds into the back door of an APC that had swerved sideways before it opened the rear door for the men to dismount. Most of that squad died inside their APC. Twenty seconds after the action started, the two leading APCs were demolished and in flames, with but a few bodies visible on the ground. Most were burned up inside the APCs.

The two trailing APCs came rumbling through the dust cloud and also ran into deadly small-arms fire. I noted a criminal neglect of training on the part of the enemy. They exited from the APCs confused as to where their enemy was.

Two at a time would jump out of the rear doors, collide with each other as one soldier swung to the right from the left door and another one swung left from the right door. To further confuse them, they just took it for granted that their enemy was up ahead of the APCs where they would have been had their drivers not swung their APCs away from danger.

It was a fatal maneuver for a loaded APC. The two APC doors flying open in the rear exposing their men inside was like telling my Yards, "Here, fire into this dark spot." The Yards massed all their fire into that perfectly marked target.

My rocket launchers managed to get two rounds off each before I gave the order to disengage. The enemy was destroyed without being able to inflict casualties on us. The entire action, from the time the first round was fired until I gave the withdrawal order, took less than four minutes.

Swiftly, we moved downward through the underbrush, leaving the burning APCs and the many enemy dead to add to the loss of the guns and their hamlet. My Yards could not keep quiet. They were exuberant, and everywhere I looked I was met with smiling faces. None of them had earlier believed that such a perfect victory would be theirs. In their childlike innocence, they gave me all the credit for the destruction of the enemy.

We had to move fast, for I believed that the unit we stopped was but a point element of a larger combat force that was heading our way. The enemy had strength in the area, and they would use it.

A few badly directed 120mm mortar rounds exploded harmlessly behind us. It reminded me that we were still in Laos and could not request counter fire. I pushed the men harder.

When I felt that we had moved far enough toward our camp to confuse the enemy, we made a 90-degree turn toward Black Face to rejoin the rest of the patrol. The camp's location was well known to the enemy and common sense dictated that we would seek the defendable barricades of home after such a daring raid. I therefore expected the enemy to go all out to catch up with us before we got to Ba Cat.

I halted our progress when we came to the freshly-filled graves where Mock had buried our fallen comrades. Earlier, Doc had given me the casualty report on our losses: eight men killed in action at the guns and the hamlet. The fresh graves, not readily discernable even though I knew what to look for and where, marked yet another little dot in our world where some had given their all for freedom.

Then I counted the graves: There were nine, not eight. One more must have died, I thought.

With reverence, we paused a moment in silent respect for our dead. Then we moved on, away from those eternal shadows of the triple-canopy jungle, where silently, and equally eternal in rest, lay yet another nine of "Our Yards".Soon afterwards we rejoined the main body. Captain Mock came to me.

"Second Platoon dey be cut paf for Black Face. Much be have bamboo. No problem. We be wait, leave creek go up Black Face. No gots enmeny up Black Face, say scouts.

"Scouts also be say many enmeny be go Ba Cat. You be call air strike planes we no be see. Kill many NVA before dey be gets camp."

Mock was almost out of breath after that long speech.

I smiled. "Planes we no see."

That was what most of the Yards called B-52s. I shook my head to Mock.

"No, buddy, I no be call...damn I am beginning to sound like you, Captain. I'm not going to ask for an air strike. I'll report the information to Booby Trap and let him decide what to do about that large force heading for the camp. I have my own troubles here."

I approached the subject of the nine graves. "Captain, how many got killed?"

He held up eight fingers. I held up nine fingers. He shook his head and again insisted on eight.

"I see this many grave." I insisted on my nine.

"Me I ask Sargy Tom. Him be stay dead Yards."

I saw Mock get a little uncomfortable. He too must have realized that Tom had no business burying dead Yards.

"Okay, Captain, we no speak more. I take care all."

Later I was going to find out from Tom about that ninth grave. I placed my arm on Mock's shoulder by way of approval.

"We be good team, you, me, Captain. Boo coo kick ass today."

"Yes be Sargy."

Mock held his blank countenance, but I knew him so well that I could detect his approval. He knew that there was something unpleasant coming.

"Captain," I looked him in the eyes. "What about the white prisoners? I gave orders for no prisoners to be taken. Only the scouts were to bring in two, if possible."

Mock started to squirm. "I be kill damn Yards take prisnor." He said, and I knew he would do so if I let him.

"No, Captain. No kill but we no forget who they be. Maybe you just kick ass the Yards take prisnors."

"Sargy, one prisnor she be white. Yards dey be fraid she. Two dey be French, one he be Nort Viet, one he be...me I not know...maybe all same Sargy but no gots green beret."

"What? I was shocked into action. Quickly I ran to where the prisoners were huddled together.

"Are any of you U.S. servicemen?" I asked loudly.

No answer. All of them just stood there, obviously afraid and confused as to what was going on around them.

Tom walked over to me.

"I got de same shock when I tought dat maybe we had liberated an American soldier. Man, wouldn't dat have been sometin."

I expressed my disappointment.

"Some day we may just be lucky enough to run into one of the many VC POW camps."

"The broad is an American and so is dat creep with de long hair and beard. Can you imagine dat, Tony. Mixed up with de enemy."

Tom spat on the ground, as if his words were distasteful.

"Two dey French and one Nort Vietnamese. Dey all claim to be fact-finders for de World Council of Churches. Now tink dat one out, Babe. To me it stinks. Dat bitch could be anoder Jane Fonda, and de creep, well...I tink we let Mock find out..."

"Okay, Tom," I cut him short. "Where is Doc?"

"Wit de wounded. We got tree. He is up ahead wit de 3rd platoon. Tony, I don't believe dat shit about de churches. I tink dey is all spies for de NVA or just plain traitors. Anyway, man, let's just do dem in." Tom wasn't happy having them there. They presented a new problem, one we could very well do without.

Around the five prisoners, a circle of curious Yards had gathered. The only white people they had ever seen wore green berets and carried weapons. The woman's long blond hair, matted and in disarray, seemed strange to them. She was the center of their attention.

The male prisoners had their arms tied behind them, and all prisoners were tied together with a rope around the neck. A Yard stood holding the rope. He looked ready to drop it and run for his life should I make a move toward him. The Yards knew how unhappy I was with what they had done.

The prisoners had obviously been pulled out of their beds. They were practically naked except for a few scant pieces of nightclothes and underwear that were badly torn by the underbrush through which our Yards had dragged them. Their feet were bloody and many scratches showed over their bodies.

The girl stood close to the men. She was not bound. Our Yards were afraid to touch her. Someone had given her a jungle blanket that she held tight around her trying to hide her almost naked body. The blanket did not conceal her perfectly-shaped figure.

I took her to be about 23 years of age. She stood but an inch taller that our Yards, had lovely blue eyes, and even through the sweat and dirt on her face I could see that she was exceptionally beautiful.

She kept her eyes on me as I walked toward the Montagnard that held the rope that was looped around her neck. He was one of the Yards who were responsible for taking the unwanted prisoners. He started to back away from me, dropped the rope and looked as if he was about to make a run for it.

"Stand still, damn you!" I ordered.

He shook with fright, but stood still. His little black eyes darted in quick jerking movements like that of a wild, caged bird seeking an escape route.

I took him by his load-bearing harness, lifted him to arms length above my head, and swung him as if I wanted to throw him into the brush. He uttered some strange sounding noises. I could feel his fearful trembling.

I put him down and unbuttoned first his fatigue jacket, then his trousers. As I slipped his jacket off him and tossed it to the girl, the surrounding Yards started to snicker. When I pulled his pants off and tossed those to her, all around us I heard ripples of giggles, and then outright laughter.

Even the Yard whose clothing I had stripped off, after he decided that I wasn't going to kill him, joined in the merriment. The girl let go of the blanket and quickly reached for the fatigues, while exposing her beautifully formed, but somewhat bruised naked body. The rough handling she had received at the hands of our Yards had left some black and blue marks on her otherwise smooth white body.

When she bent down to reach for the jacket, the blanket that fell to the ground. I saw her two lovely, firm, full breasts, holding themselves erect.

With nervous hands she quickly put on the trousers and the jacket. She was so terrified that her trembling fingers could barely fasten the buttons. Until she had all the buttons fastened she was not very successful in her effort to hide her naked body from the staring eyes around her.

I stripped the Yard down to include his boots and socks which the girl also put on. Even though he had lost his clothes he considered himself fortunate. Mock told me later that he became quite a hero with the rest of the Yards. With them, the event grew with time and with each telling, until it finally blossomed to elevate a former non-entity to enviable social status. He proudly stayed naked while he told all who would stop and listen to him that the clothes, woman with hair, all same Sargy, wore, used to be his.

The girl stood with fear and confusion plainly evident on her face. She wanted to speak to me but I waved her to silence. To me she was a communist, and no better than those VC women with their damn black-and-white-checkered scarves, or the ones that had, with great pleasure, castrated captured Green Berets and stuffed their testicles into their mouths. They had sewed the soldiers' mouths shut with barbed wire, and with delight watched them suffer.

"Shut up and move with those men," I said. "Do as you are told or die. An enemy force is following us and we have to move. You have to keep up with my men. They will help you as much as they can."

I felt no sympathy whatsoever for her.

I turned my attention to the other American.

"You the other American?" I asked the bearded creep.

"Yes, Sir," he answered in a timid voice. "We belong to an ecumenical council that is not involved with your war."

A strong and offensive smell of urine surrounded him. I did not know nor did I care what he was trying to tell me. I had to move the column toward our objective.

I slashed the ropes off him. "If you want to live, move with those men." I motioned for the 4th Platoon's 60mm mortar men to take charge of him.

The captive staggered after the mortar men, making feeble efforts to push bushes away from his almost naked body. His underpants were barely hiding his private parts. His undershirt was in tatters, and his feet were bleeding. He did not seem aware of what was happening. He was like a person who was in shock.

"You two. You French?" I asked.

"Oui, Monsieur," they answered in unison. They looked tired, disheveled, and very scared. They had reason to be. At that time there was little secret about some Frenchmen in Vietnam, and where their sympathies lay.

"What were you two doing in the 5th NVA Division area?" I asked even though I knew the answer.

"We are neutral French and demand that you release us immediately."

"Answer me, damn you. What were you doing with the NVA?"

"We work for the World Council of Churches, same as the Americans."

"What the hell are you telling me! The NVA would be the last place for bible punchers to be. You carry information on our Army across the border to the NVA?"

"No, Sir, we are God-fearing people and just want to carry the word of God from the World..." I stopped them.

"You said that before. World Council of Churches? What the hell are they?"

Tom spoke up. "They is dat commie organization dat paid for Rap H. Brown and Angela Davis' defense and also sent weapons to Biafra."

"You sure, Tom?"

"Sure, I'm sure, Babe. And besides, man, dat creep admitted it. He said...ecume...commie organization. Den dey change it to some church organization. Let's do dem in."

"Ding,' I called. "You gots friends still be gots front teeth?"

"Yes be Sargy me be gots boo coo friends be gots front teets," he answered grinning from ear to ear.

I turned to the Frenchmen. "This Yard will escort you two back to the Laotian border."

"Thank you, Monsieur." They sounded happy and relieved looks showed on their faces. None of the Yards standing around us had smiles on their faces as Ding led the two Frenchmen away.

I ordered the North Vietnamese prisoner escorted to where the scouts held the NVA officers. Only a faint nagging discomfort pricked my conscience.

I moved the patrol at a brisk pace downward along the creek bottom. I had hated the delay while I spoke to the prisoners. I peeled back the green tape from my watch. It was 1300 hours.

"Already 1300 hours," I said to Mock. "Five hours till darkness. Move them faster, Captain, or we are in trouble."

I had to clear my brain to make a sound analysis of our tactical situation. Too many jumbled-up thoughts had started to crowd my mind as soon as I had looked into those soft, scared blue eyes of the girl. Her eyes had lost their luster, like the eyes of a deer shortly after a hunter's bullet had hit it, and just before it died.

"Damn...damn," I thought. "How can one round-eye make me think like a Campfire Girl? Perhaps it has been too long since I've seen a round-eyed woman." I felt like slapping my own face.

I estimated the enemy force to be three short hours behind us, and their scouts one dangerous hour away, pushing hard to make contact with us.

"Captain Mock!" I called. He quickly came to my side while chewing and trying to swallow a big mouthful of patrol ration, so that he could answer me.

"Get us six volunteers from among the ammo bearers. I want them stay behind, stop enemy scouts for short time. Extra meat and rice rations per man, if they stop the enemy scouts."

I did not want to weaken the four rifle platoons by using one of their squads and saw no reason to use an entire platoon for such a small but important assignment.

"Why no be use scouts?" he asked after a hard swallow to clear his mouth.

"We need scouts on Black Face. I'm not going to call for artillery or air. I want to move onto Black Face without NVA finding out. We need time on top of the mountain to take up defensive positions."

Sometimes I could speak fast and not use Yard English and Mock could follow what I said. If he did not, all he had to do was look at one of the interpreters who were always required to be close to me, and he would get a quick translation.

"Me unstand. Okay. Ammo bearer they be stop enmeny scout short time. Me tink NVA big force be come fast down creek."

"You're right there, Captain. They be come fast because they be boo coo pissed off, you, Mock buddy."

"Me?" he asked in puzzlement.

"Yes, you. You be mess-up nice shiny NVA guns and hamlet. Me, I incent. Me be tell NVA when me be gets chance. Also me be tell VC, NVA, you be boo coo kill many many VC."

He smiled. "Yea Sargy. You be tell NVA. Den you be pull grenade pin. NVA boo coo blief you." We both laughed.

Six Yards with M-16 rifles dropped back and hid themselves in an advantageous firing position from which they could cover what I believed to be the enemy's avenue of approach. I expected them each to empty a

30-round clip into the NVA or their scouts, then run as fast as their short legs would carry them back to the safety of our main body. Their action could stop the enemy long enough to give me precious minutes more to instigate deceptive tactics.

My tactical plan was to consolidate my position on top of Black Face, as was required by my mission. It was reasonable for me to assume that the enemy would continue toward our camp thinking that I had headed there, too.

The next day, I expected them to realize their mistake and double back to Black Face. They would then bottle us up between those units of theirs, which I believed were at that time heading toward Black Face from the opposite direction.

I further assumed that there were no enemy units on Black Face, but if there were, I did not want to make contact with a strong NVA force closing in on us from another direction.

They had to be stalled long enough to let darkness set in, before they came to where we changed direction.

While we were on the creek bottom our progress was good, but once out, and within the mass of entangled undergrowth, the pace became painstakingly slow.

My men followed the usual precautions and destroyed most of the signs of our trail, even though I knew that the enemy would not follow in our path for fear of ambush, booby traps, or both. This, too, I hoped, would give me additional time before they closed in on us. Every minute was important.

I continued to further analyze my situation, while proceeding slowly toward the leading elements. They were two hours from the summit of the mountain.

I wondered what had taken place at our camp. With many Yards out on patrol, it would not have been unreasonable to assume that Group had acted fast and replaced most of my men with Yards from other camps. That would quell what animosity either the Yards or the South Vietnamese would otherwise have displayed. Mass transferring and reshuffling prior to the ARVN acting were what I expected Group to do. That was why I had ordered another patrol out.

I refused to have my mind dwell for any length of time on the problems that I personally was going to have when I returned to Group. They flashed through my mind one after the other without analysis.

Ordering government meat to be delivered in an unconventional manner was one problem; eleven, yes, damn it, eleven ARVN soldiers
accounted for but dead; combat operation into Laos; wiping out a hamlet
of civilians; World Council of Churches — there lay my biggest problem —
those Americans. I realized that they could tell about the French and North
Vietnamese prisoners.

Without them to carry the word back to Group, I could lie myself out
of things. But, with them there, I knew I had troubles.

With satisfaction I thought of them meeting up with an accident. Yes,
that would be the best. Then I remembered those lovely blue eyes, and I
knew Group would have to do without some of my lies.

One other way out of my problem also presented itself. The old
standby. The one that would solve all. How easy it would be for me to walk
into an enemy bullet. My mind rested on that thought. Why worry at all?
I was far from the safety of our own troops and then, too, before I did get
back, I was sure to add a few more transgressions to the already full slate.

I approached the leading elements of our patrol just as the final report
came from our scouts.

"No enemy on Black Face."

"Dats a relief, man. Wit Charlie on our ass," remarked Tom.

"I delayed them again. They're not going to know where we are until
early tomorrow," I told Tom and Doc.

Doc had just joined me. I could tell that he had something on his mind.
"Okay Doc, what is on your mind?" He looked a little tired.

"Tony, we have six Yards that need Medevac. Three were wounded,
one with snake bite, one with a busted leg — he fell down a cliff -and the
other one has some kind of serious stomach disorder. Can you do it?"

I turned to Tom. "Message to Booby Trap. Objective secured at 1600
hours — Stop — Request Medevac for six Yards — Stop — Ready for
ammo resupply — Stop — Small arms stop — 60 mike Mike — Stop —
Three point five — Stop — Ten each LAWS — Stop — Hand grenades —
Stop — Request info on enemy my area during night — End of message."

"Okay boss. On the way." Again I marveled at the speed with which
Tom could encode a message and tap it out in Morse code. He was truly
the best radio operator I had ever known.

"You said nothing about the prisoners we took and the Americans,"
said Doc.

"Oh I forgot, but they'll also be on the choppers." I lied. Tom wanted to say something but I waved him to silence. Doc noticed it, but did not say anything about it.

I called a runner, and sent him to the squad that was with the two Americans, with orders for them to get up the mountain ASAP. I made sure that Doc heard me give the order.

Then I turned to Ding and whispered, "Two American and prisoners, you be see they no be get here until choppers be left. I no be like they be get on chopper."

Ding understood perfectly. As usual he read my mind. In seconds he was away from us, then I wondered if by chance he misunderstood, and thought that I wanted them all done in. Well, I did not have time to worry about small things.

The sun was sinking fast, with a clean, cool breeze sweeping through the trees. We cleared out of the brush to move onto the area where the air strike and our artillery had chopped all vegetation into black stumps and cinders.

The entire top of Black Face Mountain was burned to a crisp with only charred stumps sticking out of the ground between shell and bomb craters. We found it extremely difficult to climb over the burned out stumps and crawl through craters. Some of the craters had fine ashes six feet deep inside of them.

"What a pounding this mountain took," I said to no one in particular as I lingered for a moment, roaming my gaze over the carnage that was wreaked on the mountain.

Group had acted fast, realizing the short period of daylight left during which to re-supply me, and having anticipated my needs, they were ready with an airdrop package when my message was received.

The sun was just ducking behind the mountain tops far to the west when the first Medevac helicopter swooped down through our green smoke marker onto the bright orange panel my men had spread over the ashes to mark the landing zone for the choppers.

I stood aside and watched with pride the true professionals going to work: our U.S. Army Medics. They literally scooped up the wounded into the helicopter, dropped 20 Mermite cans of food, ten Jerry cans of precious fresh water, and many boxes of ammunition.

Friendly arms waved to us as the three helicopters, one by one, jerked upward and engulfed us in black swirling ashes. Dirt and flying cinders scattered all around us. The choppers were in the air again and on the way back to the C-Team that handled our logistics. The entire re-supply and Medevac took less than five minutes, leaving all of us smeared with black ashes.

The first person who spoke was Doc.

"Tony," he said in a tone full of dismay and incrimination. It made me think that he had given up trying to understand what I was up to on that patrol. "you should have evacuated the Americans and the two French, as well."

"Didn't the Americans get on the choppers?" I asked, faking puzzlement.

"No, man, dey is still climbing up de mountain side," volunteered Tom at once. He seemed to enjoy Doc's discomfort.

All I could say was that I did tell them to hurry up for the air evacuation.

"Doc, I did try to get the Americans up here in time. You heard me give the order to the runner. Not my fault if they did not make it."

"And the Frenchmen, were they too, told about the Medevac?" Doc asked with a dejected look on his face.

Tom answered him. "No need to, College Boy, Ding took care of dem." Tom seemed to enjoy himself antagonizing Doc.

"You're joking?"

"No joke, man, dey is frogs working for de NVA. Dat make dem free game."

"Being French or working for the NVA?" Doc asked.

"Eider or both. Whats de difference, man. Dis aint no Sunday school picnic. Heah, we play fo keeps."

"Darn it, Tony. You can't just sentence people to death at will. You are beginning to play God."

"Who say he can't do as he want to?" Tom answered and was obviously enjoying himself being able to upset Doc, but I knew he might very well go too far. Especially when he continued.

"You should join de Campfire Girls and take up bird watching like I say befo to you."

"Okay, you two. That's enough. And who says I did them in. I merely sent them back into Laos where they came from," I said sternly.

"With Ding?" asked Doc.

"That's enough, Doc!"

Tom also acted as if he was going to say something and I pointed a finger at him.

"You too, Tom. Both of you shut your mouths, unless you want me to do it for you."

Doc picked up his medical kit and with a sidelong look at me, headed down the mountain toward where I saw some Yards struggling with the Americans. Behind Doc followed his train of assistants. I knew he would bring up the subject of the missing French again, but only when Tom was not around.

I was thankful for the hot food and the knowledge that our wounded were receiving the necessary care. It had been an agonizing march up the mountainside for them and the bearers. They were half dragged and half carried through the brush. When they were in the area where bombs and shells had exploded, their progress had been especially painful and slow.

We did not have regular stretchers, but improvised with two rifles. The Yards would fasten nylon jungle blankets between the rifles to make a practical sling. Two Yards on each side would carry the sling with the wounded soldier.

The welcome food, which Booby Trap had ordered for us, consisted of an ample supply of spiced glutinous rice and fried beef chunks with lemongrass and coriander leaf added to give them a pleasant taste. One full Mermite can was brought for Tom, Doc, Mock, and me. Of course, the socially-conscious Ding and the fast learning Mo could not lower themselves to eat with the common Yards.

The entire command was greedily digging into food cans and stuffing their mouths full, not unlike the small vulnerable monkeys who, through necessity, stuffed their cheeks full of food just in case they had to run for safety before they could get their share of the food.

The need for internal and perimeter security was forgotten. I shook my head in resignation at their unmilitary behavior. Even Mock was bending over a Mermite can, completely oblivious to the fact that we had just barely occupied our objective, and as far as the enemy was concerned, were still to be dealt with.

I saw Doc and some of his followers struggle up the mountain side toward us. They had the American man wrapped up in a jungle blanket between two rifles, and were carrying him as if he were dead. I looked at the girl. She appeared to be in an extreme state of exhaustion and just barely able to keep up with what I considered a disgracefully slow pace.

"Someone must have shot the creep," I remarked to Tom.

"No such luck, man. He's still breadin." Tom answered, his disgust plainly showing. "He just quit on de Yards. Tought you ordered de Yards to do dem in if'n dey don't keep up wid dem?"

"Not the American, I didn't. Only the NVA prisoners. And Tom, let up on Doc about the Frenchmen. Let's play it down in front of him. He is different from you and me."

"Okay, Boss. Whatever you say man, but dem two," he pointed at the Americans. "Dey is gonna cause problems if'n we let dem back into de real world, man. You tink about it."

"Okay, Babe, I'll think about it. But it is not like doing a Frenchy or a North Viet or a VC in."

We were eating with our hands directly out of the cans. The lids were kept shut as much as possible to retain some heat. Our Army Mermite cans were well enough insulated to retain their heat for hours as long as the lids stayed closed. I wanted Doc to get the benefit of hot food when he joined us.

"Hurry up, Doc. Hot chow," I called out to him.

The American creep was laid down next to us. The four Yards who had carried him looked beat. I nodded my thanks to them. In return I received four of their ever-ready smiles. Two of them had no front teeth. To them I motioned with my finger at the bare gums. Broader smiles followed, and I noticed that those two immediately shook off their weary looks.

"Sit down, Doc." I also motioned for the girl to sit down near the Mermite can.

"Water, please," she whispered barely loud enough for me to hear her. It sounded like a last desperate plea for life. I gave her one of my canteens after I had removed the screw top. She took it with hesitation and trembling hands. She was obviously very thirsty, and drank long and deeply.

She handed the canteen back to me. Her hands were still shaking. "Thank you," she said meekly.

"Have some food." I held the Mermite can lid up for her. When she hesitated, I added gently, "Yes, with your hands. Grab a handful of rice in one hand and a chunk of meat in the other. Don't worry about your hands being dirty. They'll be clean by the time you've had enough to eat. Fill yourself up. We have plenty, and there's no telling when we'll eat hot food again."

Gingerly she did as I had told her. Doc made the creep sit up and gave him a piece of meat and a handful of rice.

"You mean he is not dead or wounded, Doc?" Tom sounded disgusted. "Why de hell you carry him Doc? Can't de creep walk?"

Doc did not answer, but he showed his annoyance to the man. "Sit up, darn you, and get your own food. I'm not going to feed you like you're some baby. Because of you, the two of you were not evacuated. You missed the choppers, darn you."

I was watching the girl. Although dressed in unflattering jungle fatigues, torn in places to show white, soft parts of her body, her perfectly shaped figure was not hidden from me. What I could not see, my imagination provided. She was aware that I was watching her. I detected defiance slowly creeping into her bearing.

"This one, I'd better be careful with," I thought. I felt that she was just a little different from the type of women I'd known in the past. But then, all round-eyed women seemed just a little different to men in Vietnam after they had been in that country for awhile.

No one spoke until we had had enough to eat. Some food remained in the can. Ding and Mo were sitting a few yards from us. Somehow they had procured a Mermite can lid and had heaped more food than they could eat on it and removed themselves from the rest of the Yards.

I drew Doc and Tom's attention to them. "They consider themselves better that the common everyday Yards."

Doc smiled.

"That Ding is getting too big for his boots. Yesterday I heard him explain to an ammo bearer that he was next in charge to Sargy, Tony. I laughed when the ammo bearer apparently did not believe him and Ding grabbed him by the neck. I take it that the ammo bearer now believes that Ding is indeed the next in command."

"You should have aksed him what we or Mock is doin here," Tom said. "I bet he would have said, 'Me no be tell damn dumb Yard evrytin. Sargy, Tom, Doc, Tony all be know dats be nuff know. No Sargy, Doc, me I no be tell Yards all'." We laughed at Tom's mimicry of Ding.

"What is your name?" I asked the girl.

"Catherine, Catherine Friem," she answered softly.

"How about him? He your husband?" asked Tom in a threatening manner. She started to speak but the man spoke instead.

"No, we're not related. We merely work together for the National Council of Ch...."

"Yeah...Churches. You said dat before, punk. I'm aksin de girl. You shut up or I'll slit your throat." Tom turned back to the girl. "He your husband?"

"No." She looked at me. "What is this? You sound like Americans. Soldiers, I take it. Green Berets...and all these awful looking little dark people with hand grenades hanging from them. What are you doing in these mountains? Murdering all those innocent people in Laos this morning!"

No one answered her. She continued. "I am ashamed to be an American if we allow men like you to run wild."

"She has you pegged right, Tom. She was looking at you when she said that. You also look wild to me. Always did, and a little strange, too," Doc said jokingly, and smiled at Tom.

Tom just ignored Doc's remarks.

"Yeah, murdering, you say. Well, leastwise we murder dem dats stay awake at night lookin for ways to do us in. You and dat church of yours. You help dem NVA? How much money you give em? Maybe weapons, too."

Tom had worked himself into a dangerous mood. He did not care to have the two of them near us. To him, as to me and Doc, they represented another world. A world that we dared not mix with the one that we had to survive in.

"You are wrong..." the man started to say.

Tom had his dagger out and held it against the man's neck."One more sound out of you, creep, and I slice your neck in two. You speak only when I let you. Understand?"

Doc and I both let out a sigh of relief when Tom sat down again.

"That was close, Mister," I said, "better do as Tom says."

I turned to Tom. "Take it easy, Babe. I'm as perturbed about them as you are, but let's think things out first before..."

Tom finished the sentence for me. "Yeah, before we do dem both in."

"Let me do my own talking, damn you, Tom," I snapped back at him. "Any one gets done in right now, it's liable to be you." The girl had tears in her eyes. The strange world she was suddenly thrown into was more than she could cope with. Her tears ran clean rivulets down her ash-smeared cheeks. I felt like saying something kind to her.

"Cathy or Catherine, we are soldiers and we do what we do best, and that is making war. The way we go about it, I don't expect anyone to approve. Least of all the enemy or a member of your World Council of Churches."

She started to say something but I interrupted her. Barely enough day-light remained for her to see me waving her to silence.

"Do what you can to help yourself while you are with us. Tomorrow I'll try to get you out by helicopter. For tonight we should be safe from enemy attack but as soon as their scouts find us, we can expect incoming rockets and artillery. Tomorrow we will have to face the NVA. In the interim, I don't want to be your judge, but I can tell you, that as far as the three of us are concerned, for you to be in the enemy camp is treasonous regardless of what you consider a valid reason."

"I would like to explain," she said timidly.

"Explain what? asked Tom. "Explain dat your contact wit de enemy is helpin us? Just like dat commie bitch, Jane Fonda?"

"Well...not really, but we were only interested in gathering facts."

She sounded uncertain. She tried to wipe her tears away with her jacket sleeve, only to make a bigger mess of her face.

"And what did you find out, Miss Friem?" asked Doc.

"We...I mean, I found out that they, the North Vietnamese, are very interested in finding a peaceful solution to it all. No killings, just peaceful solutions that could be worked out over a conference table. They are not at all our enemy, really. All they want is for the U.S. soldiers to go home and the South Vietnamese soldiers to stop attacking them."

She sounded as if she really believed what she told us.

"Motherfucker!" said Tom. He jumped up and walked away. His words trailed behind him, "She just fixed it so as I don't sleep tonight. Here in Sout Vietnam, NVA pouring out of..."

The rest of what Tom said was lost to us.

A small number of Yards were creating a tumult near our eastern perimeter.

"I go be see what dey be matter damn Yards," said Mock. He disap-peared into the darkness, which by that time had completely blanketed the mountain top. With the darkness also came a hush which left each of us with our own thoughts.

In a few minutes Mock was back. He settled himself down next to me. "Recon patrol, they be bring back four our damn scout. NVA they be do em in. Sew mouth full balls same they be do always they be catch us."

They made it especially easy for us to find the bodies. Perhaps they intended their grim actions to frighten us off. Little did they know that it served to further stoke our already burning hatred for them.

With darkness having enveloped us, conversation automatically changed to whispers, as if voluntarily admitting subordination to the perils which surrounded us.

"Cathy, you can please yourself. Doc, Tom, or the Yards. That one jungle blanket we gave you will not keep you warm during the night. It is going to get very cold and it is necessary for you to remain completely still all night.

"One way we can detect the enemy, should their scouts penetrate our defenses, is by movement and noises. Anything that moves or makes a sound, regardless of how slight, is hostile to us, and we deal with it. There will be a few Yards sitting close to me all night. Anything that they see or hear they fire a poisoned arrow into, or use their bayonet on. So, seek some body heat to help you through the night. Extra blankets we have not."

She did not answer, nor did I expect her to. I wrapped my blanket around myself and settled down for the night. The stars came out, crisp and clear, and the air smelled sweet. Although my mind was troubled, I could not help but feel a sense of well-being.

The day's action had been most successful. The enemy had suffered heavy losses. I had only eight...or was it nine, killed in action, and only six wounded and hurt badly enough to warrant their medical evacuation.

The enemy had suffered the loss of material and manpower and their morale had been dealt a stinging blow. What their next move would be I did not dwell on. Even without the information that Group and my scouts filtered to me, I felt certain that they would come out of their safe haven from across the border and seek out my patrol. They had the terrain and the close proximity of the border to their advantage. I smiled with satisfaction as my mind wandered on through pleasant thoughts.

That I had to stand and fight was a foregone conclusion. If I did consider a much larger operation, with my patrol but a small part of it, then I saw the beginning of one hell of a battle developing the next day. Should that happen, many of my earlier objections, such as that of our Yards being dangerously exploited, would vanish and be replaced with jubilant self-importance.

I had no fear for what might develop the next day. I was in an area where the full support of our armed forces could be brought in for direct and indirect support of our mission.

I made a mental note to order a reconnaissance patrol out with the first sign of daylight. The area of the slate creek from which we had come earlier had assumed new importance to me. It was our only avenue of escape if things developed badly for us. Without considering other options, I knew that I would have to fight my way back to our camp when Booby Trap gave the order for us to disengage ourselves from the enemy.

It was further imperative that I vacate the eastern edge of Black Face with as much stealth as possible. My defensive plan depended on the enemy believing that I had dug in deep for defense. This I reasoned would be a normal situation for them to expect, especially on the northeast military slope. This forward slope, close to the top of the mountain, gave the best field of fire.

My best action, I assumed, was for me to spread my men out thin near that area, for that was where I expected most of their indirect fire to be concentrated.

I did not underestimate their available firepower. The guns that we destroyed, I believed, were but a small part of their total available indirect firepower. Other guns were in close proximity to the 5th NVA Infantry and infantry prior to the assault on our position. I was well aware that the communists had learned from Napoleon to rely heavily on the use of artillery.

It was not long after the surrounding mountains were covered by complete darkness and the night owls were stirring that the first expected shuffle toward me took place. First one Yard and then another, Mo and Ding, of course, moved tightly against me. Mo took one of my hands and held it in both of his. He seemed to seek the human kindness which his childhood had known so little of.

That blissful, long-cultivated twilight-zone slumber of mine engulfed me. I seemed to float a few feet above the scorched surface of Black Face. Each defensive position became a fleeting picture before my closed eyes. I pictured fields of fire, natural obstacles, clean and dirty weapons, ammunition belts for the machine guns, back-blast areas for the rocket launchers, and an endless array of items that needed the attention of Mock and me at the first sign of light.

I rested. The stars smiled down on us with friendly twinkles. Unlike the harsh sun, which sees all, the stars would always smile for they could not bridge the vast span of darkness to see the many blood-smeared bayonets nor smell the closeness of death that resulted from our nocturnal actions.

How grateful I was to know that my inner thoughts and all my actions did not lie bare for the world to see. What peace remained inside of me was there only as long as I could hide my deeds and inner feelings. If all were known, condemnation would be my only reward.

When my mind started to dwell on the things that I had done, a gentle gray veil would voluntarily move in and protectively obscure the ugly details from me. Some other person, not me, was guilty. I was absolved and standing on the side line as an innocent observer.

That strange and effective gray veil, behind which I often hid, like the coward I was, started during the Normandy invasion when I walked ashore at Omaha Beach with the 116th Regiment of the U.S. 29th Infantry Division, Maryland's famous Blue and Gray.

It also stood me in good stead when we fought a retrograde action against the Chinese from the Yalu River to south of Seoul. Once, after a terrible battle on the Imjum River where Chinese dead were stacked ten feet high, I was ordered to give an after-action report. It took me some time before I could even remember the battle.

I was just about to drop off to sleep when I heard a rustle near by. Ding and Mo rolled away from me and waited with bayonets at the ready. I felt a hand reach out for me and I almost slashed out with my bayonet. I jumped on Ding and held his arm. He, too, was just about to swing with his bayonet at the dark form moving close to me.

"Come among us," I whispered softly to Cathy and I drew her close to me. She was trembling all over from fear and the cold. She emitted soft moans that made me think that she was in shock.

The aftermath of the day's happenings were surfacing. Up until then, I thought she had stood up rather well for someone like her. Perhaps things had just piled up too fast for her to digest mentally.

Under the jungle fatigues she wore nothing. The nightgown she had had on when our Yards grabbed her was in shreds when I had handed her the fatigues. When I held her close to me I could feel her soft body shiver with cold.

Ding threw another blanket over us, then he and Mo moved a few feet away from us. Slowly Cathy became still while holding me tightly. Warmth crept back into her body. Then she fell asleep to have her tormented thoughts drift away.

While she slept, my hands felt beneath her jacket. The soft smooth feel shook me out of the combat area, and the virile strength and health I've been damned with carried me away.

I loosened my belt and pushed my pants down to my knees. Then I tripped her belt buckle and slipped her fatigue trousers down to where I could reach them with my boot and push her pants all the way down and over her feet. Still she slept.

Without waking her I spread her legs slowly, lifted her jacket and felt her breasts. Then I went on top of her and entered her. She woke with a start and screamed, but I had my hand over her mouth. Only a muffled sound escaped. There was nothing that she could do to stop me.

Immediately I felt that she was still a virgin and that thought excited me even more. I held myself deep inside her and lay still while I slowly removed my hand from her mouth. She moaned softly while I tenderly kissed her mouth.

She tried to push me off but could not. She was weak and I was too strong. She struggled in silence for a few moments and then gave in. She seemed sapped of all will or perhaps my kindness relaxed her.

Nature did not intend for a woman to suffer completely under the dominance of a man without some reward to herself. She climaxed and dug her nails into me. All too soon I was done. Her tears wet my face but she continued to hold me tight.

The stars came out and glimmered. A soft breeze gently kissed the distant treetops that silently quivered and swayed in the dark. A kindly blushing moon, that earlier had played hide-and-seek among the clouds, now lingered behind one a while.

The dawn found her still in my arms. Slowly I disengaged myself from her. I wrapped my blanket around her. She continued to sleep soundly with her sweet innocent beauty barely discernable in the early light.

She was no longer a stranger. It seemed as if she were someone I had known all my life. Huddled up in two camouflage nylon blankets, she rested under a gray sky, oblivious to having stumbled into harm's way. What a shame, I thought, she'll wake and be shocked by the ash-covered, barbaric surroundings of Black Face mountain, and the knowledge of what I did to her.

How strange and incredible were the events that had thrown us together. I felt guilty for what I had done to her, but what chance would that single act have to prick my already overloaded conscience?

"The line forms on the right," I said softly to myself.

Like two faithful watchdogs, Ding and Mo also gathered up their weapons and rolled their blankets into combat packs in readiness to follow me wherever I should go. The ammo bearers would later relieve them of their combat packs to make them free for quick movements.

The distant rumble of air strikes and artillery shelling sharpened my mind into a fast summation of the situation and what courses of action lay open for us. It seemed to me that a large operation was underway about 20 miles to the north and east of us.

I knew that the ARVN 23rd Infantry and some of our Air Mobile units from the 101st Division were in that area. I did not know if our patrol was part of that operation and could hardly believe that we were, since I had not been briefed on any operation other than that of the patrol. I woke Tom and Doc.

"Anything new come in?"

"A few reports from dat large enemy unit dat was followin' us. Scouts estimate it to be a NVA battalion. Dey saw Chinese-made heavy machine guns, bangalore torpedoes, and satchel charges. Looks like dey is heading for Ba Cat," Tom said sleepily.

It did not look as if he had had a good night's rest. Maybe that World Council of Churches did rob him of sleep.

"Get the information to Booby Trap. Specially about the bangalore torpedoes. They plan to blast holes through our camp's barbed wire and mine field," I ordered.

I smiled at the thought that maybe they'd blow those damn long-neck geese to hell, too. I did not know that Tom's assistant had not sent the message to Booby Trap that I had ordered regarding the MIKE Force. That force was always kept in readiness at Group to re-enforce A-Camps. I never did find out why he failed to transmit my message. If I had known that at the time, I would have moved to interfere with the enemy battalion that was heading toward our camp.

"De way I see it, we is gonna find trouble on our way back to camp." Tom was wideawake.

"Looks like it, Babe, but what is new? We're practically intact, ammo resupply and all." I was in good spirits, having slept well and...Cathy... My mind refused to dwell on her.

Mock approached me. "Me be smell hostipal. VC hostipal me tink."

"I also smell eter," said Tom, putting on his load-bearing harness to follow me.

"Message from scout they be see boo coo enmeny tree mile away. Dey be come Black Face," Mock said, pointing to the north of us where he believed the enemy would approach.

"It is as we expected, Captain. All ammo distributed...passed around, and did we get what we asked for?"

"Yes be, Sargy. Ammo okay now, so be water. Yards now be ready NVA."

"If I can help it, we are not going to fight them this time. We are at a disadvantage here."

Before I was finished speaking Tom was facing me.

"What you mean, man? Let's get dem. We spend monts lookin for dem and now we got dem you want to run." Tom sounded perplexed.

"Right, Babe. That's the way I see it right now. Think, man... we're sitting in the middle of an entire NVA division. If you don't believe me, just wait till sunrise and see their artillery and rockets raining down on us. Our mission is to occupy Black Face. Okay, we did, and we will remain on this mountain until Booby Trap orders us off.

"But I'm moving the men away from the enemy's avenue of approach. You and me, we stay here. When the right time comes we attack them. I want our air and artillery to get at them first. Message to Booby Trap."

Tom took out his notebook.

"Time — 0500 — Stop — Observe enemy battalion GS 105155 — Stop — Moving southeast — Stop — Expect contact with enemy at 1100 — Stop — Request air recon — End of message. Send it in the clear. I want the enemy and every one else to hear it."

I signaled for Mock to follow me. Daylight was fast spreading a ghostly glow over Black Face.

"Get a squad to find out where that ether smell is coming from," I ordered the 4th Platoon Leader who had joined us.

"Me be know where hostipal be. Also be tunnel," he answered.

Doc and Tom followed as we made our way through the many shell holes. Some of them had ashes many feet deep inside of them. Into one such shell hole I followed the 4th Platoon Leader. To the side of the shell hole there was a big gaping black hole, and a strong smell of ether came from within.

"Doc, back away from this crater. Get me four scouts, and the rest of you clear the area," I ordered.

I expected the usual dangers which were present with enemy underground positions. Some fanatic VC or NVA could make his last desperate stand. I had to clear the area fast. A suicidal situation might develop for us if I had to fight from bunker to bunker while at the same time repelling an enemy assault.

I stripped down to my shorts, retaining only my .45-caliber pistol and a flashlight. Four scouts, Ding leading them, came to me on the double, and we slid down the black hole. I caught a glimpse of Mo, but when he saw me looking at him he closed his eyes, thinking that I could not see him, and ducked behind Doc.

We encountered a very strong smell of dried blood and rotting human flesh. The nauseating stench seemed to float like a fog along the light beams of our flashlights. Blood smeared bandages lay scattered where we crawled through a narrow tunnel and entered into a large opening some 20 feet further along the tunnel. There we found an underground hospital ward.

My flashlight, and those of the scouts, stabbed through the darkness. What I saw at a glance brought down across my conscious mind that familiar blessed gray veil which had long since become the greater part of my valor, but not before the flashlights had illuminated a veritable chamber of horrors.

On makeshift cots dispersed throughout the spacious chamber lay war-wasted bodies. Some were in advanced stages of decomposition. Others had outstretched arms begging for help. Pitiful, weak, pain-filled wails filled my ears in pathetic tones.

I recognized what once had been a woman crawling toward me. Where her eyes had been, a mass of maggots crawled. In one hand she clutched her dirty blood-smeared black-and-white-checkered scarf.

"Oh my God!" I screamed. Cold shivers spread though my body. "No more, no more war, I've had enough," flashed though my mind.

Before the gray wall descended completely over my mind, I saw one of my combat-hardened scouts vomit and then back away from a crawling mutilated human being, who, in agony and waning life, begged for water.

Orange flames split through the darkness. Loud echoing explosions ripped the foul air apart. Again and again my right hand kicked back and I was distantly aware that .45-caliber shells tore through the many moving bodies inside the hospital ward.

Other .45 caliber shells were still splitting the repugnant air below when I crawled out into the clean air above to stand among the many Yards who were attracted by the shooting from down below.

"What happened?" asked Doc, looking at the smoking pistol still in my right fist. Tom reached out and took it from me.

Looking at my pistol Tom said, "Your clip is still full, Tony. You did not shoot down der." I wondered if Tom was in my nightmare or I in his.

"Helicoppiter!" shouted a Yard close to us. I looked up and there, above rifle range, were two circling helicopters. I could see in the helicopters' doorways a number of cameras with large telescopic lenses trained on us by persons other than soldiers. There were no riflemen sitting at the open doors with their M-16s trained downward.

The sun had cleared the distant mountaintop and bright rays were bouncing off the black ashes around us. The air was still and cool. From where I stood, almost level with the clouds, I could see across many miles of dense jungle. Tom pointed at the helicopters.

"Tony, see. Civilians in dose choppers, man. News reporters and high brass waiting for de shellin to start." He laughed loudly. "Oh boy, dey is gonna be pissed off wit you, Babe. Dem guns you done in was to pound us just about now." Tom was enjoying himself.

"Surely not. It's too incredible," said Doc. "When we first talked about it I was joking when I mentioned that it would be like Nui Coto."

Doc motioned for his helpers to go with him down into the underground hospital. The four scouts who had gone down into the VC hospital with me and Ding had rejoined me.

For some unknown reason, Tom was still elated about the helicopters that were circling overhead.

"Dey is not comin near us. Dey is just waitin for dem NVA shellin. Dey is not talkin to us on de radio, man. Can you believe dis? Dey is gonna write some headlines about us. Big headlines tellin de world how de bad NVA use Laos. We is gonna be movie stars."

"Okay, okay, Tom. You sure are some talking nigger. We have things to do. And any of the POWs we sent them could have told them about the enemy using Laos," I said, knowing that Group did not get the same results from enemy prisoners as Mock and Ding.

"They don't believe your prisoners. That's why you don't send them prisoners any more," Doc said over his shoulder as he went down into the shell hole. He evinced more discontent by his attitude than he did with his words.

"Anytin you don't like de way Tony take care of prisoners, college boy?" Tom sounded argumentative. Doc ignored him.

I looked at Doc as he went into the tunnel and I could not clearly remember what there was down there. It took a few seconds before I vaguely recalled the bedlam and the smell of ether and gunpowder.

I gave the order to move all but the 4th Platoon off the mountain to about 1,000 yards down the western slope. Many reports on enemy movement had started to come in through Booby Trap from U.S. Air Force observers. My scouts, too, had been very fortunate in collecting the necessary combat information I needed. I saw high above us, circling, a U.S. Air Force high-flying RC-135.

I knew that plane was clearly observing all that took place below it, and the information it gained was being instantly transmitted to a communication center and then evaluated and disseminated down to Group. If it was of interest to us, and it received Booby Trap's blessing, we would get it almost as soon as the aircraft reported it.

Something strange was taking place. Too many messages came over Tom's radio, almost too fast for him to copy.

Tom hollered out to me.

"Eh Babe, sometin I don't understand, man. Too much friendly traffic cluttering de air. Some of ma incomin messages are garbled. Sound as if de entire U.S. Army and or de 23rd ARVN Infantry is on de move somewhere."

My mind was working fast as I scrambled over stumps and through ash-filled craters to follow the main body off the mountain top. A large enemy force, estimated at battalion strength was approaching us from the north. This force was expected to hit us at noon that day. Our Army Cobra gunships had spotted them and were working them over with mini-guns and rockets.

It was a pity that the terrain made it impossible for the gunships to inflict more than nominal damage. The mountainous area gave the Cobras only short fields of fire and the heavy foliage cut visibility for the pilots.

To the south of us, another sizable enemy force was moving some-where, presumably against our camp, but I could not be sure that they had not doubled back and were at that moment climbing up the side of Black Face at our backs. If not, they could be sitting in ambush for us, knowing that we would have to retreat in their direction soon. Judging from the reported size of that unit, they might very well be capable of doing both simultaneously.

East of us, a dense black jungle stretched for 20 miles through isolated Viet Cong strongholds which nobody had ever been able to assess cor-rectly. I was not going to lead my men through that area. Command and control would vanish within the first mile if I did.

Then came reports from aerial reconnaissance indicating that the slate-covered creek at our rear was free of enemy. I had earlier ordered a recon patrol to the creek, and I was hoping to receive a confirmation on the aer-ial recon report. I dared not blunder in that direction. It was the only direc-tion I could go without running into a heavy enemy concentration of infantry. I felt relieved that the air observers did not report a threat to us in that direction.

"Tom," I called.

He was busy writing down messages which he handed to a runner to bring to me. I had rejoined Cathy and the creep. Our ammo bearers were gathered around them. Tom gave me the signal that he was free to hear me.

"Message to Booby Trap. Request air photo intel report on grid squares 10711518, 10721519, and 10731520."

The grid squares covered the slate creek and a distance into Laos. I was preparing options for us.

"Tom, tell them I need the readout ASAP."

He nodded, while his right hand beat a fast tattoo on his signal key. Communications were excellent since we had received fresh batteries for his PRC-25 radio the evening before.

It was 30 minutes after sunrise when the first enemy shell exploded on Black Face. It was a 120mm white phosphorous shell used by the enemy to zero in on us. I looked at Mock.

"Mock, old buddy, NVA be gots forward observer somewhere he looks at us, you be think scouts be find?"

He shook his head.

"Me be know white shell. But boo coo be jungle. Scout he be take long, long time find. Nudder shell be come soon."

He acted as if he were responsible for the dense jungle and thus our predicament. It would be a miracle if our scouts located the forward observer before he had completed shifting fire on us.

My Yards were moving fast down the mountain to the new positions. I ordered the ammo bearers to move the two Americans down with them, but a few minutes later, while I was busy getting dressed, I spotted Cathy close to me. She had her eyes riveted on me.

I could not tell if her attitude was hostile or confused.

I had delayed getting dressed while Ding was looking for some water for me to clean myself. There were no cans of water left so I went ahead and put my clothes on over the dirt from the underground hospital. When I was back in uniform I motioned for her to follow me.

I took her by the arm. "Soon now, the enemy will start shelling us in earnest, and within the hour this mountain will become a madhouse. Before the day is over, you will have become a combat veteran, and if you play your cards right you can fake a syndrome for a free ride through life."

The smile I gave her did not faze her. I felt guilty and wanted to be kind to her, but my words just did not sound right to me.

"Can this horrible nightmare be stopped?" She sounded serious but pathetic. Her lips were trembling and white. "Many will die uselessly, and back home we spend millions fighting capital punishment, while here, with one order, more men are condemned to die in minutes than are sentenced to death by all the courts in the world."

While she spoke she started to laugh, with glazed eyes wide open and darting around her.

"Cathy! Cathy! Control yourself. I did not start this damn mess," I apologized, feeling helpless to handle this new twist in her behavior. "And...and I am sorry about last night."

That did it. She stopped crying, rubbed her eyes dry on her sleeves, or rather smeared more ashes over her face. After that I would gladly have had her resume her former hysterics. Her soft blue eyes seemed to convey a mixture of hate and hurt.

"All I want is to get away from you and this horrible inhuman world of yours," she said very softly and with bitter emphasis on each word.

Enemy heavy artillery rounds were coming in then. The first ten rounds struck the top of Black Face with a terrible jolt. We were not far enough away from the main impact area for safety. I grabbed Cathy and threw her over my shoulder. I almost had to grab her in the air and bring her down, she was so light, just like a Yard, and I had used too much strength.

With her, I ran down the western slope where my men were starting to dig in for defense. We had to move 500 yards before we gained an area that had not been destroyed by shells. The area did offer some conceal- ment and cover for the next phase of the operation, which was to deny the enemy a chance to dig in on Black Face.

I set her down among the 1st Platoon. The 1st and the 3rd Platoons were what I wanted to use for the counterattack. I knew that I had better stop the enemy before they could consolidate and reorganize themselves into defensive positions on top of Black Face. If I was successful in that, I would get the chance to get away from the enemy — when and if I got the order from Booby Trap to do so.

The enemy was showing tenacity, determination and a strange disre- gard for sound tactical doctrine by venturing farther and farther away from the safety of Laos. They were exposing themselves more and more to our superior firepower.

Their actions caused strong apprehensions in me, especially in the face of increased U.S. Army intervention. Our Cobra gunships were joined by a few Phantoms from our Air Force, and still the enemy moved on. I felt as if my patrol was trapped.

"Cathy, move down further with those men," I ordered her, while pointing at the ammo bearers who were moving down to the slate creek with heavy boxes of ammunition.

"No, I'm staying close to you. I'm afraid to leave you." She did not sound defiant but just confused and overwhelmed by the fast-moving events.

I would have said more but just then the mountain shook as a number of 120mm artillery shells hit the mountaintop all at once. I wondered where those 120mm guns were located. If they were near the 155mm guns that we had destroyed, then I had missed a chance to get them. I would hate myself if this were true, especially because of the powerful, capable force that I had had with me.

"Enemy is clearing his own avenue of approach," I told Mock. "All our men off that area?"

"Yes be Sargy long time be off. Only scout dey be come later same area. Maybe two, maybe tree scout no more."

Then he added as if he had forgotten, "Last night me tell you Sargy, four scout they be kill. NVA cut off," he pointed at his own genitals, "sew in mouf. I be tell 2nd Platoon they be bury."

"Where you be bury them?"

"Dat side mountain," he pointed at the eastern slope.

"Men they be see bodies?"

"They no see all, Sargy. Only 2nd Platoon they be see all."

"I want all men they be see. I be want them talk about it. Tell them, better, show them, what VC and NVA do to Yards. Send for one body. No drag, they be carry. I no want Yards be think we no respect dead damn Yards. Okay, Captain?"

"Me unstand Sargy. Me be go gets one." He then left me with a squad to get one of the dead and mutilated scouts.

As I watched Mock walk off, I thought about the role I was supposed to play in the overall operation. I was there to advise him and not to run the combat operations. When Captain Blound was with us, he too often fell into the habit of taking over an operation.

It was a peculiar role for an American soldier to be in, the combat advisor. I had experienced the difficulties of advising some cultures in combat operations. One dared not sit back and expect them to adhere to the sound tactical and strategic doctrines that we had been taught in Fort Benning's Infantry Training Center. If you did, you might just as well sit back and wait for disaster to strike.

When we turned Vietnamese or Montagnards loose to do what we had trained them to do, you felt like the guy who was trying to push a chain along a road by holding onto one link.

I kept promising myself that I should interfere less with the patrol and give Captain Mock more of a free hand in running it. After all, he was supposed to be in command. We Americans could not be around forever to run the country for them or fight their enemy.

Mortar shells, some of them of large caliber, also started to land on the mountain. First two, then four, and then nine at one time exploded harmlessly on the mountain. The advancing enemy had more mortars than I had expected.

By that time The NVA were well away from their safe haven in Laos, and the use of those short-range, indirect-fire weapons indicated that they were committed to clear an advance for their forward elements.

The knowledge of the mortar fire and other reports that came to me signified that the enemy was using regular army infantry tactics. They were methodically softening up their objective and slowly leapfrogging forward with a wanton disregard for their losses. Communists seldom considered the loss of life during an attack.

Our Air Force and Army Artillery were raining death down on the enemy, but they continued their advance. Their individual soldiers were aware that the closer they came to their objective the more exposed they would become to our superior firepower. It entered my mind that in their army it must take a really brave man to run away from enemy fire.

Tom moved near me with six runners.

"Guess I better get down dis way, too. Charlie is mad at us, Tony."

He looked at Cathy and smiled. I felt as if Tom knew what I had done to her during the night.

"Got the air recon report from those grid squares yet?"

"Not yet. De photo recon plane is over de area now," said Tom.

He and his men followed me a little further down the mountain. Many of my men could still be seen among the burned-out brush and bomb-shattered trees. They had not gone far enough down the mountain.

"Move those men farther down," I ordered the platoon leaders over my PRC-6 radio. No need to take a chance of Charlie throwing a misdirected round into them.

I saw Doc and his medical helpers approach.

"If he says a ting about dat underground hospital I'm gonna smash his face in," said Tom in a hostile tone.

"Hold it, Tom Babe. The guy is okay. A little different, but okay."

"Long as he don't start dat holier-than-thou crap."

Tom at times acted too protective of me. It embarrassed me. I had no qualms about protecting myself.

Doc could hardly wait to get close to me before he asked, "Tony, did you stay long enough down in that hospital to see it all?"

"I'm not a medic." I replied. "I stayed long enough down there to make sure that there was no one down there to fight. Fighting is my business, not looking after hospitals."

I was irritated at Doc and his obsession with helping humans.

"Did you see the other wards?" Doc insisted in speaking about something I would rather have forgotten.

"Were there others?" I asked, but was not surprised that there were other hospital wards down there.

"Yes, there were others. Two more." Doc looked me in the eyes for awkward moments without saying a thing.

Tom spoke up.

"Doc, if you have sometin else to say, say it and den shut up about dat damn hospital."

"Yes, I have something to say," he pointed a finger first at me then at Tom. "This is the last time I go on a patrol with either of you two. The two of you have turned into animals.

"I want to save lives. I have to or I would go stark raving mad because of the guilt I feel for having killed one person. But you two, don't you feel guilt? Especially you, Tony." Tears were shining in Doc's eyes.

Tom and I could say nothing as Doc continued.

"An innocent girl died because of me and I feel her death. You two can slaughter many people and still close your eyes and sleep while I have not slept peacefully for years. Someone should kill you, Tony. I wish I had the guts to do it. But, I am here and..."

"Shut up, damn you, Doc." I ordered, jumping up. There were enough problems on my mind without Doc adding to them.

"This is not the time nor the place to voice disagreements. Just shut up! When we get back, if we get back," I emphasized the if. "I'll let you go see the chaplain and have your Tough Shit Card punched. You can also fake one of those damn phony Vietnam war syndromes if you want to, but for now just don't fuck with me, unless you want to find out just how much of an animal I can be."

Tom laughed.

"And Doc, look behind you. See what animals de NVA and de VC is, man. You damn Yards, you put it down here so Sargy Doc he be see."

The four riflemen who carried the dead scout that they had exhumed, laid it down near us and uncovered the body so all could see the gruesome spectacle. The dead scout's eyes were open and seemed to stare at us. His mutilated face was clean. Someone had rinsed it off with a canteen of water.

The lips were roughly sewn together with barbed wire. Parts of his genitals protruded from the sides of his mouth.

"Dey did dat to him, Doc, while he was still alive. Look good, college boy. Back dere," Tom pointed at our eastern perimeter, "is tree more. Dey gots de same treatment. Pretty, eh man?"

To my surprise Doc said nothing. He just sat down, where he was, hid his face in his hands and started to sob softly.

"God, dear God, forgive us all," he pleaded between sobs.

Cathy went into hysterics and made shrill hiccuping noises.

I shook her but she did not notice me. Her eyes were glued to the small scout's dead body. I slapped her hard across the face. Then she stopped and turned glaring eyes on me as if she only then saw me for the first time.

"Shut up, woman, or I'll punch you out! I've heard enough of this damn shit. Captain Mock, move this down to where other damn Yards also see. Also, Captain, you tell them, before day be over, we be make VC and NVA pay for torturing our men. Stress the our — I'm one of you."

Mock nodded and gave me one of his smiles and said, "Yes be Sargy...we all be know. Me no need be tell damn Yards. They be know you be one us."

Doc had gotten control of himself again.

"Tony, will you sent a message to Group and inform them that there are dozens of enemy wounded in that underground hospital and if we could stop the shelling and get a Medevac, we might still save some?"

"No Doc, not this time! I don't want anything to stop now. The 5th NVA Division is partly out of Laos and I'm going to do everything possible to draw them out further."

I had begun to understand why Booby Trap had ordered us to move onto Black Face.

Other indications came to me to support my changing beliefs. A dull rumble came from the north of us as air strikes and artillery lit up the sky like flashes of lightning.

We were in a battle, with our patrol playing a small part.

Doc did not argue with me further. He took out his notebook and read out to me.

"Losses so far: eight killed in the attack at the guns, six medevacuated, and then the four scouts the enemy caught. Makes eighteen casualties thus far."

124 Honor and Sacrifice: The Montagnards of Ba Cat

"Eight killed at the guns? I saw nine graves," I said, while looking at Tom as he slowly walked away from us, pretending to be busy with his microphone.

"Must be a mistake, Tony. There were only eight bodies laid out for burial when I left with the wounded."

"No mistake Doc, damn it. I can count. I saw nine freshly filled graves."

"I don't care! I left eight bodies for Tom to bury," Doc said with finality.

"Tom? What the hell was he doing with the dead?"

"He told Mock to move on, and that he and his squad would dig the other grave and do the burying."

After that, Doc and I just shook our heads. We had no answer as to why Tom had got involved with the matter. I made a mental note to ask him later.

The mountain trembled under an incoming barrage. Black ashes, sulphur, steel, and fire flew through the air while deafening thunderclaps reverberated through the mountains.

"Captain Mock, warning order to 1st and 3rd Platoons. Prepare for attack," I hollered to Mock who was sitting peacefully on a burned-out stump close to me.

He waved his acknowledgment of the order. Runners immediately left to carry the orders to the two platoon leaders.

My tactical plan was to let the enemy continue to pound the area where their forward observers believed my men were dug in to defend the mountaintop. In the interim, we were at least 500 yards removed from the military crest. My men were waiting in readiness for the assault on the opposite slope where the enemy least expected us to be, since they believed that we wanted to repel their assault on the mountain.

This defensive tactic of mine could not have been justified prior to the advent of the Vietnam war. Before that time, weaponry had not advanced enough so that overkill with pinpoint accuracy was possible. The mass delivery means for close support of our Infantry units in direct contact with the enemy were also readily available now.

When it came to close support of our Infantry, the Navy and Air Force had also become experts in joining the Army in having nearly wiped out an attacking enemy before they had reached the assault phase of their attack.

I had to time the enemy's movement just right. I planned to move against them after they had lifted their fire. From other contacts with the NVA, I had learned that they did not, as we did, shift their fires over the objective to interfere with reinforcements and counterattacks.

It was a dangerous assumption for me to make, but then, what alternatives were there? I had lived a life where little to no alternatives had often been the norm.

My tactics constituted a counterattack without having had my own position overrun. That in itself had advantages, but only if the rules of sound infantry tactics were disregarded by the enemy. It also depended on the enemy not becoming aware that they were expending ammo and energy against unoccupied positions. Much depended on the assumption that the NVA, for strategic and tactical reasons, could not let us stay on top of that mountain. Black Face Mountain straddled a main infiltration route for supplies from Laos into South Vietnam.

It often happened that we, at A-Team level, were not briefed on a larger operational plan, even if we were a part of it. Perhaps higher headquarters did not trust us or just considered us too dumb to grasp a large tactical operation. Again, I must have given Booby Trap ulcers, because his orders were for me to occupy the top of Black Face. I did not occupy it and I was sure that, with all the aerial activities that went on, the information must have been made available to him. Other things, of greater importance, were on my mind.

A tactical advantage could develop if the enemy were not given respite to dig in for defense once they got to the top of the mountain. I had to time things right or lose many men.

Tom was about 20 yards from me. "Tom, message to Booby Trap!" I said loudly.

"Go ahead!" he hollered back.

We had always understood that we should keep ourselves separated during incoming rounds. We did not want one shell to kill all the Americans that were on a patrol. We had to leave at least one of us alive for Booby Trap to blame.

"Request Spooky or Cobras strike the northeast slope — Stop — Stand by for close air support on my green smoke signal —Stop — Will mark target with two green ground bursts — Stop — End of message."

"On the way, partner!"

Tom sounded in his glory. Within a few minutes Tom again hollered back to me, "Message from Group. Two cobras fully loaded overhead standing by for your green smoke signal to go to work on Charlie."

"Thanks, Babe!"

I did not feel alone anymore. Matters were slowly shifting in my mind. It had become more and more evident that we had some large Infantry units involved in the operation. A big battle was shaping up about 15 miles north of us. I could hear heavy gunfire without letup. Also a few attack jets were screaming overhead, firing rockets into a concentrated area many miles away from us.

At the time I thought that it was our powerful 23rd Infantry Division, the Americal Division, that was on the move. Later, I found out that it was the 23rd ARVN Division that had gone into action against units of the 5th NVA Division near Dak Kon about 15 to 20 miles east and north of us. I could hear the dull rumble of gunfire in between the explosions taking place around us.

The ground beneath our feet trembled, and then shook violently, as four U.S. F-104 fighter bombers streaked overhead so low we felt the heat from their jets. Then streams of rockets shot out ahead of them, blasting channels through the heavy brush toward the unseen advancing enemy. A lump formed in my throat.

"Thank God," I muttered. "Our Armed Forces, the regulars, have joined us in the fight."

Eight-inch, 175mm, and 155mm artillery shells were swirling overhead, to blanket what was left of Black Face and the northeastern slope. The U.S. Army Artillery was firing high explosives and air bursts as fast as the gunners could feed the shells into the guns.

The airways were cluttered with radio transmissions from pilots, both Air Force and Navy. Tom screamed to me through the deafening cacophony.

"We got the Navy in on it too, Tony!"

He pointed to two jets approaching low over us. In a split second, the two had dropped the first napalm. The silvery napalm cylinders tumbled, then hit the earth to spread a fiery path of death the size of two basketball courts, and beyond that spattered burning particles which could disfigure a human for life.

Then came two A-6A Intruders to drop their 500-pound bombs. They were followed by four Marine F-4B Phantoms that I thought were going to plow themselves into the mountain, they came so close to the ground to drop their loads.

Behind them came two more, then two more, and on and on they screamed over our heads to tumble their hot messengers of death down the mountainside, well away from us. It seemed to me that we were no longer the center of what was taking place. Most of the action by our Air Force and Navy was miles away, while Army artillery was supporting me.

It was a crazy development, one I did not understand and had little time to think about. The enemy was determined to reoccupy Black Face mountain while, at the same time, they had another battle in progress about 20 miles to the north of us.

"What the hell is going on?" I asked Captain Mock.

"Me also be boo coo fuckup, Sargy. We be gots noder war be go," he answered, while pointing to a massive black fire and smoke cloud shooting skyward some ten miles away from us.

On Black Face, the enemy was supposed to lift his fire, but he kept up his sustained fire from Laos. I could wait no longer. I ordered Tom to transmit my signal for shifting our support fire, and, at the same, time gave the signal to the 60mm mortars to fire the green smoke shells.

"Captain Mock!" I screamed, and could hardly hear myself. "You stay with main body. Only 3rd Platoon! Only 3rd Platoon!" I repeated to make sure that he understood my command, "Attack! Attack!"

I jumped out into the open with Ding at my side, and headed for the eastern slope. The enemy advanced toward us with as much bloodthirsty hatred for us as we had for them.

Behind and from around me came many screams of "Nui Coto kill! Kill! Nui Coto kill!" Our loud and maddening screams blended in disharmony as we stumbled into the flying shrapnel of enemy artillery. Our supporting fires had stopped, but not those of the enemy.

NVA shells were bursting all around us. Small Montagnard bodies were blasted to bits, not by accuracy but by the shear volume of enemy artillery rounds that were fired from Laos — a mere five miles away, but completely safe from counterfire. Nui Coto, yes, indeed. It was another Nui Coto.

The 400 yards became a gauntlet, where fate, the devil's sword, had ruthlessly turned against us. At 200 yards from the enemy, only the short bursts of M-16 rifles from half the 3rd Platoon sounded around me.

When we closed with what remained of the enemy's forward element, my 3rd Platoon was no more, but neither was the enemy. There was but little need for the bayonet and the bullet. The real killers were behind gun carriages of heavy artillery.

I had once heard an artillery man say, "Artillery lends order and reason to a battle which would otherwise become nothing but a chaotic melee." How true.

A strange silence descended over the battlefield, broken only by the pitiful wails of the wounded. Never during a lifetime can man experience a deadlier silence than that which follows the last explosion on a field of battle.

Pieces of human bodies torn out of their uniforms, broken weapons, and smoldering ashes littered the area. Man had marked yet another small spot on earth where he had abandoned all reason.

"Pull back! Pull back!" I ordered the few Yards who had gathered around me. We had penetrated to the northeast slope and had encountered but a few enemy soldiers. I saw no VC women with their black-and-white-checkered scarves during the attack, only uniformed NVA.

With arms held high in surrender, the wounded enemy soldiers unsuccessfully begged for mercy. All of them were out of ammunition, hungry, tired, and so disoriented that they fell easy victims to our bayonets. In reality, the battle was over as soon as we had closed with them. Those 5th NVA Division soldiers had gotten their wish — Born in the north, die in the south.

First four, then six, then two more Yards came to me out of the sulphur smell and low drifting smoke. I led them down the mountain.

Is this all I have left from the 48-man 3rd Platoon? I asked myself bitterly.

The full knowledge of the mistake I had made in my timing came to me, but that sweet, gray mental veil blessedly obscured reality. Again, I found myself standing on the sideline, quite free of guilt and conscience.

"Captain Mock," I called over my PRC-6 radio. "We took a beating. Prepare to go down into the creek bottom."

"You okay, Sargy?" came his anxious voice.

"Yeah, I'm okay, but 3rd Platoon is all but wiped out."

"Me wait you, but be send all 2nd Platoon and medics to Sargy."

"Okay, but you be push them. I want clear this area ASAP."

Tom's voice came over my radio.

"Booby Trap order you to proceed to checkpoint zero fiver."

"Got you, Babe, wait for me." I knew that Booby Trap would want me off the mountain. It must have been obvious to all that the NVA was going to take that mountain at all costs, and occupy their underground bunkers again. The strength that remained to me could not stop them. Later, in the darkness, they would sneak out of the cover and concealment the jungle afforded them and retake Black Face.

High above us and to the side, away from possible enemy fire, circled two helicopters. I could see many civilians crowding the doors with large, long-lens cameras trained on us. They recorded, for all the world to see, how our friendly forces once more heroically repelled another communist assault on the free world.

Some time later I heard that there were complaints uttered by news photographers about the poor quality of the pictures they took, which was caused by the black ashes that obscured much of the battle area. Some of the reporters wanted the Army to correct that situation in the future.

One story that appeared on U.S. newsstands about us was so flattering that Booby Trap was decorated for the splendid performance of his command in the face of the enemy.

As I looked up at the civilian spectators I spoke out to the otherwise empty sky, "The show is over, now you can go back to your evening cocktails and white bed sheets. I've performed for you. Hope you enjoyed the show." I could not help but add, "You bastards!" It was more than just a coincidence for them to be up there.

For them, the scattered blood-smeared actors and the pitiful cries which came from among the many pieces of strewn human flesh and bones, would all be forgotten with the downward ring of the curtain, and in their pursuit of other headlines.

We walked out of the smoke and fine black ash that had acted as a screen between the battlefield and the rest of the patrol. Ding was by my side as he had been all through the action. I wondered where Mo was. I saw him later near Cathy. When he saw me look at him he quickly closed his eyes, as I had seen him do before, believing that I could not see him then.

Cathy started toward me, then stopped. The white pallor of her dirty face was about the only distinction between her appearance and that of the surrounding Yards. I noticed her breasts even though she was covered with black ash the same as we all were. Her bosom rose and fell with unnatural jerking motions.

"Take it easy, Cathy. We still have a long way to go and no chance of getting an air evac. Pull yourself together."

I could not sympathize with her pitiful predicament. I had other matters on my mind.

She wanted to speak, but all she could say was, "I, you, please get us out of here." Her voice was drowned out by our Air Force jets that streaked low over us on their way to unload their heavy ordinance.

The enemy was hidden in the heavy foliage a few miles north of us, where they could not be detected by the naked eye, but only with electronics. I assumed that the enemy was getting ready for another assault on Black Face.

I took Cathy by the arm, and dragged her at first, then just picked her up and threw her soft body over my shoulder. This time I was prepared for her lightweight. With her over my shoulder, I ran down the well-traveled footpath to the creek bottom where the main body was assembled.

I hated the situation that I found myself in. The heavy losses I could cope with, but the lack of alternatives played heavily on my mind. I was being driven into actions I couldn't control or influence.

There existed but one avenue of retreat for us. Booby Trap must also have realized that, for checkpoint zero fiver was about the only area close to us from which we were not receiving information on enemy movement. For how long was anyone's guess. I estimated that we had 30 hours, at the most, to get re-enforced, or air evacuated, or trapped.

We are ready for you bastards, I said to myself.

Cathy wiggled on my shoulder and muttered something. I gave her smooth, soft bottom a pat, took a handful, shook it to make sure it was real, then gave it a good pinch.

"Shut up, and relax," I ordered as I jumped with her over a burned out stump. She mumbled something else, but I paid no attention.

I rejoined Tom, who had slowed down to wait for me.

"Tom Babe, message to Booby Trap. Approximate 300 NVA KIA on objective — Stop — Friendly losses three zero — Stop — Scout report enemy battalion size unit five miles south my position — Stop — Recon patrol report will follow — stop — Request small arms ammo drop check point zero fiver — End of message."

"On de way, Babe," answered, Tom. He sat down where he was, and tapped out the message on his transmitter key. At the same time, he smiled at me as I walked off with Cathy over my shoulder.

Soon Tom caught up with us.

"What dat you gots over your shoulder, Babe?" he said and grinned.

"Message from Group." He held his hand over his earphone while we moved fast through the underbrush. "Booby Trap want to know if der is U.S. casualties."

"Negative."

I thought of Doc.

"Where is Doc?" I asked over my radio.

Doc's voice came back over his radio immediately.

"In the back of you, tending to wounded. Second Platoon with me — Out." I did not object to the out. He was busy, I knew, and would not like it if I gave him orders just then, although proper radio procedure exercised by the Army precludes the station which was initially called from cutting off the conversation.

Cathy again wiggled on my shoulder and kicked her feet. I gave her buttocks a good pinch and heard her utter "Ouch!"

The main body of the patrol had halted in a semi-clear area, well removed from the dangerous top of Black Face mountain. The ground was on the steep side of a cliff, with good fields of fire in two directions, and at a quick glance, I decided that we could defend the area for a while if discovered by the enemy.

The 1st Platoon leader came to me when I signaled for him.

"Lieutenant, you be responsible for security. We stay here tonight. Keep close-in security. No spread out too much."

"Yes be, Sargy." He gave me a smart salute, and hurried off to carry out my orders. No matter how many times I told them not to salute me in the field, they still insisted on giving me that sign of respect. At least I hoped that they saluted me for that reason, and not for the same reason that I saluted Booby Trap in the field.

I gave orders to the 4th Platoon Leader to clear an area and mark it with our bright orange panel, in readiness to receive the ammo Booby Trap would order to be dropped. Scouts combed the area around us for possible enemy movement.

A few minutes after I had given the orders to the 4th Platoon leader, a scout ran up to me and in an excited babble told me something so fast that I had to get an interpreter.

"Big snake!" said the interpreter excitedly.

"Colonel Richard Paegel's request? Oh yeah. He wants a snake. No problem," I thought. We had the time, since I did not expect to make contact with the enemy again until the next day.

Close to the clearing that the 4th Platoon had made for the orange signal panel, I saw it. It was an exceptionally large boa constrictor. It looked about 30 feet long, and big enough to swallow a Yard.

About 50 Yards were surrounding it. The snake was slowly moving his head from side to side keeping his green beady eyes on the Yards. Most of his body was on the ground, but part of him was still wrapped around a nearby tree trunk.

Mock stood a few paces from me looking me over and I could tell he was puzzled. He wanted to see what I was going to do about the snake. To his consternation he soon found out.

"Captain Mock, tell Yards we be tie snake up. Helicopter be come he be take snake to Group."

Then I called out to Tom. "Tom, radio Group directly. Priority — Action — Colonel Paegel — Large boa ready for transport at checkpoint zero fiver."

It was one of the few times I saw Mock laughing out loud. He slapped his knees and bent over with mirth. Then he looked at me. "How be do, Sargy?" He could not believe that I was serious.

Some babbling took place among the Yards and with the word having been passed that I was going to wrestle the snake all by myself, screams of laughter rang through the brush. Many Yards gathered in as close to the snake as bravado made possible.

The snake must have felt that it was about to be attacked. It hissed loudly and its forked tongue darted in and out of its mouth. Having sensed danger, the snake was getting ready to cope with it.

Tom also started to laugh, then said, "Group's message. Boa property of U.S. Army — Stop — Safeguard and ready it for helicopter transportation — Stop — Helicopter on the way — End of message."

Slowly at first and then abruptly all laughter stopped. The Yards that were standing around started to back away from me and the snake. A few of them ducked into the surrounding foliage, and I could hear them scrambling through the brush as they tried to get away from me.

Aloud I ordered, "Everybody stay in place. Captain Mock, you be gets two squads from 4th Platoon. Cut sticks, cut our mountain ropes in short pieces. I want snake tie up ready for chopper."

I thought about the helicopter coming over us, exposing itself to possible enemy fire, so it was up to me to see that it could get in and out with a minimum of delay.

Two squads shuffled reluctantly toward me. Their ash-smeared faces were fearful. Each man carried either a four-foot-long stick or a piece of nylon mountain rope about ten feet long, or both.

Captain Mock had explained to them what was going to happen. The way they approached me with the rope and sticks, not one of them really believed that I was going to order them to attack that snake. At least, they were hoping that I would not.

My plan was for the Yards to slap the sticks against the snake's body, wrap the rope around the snake and the sticks and, bingo, the snake would be immobilized. After that, we would load it into the chopper, and I would make a full colonel happy, and stack up points with him for future use.

I lined the 22 riflemen up in a row facing the snake. Through an interpreter I ordered them to jump the snake at my count of three. They looked at me, at Captain Mock, then at their platoon leader. From none did they get support or sympathy.

I counted, "One, two, go!"

They did not go for the snake. For a moment I thought they were all going to run away.

Captain Mock, slowly, but with deliberate steps, walked up to them. I do not know what he said but I saw a few Yards starting to shake nervously.

I took my load-bearing harness off, grabbed a stick from one of the Yards, and drew a line on the ground.

"Captain Mock, you tell damn Yards. I be count one more time. All no jump snake be shot.

"Ding!" I called. "You be stand here. M-16 ready full automatic. Shoot all no jump snake."

I joined the two squads with Captain Mock next to me. Ding had given the necessary orders to a Yard, and he also came next to me with a rope he had jerked out of someone's hands.

Overhead I heard a helicopter hovering.

"Tom," I called. "Talk the chopper down onto the signal panel."

All humor had disappeared. I had to suppress my fear of snakes and tend to the matter. I counted.

"One, two, go!" All of us jumped the snake. I landed two feet from its head and with all my strength squeezed his body, while ropes, sticks and Yards flew in all directions as that snake first shot straight out and then wrapped itself around a number of Yards.

The cold scaly skin that I grabbed stayed between my hands, but the snake moved inside its own skin, and I felt it pulsating at a rate of one to each two of my heartbeats. With each pulsation, the snake became harder and harder until we could not bend it anymore.

I saw its open mouth inches from my face. A Yard stuffed a large piece of dirt and grass into its mouth and another Yard was ready with more grass that had a lot of muddy dirt stuck to it. The snake could not get rid of the grass and earth fast enough to bite anyone. Ding wrapped rope around the snake's head until the thing could no longer open its mouth.

I heard a few shrill screams from Cathy. I looked to see what the hell she was doing with the snake, but she was looking us over from a safe distance.

Once I saw two Yards lifted several feet in the air, inside a coil of the snake. Some Yards were tangled up with the snake and rope. They had entangled themselves with the sticks against the snake. Others were working desperately to free them.

After what seemed hours, but was really only five minutes, we had the snake immobilized. I stood back and fought to stop shaking. I was glad that no one apparently noticed how shaken I was. Each Yard had his own nerves to soothe.

Mo came to me and handed me my load-bearing harness. He was shaking worse than I was, even though he had stayed well away from Ding and me. He mumbled something that I did not want to hear. I did pat him kindly on the head when I felt like kicking him in the loincloth instead.

The helicopter had landed while we were struggling with the snake. The pilot walked up to me.

"What the hell is going on here? I thought we were to take some people out, and now we're told it is a damn snake. Damn, Sergeant, have you Green Berets flipped? When we climb up and out of this jungle of yours we're likely to get fired on, and all for a darn snake."

I just gave him a sympathetic smile and said, "Things are rough all over. But look at it from the snake's point of view. You'll go home some day, free to do as you wish. But that poor snake will be locked up for the rest of its life, and all because you brought your chopper to take him in."

I had stopped shaking.

"You're some kind of a nut? Now get him on my chopper," he ordered curtly.

"I want to get away from you crazy people."

I had to have more fun with the young warrant officer. "Sorry, Sir. He is yours now. We have an enemy to think about."

For a moment he thought I was serious. Then he burst out laughing and jokingly hit his co-pilot on the shoulder.

"I'm going to remember this day for a long time," he said, shaking his head as he walked back to his helicopter.

We lifted the wrapped-up snake and deposited the thing on his helicopter floor.

We were surprised how heavy it was. It took more than 15 Yards to carry it.

The two door-gunners and the crew chief kept a respectful distance from the snake as the chopper stirred the ground around us and quickly shot up and away. The last we saw of the crew was when they gave us the finger, in a crude but friendly goodbye.

I spotted Cathy next to Doc, and it looked as if she was completely perplexed. She was waving her arms at us and the surrounding Yards while her lips were moving fast.

Doc shook his head every so often at her. When I approached the two of them she became silent, and backed away from us.

I asked Doc what she was so excited about. He would not tell me, but said, "Better you don't know, Tony." Doc then added, "One thing she did say, though, was that you were the strangest man she had ever known. I also think that you are a little strange," he added, smiling.

My headquarters section had picked a cave-like area the size of a basketball court for us to spend the night in. On two sides, we were partly sheltered from the cold night wind. It was also just about impossible for the enemy to approach us from those two sides.

The sides consisted of perpendicular cliffs that were not easily seen, for they were covered with two-foot-thick clinging vines. I was satisfied that they presented an unnegotiable barrier, therefore fewer perimeter security problems existed.

One of the open sides led to the dry slate creek, which for 200 yards would be occupied by the 2nd Platoon when they rejoined us. Doc had again walked up to the top of the mountain where the 2nd Platoon was helping the medics take care of the wounded, and burying the dead.

All around us, light from the setting sun managed to filter through the thick overhead branches. It made strange bright streaks over the moss-covered ground. The patterns it cast looked as if a deranged artist had been there before us.

Not far from me stood Cathy. I could feel her eyes on me. It seemed to me that she followed with some interest the orders I gave to the Yards. Captain Mock had gone to the 2nd Platoon to hurry them, so I took care of setting up the necessary security.

I gave words to my thoughts. "We have 188 men left. Some walking wounded can still fight. Ammunition? No problem, if Booby Trap acts before darkness sets in."

I looked at Cathy. She just stood there staring at me, as if she was hard-pressed to find a niche wherein to file me. I felt her eyes burning into me, and if Mo or Ding had been nearer I would have kicked them both.

She showed enough life that I thought she would make it for one more day if our Yards continued to help her. What was going to happen to her after that? I hated to think of her mixed in with us in a close battle with the NVA, which was what I expected if we did not break away from the enemy.

We were trapped, and no matter what, I'd never run from the enemy unless I was ordered to do so. My thoughts were not inspired by heroics. It had more to do with staying out of the dark side of honor. I wanted Booby Trap to give me orders before I screwed up further. With those uncomfortable thoughts sloshing through my mind it became easier for me to cope with Cathy and the American creep. I had to do something about them. If I air evacuated them to Group I would be in trouble. She and the creep would talk. Questions were going to be asked that no one would like answers to except the World Council of Churches, the French, and some other do-gooders. Then I thought of what our hostile press could do with the story.

Damn, I whispered to myself, to hell with it all. My job is to kill commies, not worry about the small stuff. Let Booby Trap develop the ulcers.

I had no one to speak to, so I turned my thoughts to Cathy and said, "Yes, little girl, we still have fighting strength left. Enough ammo, rations and manpower to kill many communist bastards if they try us again."

"Is that good?" She seemed to spit her words out in a combination of bitterness, sadness, dejection, and hopelessness. It was a response that I did not expect. She got my attention then.

"You another Jane Fonda? If you were that bitch, you would have been killed when we first caught you," I shot back at her with equal venom.

"Like you killed the other Council members?"

I had no ready answer for that. I could not even summon the soothing gray veil behind which I could usually find solace. I looked at Ding and Mo who stood a few feet from us. They both had backed away from me. Having read my discomfort, they were afraid that I might very well shoot them instead of just kicking them.

I laughed it off, saying, "Don't be so upset, Base Plate."

"Base Plate?" she frowned.

"Yeah, that's what our Yards call you."

The Yards, in their primitive understanding of sex, must have humorously associated her with the center hole in the base plate of a 60mm mortar where the bottom round knob of the mortar tube fits in.

It was a vain attempt on my part to inject a measure of humor. I could tell by her defiant attitude that she would gladly disregard whatever Christian benevolence she might have gathered while serving God, and use an M-16 rifle on me.

Captain Mock saved me from further complicating matters. He approached, looking physically worn out. He told me that all the dead were buried on top of Black Face and that Doc remained with the wounded higher up the mountain.

"Doc, him be stay Black Face wit wounded," Mock said it nervously, expecting me to object to Doc remaining there.

"Bad decision, Captain. We need him here. Is the 2nd Platoon off the mountain?"

"No all. Me leave two squad take care Sargy, Doc."

"No go, Captain."

I did not want to embarrass him with another bad decision. After all, he was in charge of the patrol and I was only his advisor. At least that was what the Pentagon decided on when U.S. Army SF were injected into the mess in South Vietnam a century ago.

"We need all men close in before darkness, Captain. Please see to it." I touched him on the shoulder to convey my affection for him. He understood, and shrugged off some of his weariness.

"Okay, me be bring all damn Yards off mountain. Runner, he be fetch squads. Sargy, Doc, him be say you be get Medevac."

"Wait, I write message for Doc."

Motioning for the runner to stop, I scribbled a note to Doc telling him to leave the wounded and return to me ASAP. He was to bring only the walking wounded. I handed the note to Mock to give to the runner.

"Captain, you, Tom and me, we be talk. Make plan, okay?"

As we walked away, I saw Cathy follow us while stripping the skin off a patrol ration. It flashed through my mind that I might as well scratch another hope, which was that she would die of hunger, thereby saving the U.S. Army embarrassment. The moments I spent thinking of what I should do about her always came up blank.

I had the option of sending Cathy and the creep out with the snake helicopter, but had ruled against it. Luckily the helicopter crew did not recognize her among the Yards, thanks to the black ash which was smeared over all of us. One hope was, given the mess we were in, that none of us would walk away from there.

"Damn, I wish she were Jane Fonda." I muttered to myself.

Tom joined us. He looked well rested and alert as usual; strong, tireless and unworried. As always he made me feel better. He was a good man to have close to me when things went wrong.

Cathy stood a few yards from us, slowly eating the patrol ration. She stood staring at the damp, moss-covered ground, looking pathetic, tiny and dejected. Black ashes, mixed with sweat, were smeared on her face. A few white streaks showed where tears had streaked down her cheeks.

Her once shiny blonde hair was matted with leaves and had some small sticks entangled. She was probably aware that she did not then fulfill women's natural role in life of presenting an appearance pleasing to men.

"Damn, damn," I whispered to myself. "Why do I care? She is no different from any one-night stand, and a commie."

She must have felt my eyes on her. She turned and looked at me like a small frightened deer. The spot I stood on became so uncomfortable that I would have welcomed a few enemy incoming rockets.

I knew then that no matter how much I lied to myself, I could not simply shoot away the problem she laid at my feet, not with that look she gave me.

The setting sun continued to lengthen the shadows and reminded me of football games back home. Often I had sat in bleachers and marveled at the long autumn shadows slowly creeping across the field. How far and long ago that was.

I had to shake off this nostalgia. Tom and Mock were sitting close by patiently waiting for me to speak.

"We'll wait till Doc gets here before we analyze our situation to come up with some workable plan. But before he gets here, I want you two to try and agree with me on one thing."

Hesitantly, I approached a grim decision that I had made. "We have to leave the wounded where they are. I can ask for a Medevac, but it is extremely unlikely that we'll get one. By morning the NVA and VC will be all over Black Face. And unless our side suppresses the enemy fires in Laos, any further Medevacs and aerial resupply would be suicidal."

No one spoke.

"Yards find we be leave wounded to NVA dey boo coo no be like," said Mock. After having made that statement I knew he had said all that he was going to say about the subject.

"How about you, Tom?" I asked knowing what he would say.

"If we leave dem to de NVA dey'll be tortured de same as dey always do, like dose four scouts."

While speaking Tom placed his hand over his ear, listening to an incoming message. "Caribou on the way with ammo and food. Pilot has sighted the orange panel and will make a low pass for the drop."

I motioned for Ding. "Tell 2nd Platoon Leader, he be take care all ammo, and food he be take care."

Off Ding sprinted as fast as his short legs could carry him. Mo followed him. He had learned one American word — food.

There was an awkward silence. Cathy had moved closer. It made me uncomfortable not knowing how much she had overheard about the wounded.

I hated myself and I hated the world where I was forced to blunder from sin to sin because of the simple fact that I was there. I was there, and I was the ranking man.

Of course I could drop all the problems wherewith I was faced directly into Captain Mock's lap, and conveniently pull a Booby Trap — blame that man — and sleep with a clear conscience.

No, I reasoned. That I could not do. Mock was a good man but incapable of coping with many bumps and pitfalls.

Neither Mock nor Tom was willing to dwell on the inevitable solution with regard to the wounded. I resented Tom's position. He did not have to make the decision. It was not his responsibility. I was stuck with it.

As to Captain Mock, he just naturally waited for me to give him orders. I would have felt better had he been an ARVN officer. I would have remained in the background and fulfilled my mission as an advisor.

"You two, can you make a recommendation?"

"Me no speak. You be order me be do."

Mock said this in a tone which might as well have had two period stops after it.

"Same wit me, man. You're in charge."

"Thanks a lot, you two."

Sarcasm was in order. All my earlier fears, apprehensions, and foreboding came down to a single phrase, "Fuck it."

"Yeah," said Tom. "Dats what I said all along about dis fucking patrol."

I got up to leave. Tom stopped me.

"Message from Booby Trap coming in."

With his notebook on his knee he copied the message.

Within seconds, he handed me the decoded message.

"Baker zero six to Moonlight — Stop — Consolidate your patrol at checkpoint zero fiver ASAP — Stop — Close perimeter defenses tight as possible — stop — Request time lapse till comply."

"Tom, acknowledge. Send, time lapse two hours." I turned to Mock.

"Captain Mock, please get command close in on us. I be think maybe B-52 strike or saturation shelling on Black Face be come boo coo soon."

He left with two of his runners.

"Tom, message to Booby Trap: Terrain impossible to confirm exact location of checkpoint zero fiver — stop — Request air observer plot my position — stop — Will fire two red flares over position at 1800 - Out."

I signaled for a runner.

"You be gets 60 mortar ASAP. Also ammo bearer be give two red be flare signal rounds."

The runner sprinted out of sight to carry out my orders. No matter what the future would hold for these mountain people, the acronym, ASAP, would forever be a word they would remember us by, just like the German POWs in World War II remembering us by "Hurry Up."

Again I saw Tom copy a message.

"Booby Trap says to fire the two red flares only on his command and be sure they are directly over your position." Tom smiled and added, "The bastard is getting nervous."

Ding rejoined us. He gave me a nod which meant that all was taken care of. Two mortar men were behind him and stayed a respectful distance from us important headquarters people. Ding saw to protocol.

A black shadow, followed by a terrible noise, swept over us as a Caribou's twin engines screamed under full power to clear the mountainside after a parachute had jerked four pallets of food and ammo out of its back door.

The pilot had slowed to stalling speed before he let the chute jerk the load out of his back door. He took the chance of not clearing obstacles ahead. Those pilots were totally committed to supporting us and often disregarded their own safety.

When the sudden unexpected Caribou's noise hit us, Cathy threw herself into my arms. She shook violently with fright. I enjoyed the feel of her soft body, but her nerves weren't going to take much more.

"It's okay," I soothed her fears. "It's our ammo and food the aircraft dropped."

My right hand moved under her jacket as I spoke and I stroked the smooth curve of her back, then to her side and up front to cup my hand over one of her small breasts.

I felt the nipple harden. She lifted her open mouth up to me and I kissed her with my tongue going deep to her throat. Momentarily her body stiffened and she dug her nails into me. I felt the trembling of her body as I pushed her tenderly and reluctantly away from me. We were not alone.

She gazed at me with glassy eyes and a look that conveyed surrender to the inevitable. She seemed puzzled as to what had happened to her while I held her close. Perhaps she would have preferred to remain in my arms. Wishful thinking often marred my common sense.

Again tears were rolling down her face. Crying was the only way that she could express the hopelessness and confusion. She had lost that blank look that had brought back memories of Korea.

Cathy reminded me that during the Korean war, when the Chinese entered the so-called "Police Action," and drove us from the Yalu River to south of Seoul, young American soldiers who were poorly prepared for combat, especially in physical conditioning, had just given up. They died on their feet, mental and physical wrecks, devoid of feeling and cares. I remembered the same blank look on their faces. Perhaps it was nature's way of making death easier to meet. I wondered if Cathy was also going to give up and die on her feet.

Because she came to me for protection when the Caribou scared her, I felt differently toward her. It was that natural instinct to protect.

Not unlike the fabled knights, with their clumsy shiny armor, protecting their damsels, I too wanted to protect this woman. The feel of that firm breast with hardened nipple held a promise, and I was not about to let some dragon do me out of the chance to explore both breasts.

You bastard, you, I said to myself while thinking of the knights. I smiled at the thought of them struggling out of their awkward armor to collect a reward.

"Mo, you come here," he sensed my agitation, as Ding usually did, and acted scared. He understood that I wanted him to come close, so he approached me at an angle, with his eyes darting around for an escape route.

"Captain Mock, please tell that Mo to come to me or I'll skin him alive. He has to take care Base Plate. He and Ding. Tonight it be boo coo cold. They be take care she."

After Mock spoke to Mo, Mo's face broke into a terrible broad grin. Dried blood, swollen lips and the missing teeth combined to make his attempt at a happy smile rather pathetic. Some babbling came from Mo.

"What is he saying, Captain?" I asked, not too sure that I wanted an answer.

"He be say Base Plate she be okay, Sargy. Damn Yards be built hootch, Sargy, Base Plate. Fire night hootch be stay warm."

Yes, I thought. I should have known. Mo's reference to the "damn Yards" showed how much he had learned from Ding.

I knew little about the American creep who was causing many problems for our ammunition bearers. I was told that the bearers were carrying him on a makeshift stretcher and with difficulty making their way through the brush toward us.

"Cathy," I said with some kindness in my voice. "What about the man who was..." I did not want to use the word "captured" since it no longer fitted her, "who was with you in Laos?"

"His name is Bob Gates," she said feebly. Then she looked up at me, and with some defiance creeping back into her bearing and voice, asked, "What about him? Where is he?"

"He can't keep up with us. The Yards are carrying him."

"Perhaps if you gave him boots and clothing as you gave me." She almost hissed her words.

It seemed to me that I had lost all the ground I had gained earlier.

"What a cruel world we men live in," I thought, while I wished some dragon would jump up so that I could fill the beast's hide full of M-16 slugs and then be rewarded by her.

"Only boots available are those off dead Yards. Sizes four and five. They wrapped rags around his feet but still the bas..., he can't keep up. The guy is just not capable of staying with us. Tomorrow will be a hard day. I have to move this patrol far."

"Neither can I keep up with you."

"That is different. We'll help you and you know why."

"No, I don't know why!" She shot back at me. "Is it because you raped me?"

I had hopes for her then. She had come out of her shell at last. It did not make me feel comfortable, though. I would have given much not to have had to look into those sad blue eyes.

I wished for incoming enemy rockets instead of stupid dragons. The best I had to settle for was a badly aimed kick at Mo. He somehow expected it and ducked behind Cathy just in time, and clung to her for protection.

Confusion spread over her face. Then a strange transformation took place in her face. Some deeply embedded motherly instinct surfaced. She put her arms around Mo to shield him.

"You leave him alone!" she snapped at me. "He did nothing to you." She was in open defiance. In confusion I backed away, not prepared to deal with her reaction.

She and Mo stood there like two small scared children who had done something wrong and were expecting punishment from their mother.

Tom and Mock, having witnessed the sideshow, pretended to find their own weapons of great interest. To someone who did not know them, it would have appeared as if they were seeing their M-16 rifles for the first time.

I took a short walk among our Yards to observe their preparations for the oncoming night. Amiable nods and toothless smiles greeted me whenever our eyes met. Most of them were digging in. The soft, moist earth yielded freely to their entrenching tools.

From platoon to platoon I walked. At each platoon area I was met by the platoon leader and platoon sergeant with salutes and then was followed through their area.

I felt at one with them, comfortable, and in my element. It was a field for which I was trained. The rugged, thorough, and valuable infantry combat training I had received in Fort Benning and Fort Bragg stood me in good stead. I had no qualms about planting my feet firmly on the ground, wherever I might be.

Here and there I corrected defensive positions: rocket launcher's backblast area, a restricted field of fire for an M-60 machine gun, sticks that marked nighttime fans of fire, areas to cover in final protective fire, and other things to increase our chances for survival.

It was about an hour before we would start yet another restless night. Again we would pit inadequate senses of smell, sight, and hearing against an enemy who was equally handicapped. Neither they, nor we, would for a moment harbor a wish for a truce or a retreat. Fate had ordained that we should seek out and kill each other. Nothing else mattered.

Tom, Doc, and Mock were waiting for me. I could immediately tell that Doc was upset. Close by them, I saw ten Yards with fresh bandages on arms, heads, and legs.

They were the only walking wounded. Eleven non-ambulatory wounded left on top of that mountain, and who was going to be their executioner? Worse, who was going to carry the blame through life for their death.

"Thank God, for that gentle gray veil," I thought.

"I'm back, Tony. Now what?" Doc did not hide his bitterness.

"Easy, Doc. We have things to talk about." I felt his eyes burning into mine. Doc, I thought, you'd better not push me.

Aloud I said, "I know what you are thinking, Doc, and we'll get to it soon enough. For now, forget all animosity. We have troubles."

I sat down and opened my 1:25,000 map. The four of us bent over the map.

"We are here." I marked the spot with my pencil. "Enemy battalion here, enemy regiment here, and I presume that the enemy has its scouts scattered all through the area looking for us. They would want to determine what route we'll follow to get back to our camp. They are going to ambush us for sure and use every tactic to destroy us.

"As far as the enemy is concerned, we are trapped." I waited for one of them to make a comment but none did.

"In the final analysis of the enemy situation, you guys, they are all over the place in strength.

"Now, our situation. We are still a strong, company size, combat patrol. There-supply we have just received, since Booby Trap okayed my request, indicates that he expects us to fight our way out of the encirclement and into an area where Group can better support us, and also out of the range of the guns in Laos. I expect orders from Booby Trap to that effect.

"Another important consideration, as far as the friendly situation is concerned, is what we hear to the north and northeast of us. Our soldiers are in contact with the enemy that has been lured out of Laos. Either that, or our U.S. Army has moved into Laos."

I looked at each of them in turn, hoping for some comments, but again, none came.

I continued, "Since you guys seemed to have lost your tongues, I'm going to make a last observation and I don't want any smart-ass remarks or comments on it. Here it is: the only open area for us is west and also it is the last direction the NVA would expect us to take. In short, back into Laos."

Doc opened his mouth to speak.

"Shut up, Doc!" I ordered. "Now that we have all that out of the way, and you agree that back into Laos would be a sensible direction to go, we can get to the next item.

"If it concerns the disposition of the wounded, I don't want to be part of it unless it's a Medevac," said Doc. He stood up and wanted to leave.

"Sit down, Doc," I ordered. "You'll listen whether you like it or not, and you're part of it whether you like it or not. I've warned you once to go easy. I'll not do it again."

"Yes, the wounded. Nineteen, right, Doc? Eleven can't walk?" "Right. There are 19. Two I don't expect to live till morning, unless we get them to a hospital." Doc did not sound affected by my strong admonition.

"Tom has been in contact with Booby Trap and Group requesting Medevacs," I lied, and Tom helped me out.

"Yeah, dey say maybe. If'n it was U.S. wounded dey would have been heah by now."

Our call sign came over the air. Tom took his notebook and muttered under his breath, "Damn, damn," in bitter tones, while he copied the message which read: "Be advised Ba Cat fell to enemy — Stop — Keep tight security and stay in place — Stop — Standby to mark your location for air observer — End of message."

After I pondered over the message, I ordered Tom to send the following message to Booby Trap. I spoke slowly so that Tom could copy it exactly for encoding.

"Acknowledge — Stop — Request urgent intel enemy activity in slate creek west of my position — Stop — Imperative I seek escape route — Stop — Still company strength and well supplied — Stop — Terrain impossible to direct close support fire — End of message."

The Morse key on Tom's knee moved so fast I could not distinguish between the dots and dashes. Within seconds he handed me another message already decoded.

Cathy stood close to me. In an impulsive move I handed her the message.

"Read it to me. I'm studying the map."

I made my words sound as if it was a normal order. I had the 1:25,000 Army map spread out on the ground in front of me.

She was a little hesitant at first, but read it to me.

"Two hour time lapse for intel on Slate Creek — Stop — Large enemy concentration six miles north your position moving south — Stop — Air Ops report scattered squad size enemy units movement your area — End of message."

After reading the message, she handed it to me. I stuck it in my pocket with the many others, thinking that I should not forget to burn them all the first time we got near a fire.

"Tony." Tom approached me. "Do you know if anyone else, other dan us, Group, and Booby Trap has our One-Time pad? Fo man, I gets interference and I picks up orders to Group and Booby Trap ever so often."

"Maybe, Tom. I think higher headquarters, such as Eighth Army and Military Advisory Group Vietnam (MACV) in Saigon, sometimes want some entertainment, like in a radio mystery story of old time, like the one, *Only the Shadow Knows.* Then they get our One-Time pad and have some fun listening to us."

"Nudder message," Tom said. "Booby Trap must have diarrhea of de mouth." He handed me another message.

"At 1900 fire two red signal flares overhead your position –— Stop — I say again 1900 — End of message"

"Acknowledge."

Tom put his transmitter down.

"Booby Trap out." He sighed.

I drew Mock's attention.

"Captain, please runners report as soon as entire patrol closed in. Bring perimeter security in as tight as possible, ASAP. Tell men Medevac took place Black Face." He glanced at an interpreter, a few Yard babbles were heard, and off went Mock. Doc stood some short distance from me. He had heard me lie about the Medevac but said nothing. His head was hung in total dejection. I had to snap him out of it.

"Doc, where and what have you done with the American creep?" I asked sternly, wanting him to think that I was holding him in dereliction of duty, not having the creep with us.

"I'm not responsible for him. He is somewhere with the 2nd Platoon," he snapped back at me, and it made me feel good.

"The last time I saw him he was in a fetal position and looked as if he would stay that way for the rest of his life. As far as I am concerned, he might as well do that."

I walked over to Doc and put my arm on his shoulder. "Eh, Babe, many things we do, we do not like. Let's fight this one the way we fought so many others. Okay, Babe?"

He nodded his head.

"Enough on your mind, Tony, you can count on me, so do what you think is necessary."

We looked each other in the eyes, and I knew we were a team again.

I was just about to speak to Mock alone when Tom called out to me. "Another message. It is priority." Then he added. "Damn, damn, Tony. Read this."

He gave me the scribbled message. It read: "Operational control of combat patrol forthwith ARVN responsibility — Stop — ARVN advisors will take charge — Stop — U.S. personnel standby for air evac 0500 next — End of message."

Tom and I looked at each other for a long time without saying a thing. It almost seemed as if we read each other's minds. When I did speak, Tom did not utter a word. He agreed with what I had quickly planned.

Mock reported, "Patrol closed in."

"Thanks, Captain, and now you get some sleep. Tomorrow is going to be one hell of a day."

I remembered the American creep. "Captain, please see that the American gets to me ASAP?"

"Yes be, Sargy," he answered with a smile. "Dat man be boo coo candy ass."

"You're learning English fast," I thought, wondering where he had picked up that new adjective. I walked away from the hootch. I needed time to myself to sort out the new situation Booby Trap had sprung on me.

Back in the hootch, Doc, Tom, and Cathy were silently waiting for my return. I spoke to Doc first.

"Doc, the order says that we are to be extricated at first light tomorrow."

"Praise the Lord for that. Finally we can terminate this stinking patrol. There was no reason why we should have gone onto Black Face in the first place, and then that ordeal against the hamlet in Laos..."

Tom interrupted. "You finish, honky? Fo if'n you aint I's gonna slit your throat."

Tom's tone of voice was dangerous.

"Easy, you two," I ordered. "As soon as the creep shows up I'll outline the plan. In the meantime, Doc, you'll have more to complain about when you find out what else the message said."

"Okay, lay it on me," he answered belligerently.

"Group informed me that Ba Cat is now ARVN responsibility, and get this, Doc," I made sure that he gave me his full attention, "We three, you, Tom, and me are the only ones ordered out."

"What!" He almost choked on a piece of half-chewed meat. He swallowed it whole, and burst out, "What about the patrol?"

"Listen, you two. The NVA has the camp. The ARVN is responsible now. Group wants us the hell out of the picture so that ARVN retaliation for the killing of the eleven ARVN SF will exclude any U.S. personnel. Be most embarrassing if the ARVNs got a hold of any of our SF Team. Especially me."

I stopped to see what result my quick summation of the situation had on the two of them.

"That is why our people let the NVA take our camp. I hope that they acted fast enough to get the rest of our A-Team out," Doc said as if talking to himself.

"What about de patrol, Tony?" asked Tom.

"Yes, what about the patrol?" Doc also wanted to know.

I knew that I again could depend on Doc's full cooperation, for as always, when things crowded us, all personal likes and dislikes vanished. That was what made us an effective team.

"The message said the ARVN will take charge. We can forget that. No South Viet will drop close to us to take over. Terrain and the enemy situation wipe that stupid thought out. I am surprised that Booby Trap would even send such information to us.

"The poor bastards will have to fend for themselves, by reverting to what they were before we came. They cannot return to the camp or their hamlet. If they do, they will run foul of both the ARVN and the NVA. It would be just a matter of time as to who got to them first."

I had no sooner said that when the full gravity of the situation dawned on me.

"Yes, that is it," I reflected out loud. "A perfect way for our people to wash their hands of the killing of the ARVN SF A-Team. If Group did not take that route, we could get ourselves involved with a nasty situation. The ARVN has to save face. They are not going to let half-dog, half-humans wipe out an entire SF A-Team of theirs and live to brag about it. They will kill them all, even the women and children. That way they can save face."

Doc added sadly, "In the process no one will ask, nor care, how many innocents will be killed."

"You have something to add, Tom?" I asked.

"Yeah, I got someting to add. But not wit a lady present."

"Thank you, Tom," Cathy said softly in a sweet voice.

I saw Tom become uncomfortable. With those three words she had won Tom over.

"I...I," stammered Tom, "More meat?" he finished roughly.

Doc and I looked at each other and exchanged smiles, knowing that Cathy need have no further fear of Tom.

"Tony, have you seen Don Gates lately? He is in a sad state," Doc sounded as if he did not care about the man.

Cathy was close enough to hear Doc. She turned her eyes on me. Some animosity seemed to have left her, but I had a feeling that I was treading on thin ice.

"Don't blame me," I said. She made me feel guilty. "We are doing what we can for the creep." Everything seemed to have dropped on me as if mine were the only empty lap.

I pulled Tom aside.

"Fake a message and hand it to me in front of Cathy. One that reads that an air evacuation took the wounded off Black Face. She and that creep can do us much damage when they get back without also reporting about the wounded."

"Den why let dem get back?" Tom asked.

"Easy, Babe, just let them think that we evac the wounded."

"What are you gonna do about de wounded? You can't just leave dem for de VC and NVA, man."

Tom was right. I could not leave them for the enemy to find. We could not move them. We could not get them evacuated. There was nothing that I could do.

"Think, Tom, why did Booby Trap order us to tighten up and give signal marker on our position? The Air Force is going to move Black Face into another dimension, and the wounded with it."

"Mother! You sure? B-52 strike dis close to us. Fuck it, man. I'm getting scared of you."

"Why me, you nigger! I'm not Booby Trap. I'm not asking for a B-52 strike on Black Face, and even if I did, Group would laugh me out of Vietnam. If it happens, then we blame Booby Trap for doing the wounded in."

I was getting real upset with Tom, but the thought of having something to blame Booby Trap for eased matters for both of us.

"Okay, okay, Babe, now I gots it straight. No problem. We blame Booby Trap. He's the mother."

As soon as we rejoined Doc, who was dishing up some food from a Mermite can for Cathy, Tom said, "Another message coming in."

He held his hand over his ear and receiver. Then he scribbled a message for me and handed it to Cathy, "Give it to Tony, another one coming in."

I had my hands full with a ladle of food when she wanted to hand me the message.

"Read it to me, please," I said.

She timidly read the message, "Medevac for wounded Yards on objective on the way — End of message."

I nodded my thanks and took the message and stuck it with the others in my pocket. Doc stood up to go up the mountain. I stopped him.

"No need for you to go Doc. The chopper's medics can do it."

He sat down believing that all was not as it should be.

"So what," I thought, and washed the entire matter of the wounded from my mind by ducking behind my gray veil.

One by one the runners reported to Mock that the patrol had closed in on us as Booby Trap had ordered. By 1800 the final report came to me. The patrol was where I wanted it. A 60mm mortar with the necessary rounds was brought to a small area that was clear overhead.

The hot food raised our morale. Even Cathy had a healthy appetite. She had a piece of chicken in one hand and a handful of rice in the other. Dirty hands no longer seemed to bother her.

A persistent, gnawing guilt regarding to Cathy caused me to speak to Mock. He and Cathy were sitting next to me. It was unlikely that she would get back to where she could carry damaging information. However, I still thought it my duty to try and win her heart and mind.

"You listen too, Cathy, and no comments from you. It is merely my knowledge of our Yards that makes me put it the way I am going to."

I spoke to Mock. "Mock, old buddy, me be worry Base Plate. Tomorrow, we be fight like hell VC, NVA. I no can take care she. She blong me same you woman blong you. You be speak Yards take care she I be catch VC bullet."

"Yes, be Sargy. All Yards be know Base Plate blong Sargy. All be take care she."

That out of the way, I had another matter to take care of.

"Captain Mock, you tell me. I see U.S. money with Yards. Scouts tell me. Now you be tell me where come U.S. money."

Mock looked uncomfortable. He gave me one of those famous Montagnard shit-eating grins, exposing toothless gums.

"Me no like be speak," was all he said.

"You be speak me, Captain. I want to know where the hell the money came from."

My tone wiped the grin off his face and Cathy moved away from us.

"Sargy, Tom he be have much, much money me no be know he catch hamlet near guns."

Mock pulled out of his pocket a bundle of U.S. hundred dollar bills and a bundle of U.S. dollar bills and handed them to me.

"Sargy Tom also he be have much, much ring, gold, money."

"I'll be damned," I exclaimed. "Where he keep all? I no see he carry."

"Me I no know." Mock answered. I knew that he was not lying.

"How many Yards be buried after the guns?" Mock held up four fingers of each hand.

I held up nine fingers.

"No be, Sargy." And he held up eight fingers again.

"Okay, Captain." I put my arm on his shoulder to show that I was not upset.

"We no be speak more. All we forget, you, me." He understood and looked relieved.

"That ninth grave. Just perhaps," I thought. "The World Council of Churches may still have things to explain." I had scored a point.

United States money was used to support the Viet Cong. Whatever they needed was available on the black market in any South Vietnamese city. The U.S. money was found where those Council members were found.

Just maybe, two plus two still makes four, I thought.

Cathy, who was watching us from a little way off, slowly came back to sit close. A make-shift shelter had sprung up around us with Ding and Mo supervising some Yards on the project. It was cozy, with a small fire that cast a friendly glow in the slowly fading afternoon twilight.

The creep was brought into the circle and laid down on a jungle blanket. He remained in a fetal position. To me it was a disgusting state for a man to fall into.

Tom and I were perhaps the only ones that expected all hell to break loose within an hour or so after we fired the markers. The flares would explode above us for an air observer to see. It was 1900. We waited for Booby Trap's order to fire the flares.

While we waited I felt Cathy's eyes on me. It created distracting thoughts that could have gotten me killed.

I had to tend to matters that were best taken care of with an uncluttered mind. My responsibilities to my men came first.

Damn, I thought, "what is she doing to me?

Seldom did I have sex with a woman and come back for more from the same woman. The conquest and personal gratification usually left me with no complaints. Then Cathy came along.

Maybe it was because she came from a walk of life that I was rarely identified with. Also, there in the stinking jungle she stood out as an embarrassing reminder of a world where people merely read about the war. By contrast, I found myself in a war I did not start, a war whose rules I did not make, a civil war at that, which, by its very nature, always brought out the worst in man.

Tom called out. "Here it is. Fire de flares."

I gave the signal, and up shot two mortar shells in quick succession. Our position was marked with pinpoint accuracy for an airborne observer to report to Group's Indication Center.

Within a few minutes after we fired we received eight digit coordinates of my position.

"That's fast," Doc said.

"Yeah, seems we is getting VIP treatment. More garbled messages on our frequency, and our one time pad is bein used by anodder station. Crazy, man. The bastards cut us off."

Tom was puzzled, and so was I. Our radio traffic was being monitored and interfered with by other friendly stations.

An 8-inch in support
of an A-Camp

Montagnards at
author's A-Camp,
Ba Cat

Author's bunker at
A-Camp, Ba Cat

105-mm howitzer in support of Infantry

Captured Viet Cong weaponry

Author and Mo (bottom center). All others were killed on Black Face Mountain

ARVN SF (Army of Republic of Viet Nam), our counterparts, who were killed by the "Yards" in Ba Cat

Author consoling a Montagnard's wife

House in
Chau Doc

Author (left) returning to Chau
Doc after another long night on
the Vinh Tay Canal

Author and street urchin in Chau Doc

Houses along the Vinh Tay Canal

Livestock transport on the Vinh Tay Canal

U.S. Navy River Patrol Boat on Vinh Tay Canal

Common daily traffic on Vinh Tay Canal

Always the question, "Are they hostile?" They could be Viet Cong moving supplies on Vinh Tay Canal

Vietnamese cargo vessels on Vinh Tay Canal

Author ready to return enemy fire

Author on his yacht after retirement from the Army

Chapter 6

Orders to Evacuate

The tropical evening twilight soon gave way to another black, cold night. The small flickering fire within our makeshift bamboo hut cast a friendly glow around us. Near us, the jungle's familiar night sounds started their crescendo.

My roving scouts and the silent stationary listening posts strained their well-developed natural senses. They were like a starving leopard and his vulnerable prey, the monkey. Both of them determined to stay alive.

All around us men were rolled up in their nylon camouflaged jungle blankets. I waited. I mentally pictured our B-52's pilots, their eyes glued to red and green dials tens of thousands of feet up between the clouds and the stars, heading from Guam, deep in the Pacific Ocean, toward their target.

I wondered what went through their minds just prior to the release of such an awesome devastation on the ground below them. A small piece of earth, over which they traveled for but a split second, would be left with everlasting, horrible scars of death and destruction.

Three hours after we had fired the two mortar marker rounds, all was still normal. I had started to doubt the possibility of a B-52 strike or a saturation shelling from the artillery pieces that we had within range of Black Face. It bothered me to think that the enemy had occupied Black Face and was torturing the wounded that we had to abandon.

Tom further disturbed me.

"Babe," he said. "I just got dis dis message from an unknown friendly station." He handed me the message.

I read it out loud. "Battalion size enemy concentration electronically detected at..." The coordinates it gave placed that unit nearly on top of Black Face.

Tom handed me a message from Booby Trap. It was short and singular, as if he was enjoying himself at my expense. It read, "Take cover."

Five minutes after that last message, it came — first a blast of hot air that shattered our flimsy hut and swept it away in a blinding flash. The earth shook as deafening explosions ripped open the belly of Black Face. The terrible destructive power of thousand-pound bombs kept raining down in such endless agony for the enemy that it could only be described as an Armageddon. Black Face Mountain became engulfed in an inferno of flying shrapnel and flames. Our B-52s were bringing down the curtain.

Wherever B-52s struck and then flew on, only silence remained. They not only obliterated the enemy's will to continue action in that area, but also made raving maniacal basket cases of any who might have been unfortunate enough to survive the strike.

At the first blast of the holocaust, Cathy threw herself into my arms. She clung to me in terror. Her body shook with fear.

Most of us had experienced such a strike, but never that close. Many of our Yards were terrified. Some of them called loudly to their long-departed ancestors for help.

The explosions seemed endless. The earth around us started to climb up in the form of heavy dust that almost suffocated us. On and on the terrible thunderclaps of explosions compressed the air until it hurt our ears.

When the silence finally came, it was a strange silence. The entire jungle held its breath. For a few moments, no one moved. As if a still picture had been given motion, things slowly came to life. Eerily at first, then normally.

Cathy seemed reluctant to leave my embrace where she must have felt some small measure of safety. I stroked a matted blond curl from her face. She did not move away from me. Neither did she object when I lingered my palms over her firm breasts. Poor thing, I thought. But that thought did not deter me from enjoying her closeness. My hands wondered further over her body and she did not push them away.

The B-52 strike had effected me so much that I had to jolt myself back to reality.

"Ding, get the damn Yards to scat. All be back normal now. Base Plate, she be want hootch rebuilt, also she be want water for to wash clean. You be gets. Also, you be gets clean uniform that be fit she."

He wanted to say something, but I shut him up. "I no be care where you be gets clean uniform. You be gets!"

Cathy let out with a nervous giggle, and muttered, "You be gets?" She managed to smother another sound with both her hands on her mouth.

"You dumb Yards, Base Plate she be say scat." I waved them all out.

That did it. Base Plate seemed the magic prod that shook them all out of their earlier fear. Ding let fly with some Montagnard cuss words and used his boot to one unfortunate ammo bearer. Activity sprang up around us. Forgotten was the B-52 strike, which had a few minutes earlier befuddled their minds. Throughout the command, nerves were a too tightly strung for the Yards to crawl back into their sleeping positions. Some gathered firewood. The building of fires did not disturb me since all enemy activity would cease temporarily.

I walked with Mock among the Yards. Smiles met us wherever we stopped to say a few encouraging words. Mostly, we promised them some easy action for the next day against an NVA village.

It had become an obsession with me to strike again into Laos. I planned to attack a hamlet a few miles inside Laos along the Ho Chi Minh Trail. I hoped I could disturb the 5th NVA Division's rear.

I noticed that Mo was following Cathy everywhere she went. I called to Doc.

"You can do this better than I, Doc. The girl must have need of some privacy...you know what I mean."

"Yes, she needs to relieve herself as all of us do," Doc said with some bitterness. "I'll take care of it."

After about an hour, Mock and I returned to the headquarters area. I saw Cathy's head bobbing above a screen made of jungle blankets. Mo and ding splashed canteens of water over her. I saw a number of empty canteens laying around. I learned that all the Yards of the 2nd Platoon had to donate their drinking water.

I smiled at the thought of what Fort Benning's Infantry Training Center would say to what was taking place — within an enemy controlled area men were using precious drinking water to bathe a female who was far from being an asset.

How the nearly clean fatigues came about, I did not want to know, but she was in receipt of a new-looking set that fit her. When she stepped out from behind the screen and into the firelight, many Yards were there to express their approval.

Her face was the only face around that was not smeared with black ashes or streaked with sweat.

The ease with which such a trifling divergence beguiled and tickled the Yard, even out here in enemy territory, would have caused Napoleon to turn over in his grave.

In defense of their childish actions, one must realize that Montagnards had not left their home to move against the enemy. They were at home, and the mountains and the jungle, with their inherent dangers, easily absorbed the additional dangers the Communists injected. Consequently, they did not take the war as seriously as we did.

"Captain Mock!" I called. "Unless these dumb Yards shut up and start behaving like soldiers, I'm going to trade them off for NVA and VCs."

Again I regretted my words. As soon as Mock translated what I said, the mountain rang with happy laughter.

Tom and Doc shook their heads.

"De guy is gonna to get us all killed or committed to a nut house yet," said Tom.

"Fort Benning or Bragg ever hear how he runs a patrol inside enemy-held terrain, he'll be transferred to the Marines, and maybe us with him." Doc sounded in better spirits.

"Captain Mock, you and Ding come me. We be speak North Viets." I wispered to Ding, "You be gets them away from here. I no be want Base Plate hear scream of prisners." He nodded and disappeared into the dark.

"Cathy, I'm going to speak to the North Vietnamese civilian before I release him to let him return to Laos. Can you tell me something about him?" I asked in a friendly manner.

She did not answer me immediately. Her moods seemed to vacillate between wanting to shoot me and love me.

"He was assigned to us as a guide and interpreter We were in Attapue, a village about 20 miles from where you...found us."

I silently thanked her for not using the word captured.

"Is he a civilian?"

"I don't know, maybe. I think he is, though. He did not have a uniform on at any time that I have known him."

"For how long did you know him?"

"Two weeks. From the day that we arrived in Attapue until you..."

"I understand. Only one more question. Did he say that he too belonged to the WCC?"

"Yes, he did." With those three words she condemned him.

"Please be nice to him as you were to the two Frenchmen. They are really good people." Again she sounded dejected.

"Yeah, I'll be good to him," I answered with compunction, and walked away. I was relieved to hear that she believed that I did indeed sent the two French back to Laos. It was a worry off my mind.

"I want the civilian first." I told Mock, who had four of our scouts sitting near him.

He was a man of about 45. The short period that he had been with us had taken a terrible toll on his physical appearance.

"Can you speak English?" I asked.

He just shook his head as if he did not understand me.

One hell of an interpreter, I thought.

"Captain Mock, you ask him where he comes from, what he was doing with the Americans, and anything else you want to hear. Me, I no care what he say. He be damn comnis. You be do him in."

Within a few minutes after Mock had asked him the normal questions, he turned to me and said, "Sargy, dis man he be say he man of church. I be say him one big fuck lie, Nort Viets no be gots church. I be give he to Ding? Okay?"

I shook my head. "No, Ding, not here. Take him away first."

I had to speak fast. Ding almost had his bayonet into the man. I was afraid of screams. We were too close to the hut.

"Tom," I called him to the side. "Fake a message that the wounded were evacuated from Black Face prior to the B-52 strike. We may as well make sure that no one believes that they were still on the mountain when the strike took place. Read the message out loud in front of one or two interpreters. They'll spread the word around."

"Okay, Babe. I'll take care of it," said Tom.

One of the North Vietnamese officers was brought before us. He appeared arrogant and not too badly off for the period that he had been our prisoner. He acted disdainful of all Yards. It was a typical Vietnamese attitude toward Montagnards.

His eyes were on me, and I knew that if Mock or any of the other Yards were to speak to him, he would ignore them.

"I don't want to waste time with you," I addressed him, taking it for granted that he understood me. The North Vietnamese officers were mostly educated, and I had found that most of them spoke English fairly well.

"If you answer my questions, you may live. If not, you die."

He said nothing. A blank, defiant look was all I received. I knew that were I his prisoner, he would thoroughly enjoy torturing me, perhaps doing to me the same as had been done to our four scouts.

Mock slowly walked closer to him. I saw the hatred in Mock's face.

"Me be do same he be do our scouts. Afta dat he be speak boo coo much."

"No, Captain. Just wait. I want to find out about this one." I had to speak quickly for it looked as if Mock was going to kill him right there on the spot.

I came close to the prisoner. "You have a chance to live if you give me a few answers." I said in a kind voice.

The man spat in my face. Ding and Mock jumped to get to him so fast they threw the two scouts that were holding the prisoner down on the ground. I grabbed Ding and threw him so hard against Mock that both of them sprawled on the ground well away from the prisoner. Both had bayonets at the ready and the man would have been dead had I not acted fast.

"Hold it, both of you!" I cried. "And I am sorry, Captain. I just wanted to stop you two. Are you okay, Captain?"

I picked the confused Mock up and dusted the dirt off his uniform.

"Please forgive me, Captain." I was genuinely sorry for having done that to Mock.

"It be okay, Sargy. Me I sometime be damn fool like all Yard. Sargy he be speak me unstand." Mock had recovered his composure.

"You be trust me, Mock old buddy, I want this one to go. I gots very good reason.

I be tell you later." I whispered to him. Mock slowly nodded his head. He trusted me.

Ding came to me with his water canteen in one hand and a rag in the other while his eyes were riveted on the prisoner. He wet the rag and slowly washed the spit off my face, or rather smeared it, for his eyes did not stray from the prisoner while he was doing it. I saw something in Ding's eyes that I had not seen before. It surpassed hatred. I put my hands on Ding's shoulders and shook him softly.

"Ding, look at me." I said. "We, you me, we be solder."

It took Ding a little while before he answered.

"Yes, be, Sargy. We be solder." But he did not look at me. He kept his eyes on the prisoner.

I turned his head so that he had to look at me and said quietly, "Okay, we be solder. You, me, Captain Mock. We be solder. Solder he be like be take order, okay."

"Yes be, Sargy, solder he be like take order." I could tell that he was starting to pay attention to me. He looked into my eyes like a child baffled about what was going on, and wanting someone to tell him.

I called for Doc and ordered him, "Go with this prisoner. Take two scouts and safeguard him until he is out of our perimeter. Once safely away, cut him loose and let him find his own way back to his unit."

In the dim light I could not see what effect my order had on Doc, but he put his hand on my shoulder and gave it a gentle squeeze. He and two scouts led the prisoner away.

The reason I let that North Vietnamese Army officer go was not clear to me. I did, however, feel that the man had as all-consuming a hatred for his enemy as I had for mine. We had something in common. Whatever the reason, I knew that I had done the right thing. He was a soldier, and any man that had the guts to spit in my face under those circumstances would not be the type that would torture a prisoner of war.

I turned my attention to the other officer. I had assessed him while I spoke to the first one. He acted nervous and I was sure that we were going to have no trouble getting him to tell us what we wanted to know.

"You understand English?" I asked in an amiable manner. He nodded his head. His fear was plain. Blood had drained from his face and I noticed in the dim light that he was shaking.

"Four of our Montagnard scouts were tortured by you yesterday. The same way you always treat our prisoners. You personally ever done that to one?" I asked as if it was but a small and insignificant matter.

"No, not me. I go by Geneva Convention," he answered in fluent English. His accent was French. With my opening question, I established that he was aware of what they did to Green Berets and Yard prisoners. That he did not deny knowing about it was important to me.

"You must understand that I am the only person here who can stop the Montagnards from doing the same to you. They take orders from me. Right now," I pointed in the direction the other man was taken, "your friend has a rag stuffed into his mouth and they are cutting his balls off and sewing them into his mouth. I won't let them do it to you. I'll send you to a POW camp run by the U.S. but you must cooperate with me." He started to say something, but I waved him to silence.

"Don't speak yet. I want you to understand that we already have the answers to the questions I am going to ask you. Our airplanes had already taken pictures of your tanks in Laos. So don't lie to me."

I walked over to Mock and took his cigarette pack out of his pocket. I shook one out, lit it, and put it in the prisoner's mouth. He took a strong pull and inhaled it. I gave him another chance at the cigarette, then stamped it out under my boot. With my bayonet I cut the lashings off his arms.

"Now, my friend. How many tanks are directly across the border?" I asked in a soft, friendly tone.

"Seven Sir, only seven." He was still shaking with fear.

"Where are they?" I had spread my map out for him to see and I handed him my flashlight. For a few seconds he played the light over the map, then kept the beam on the Laotian town of Attapue.

"There."

His shaking finger settled on a flat area ten miles from where we were, close to a dirt road that I knew was used by the NVA to infiltrate supplies into South Vietnam for the VC."Where are the headquarters of your Fifth Infantry Division?" He did not know. According to him, the entire division was still on the move from where they had been in Cambodia. He also told us that information had been passed on to them that the U.S. and ARVN Forces were expected to move into Cambodia, and that was why they took the countermeasure of moving out of Cambodia.

I received all the information needed to support my belief that I could strike into Laos, destroy the tanks, and disappear once more back into South Vietnam. The prisoner was sure that there were no infantry units near the tanks. He could not tell us who the spy within the ARVN was that passed the classified information to them regarding our impending invasion of Cambodia, until I thought of something.

I asked him, "Do you know who General Tran Do is?"

I saw a twitch in his expression that triggered a suspicion in my mind. I took a chance that he knew the general. General Tran Do was the deputy VC Commander, and it was common knowledge that he was headquartered somewhere in Cambodia.

"No, I do not know him," he whispered nervously with his eyes darting anywhere but into mine.

Softly I spoke to him, while shining my flashlight into his eyes. "I can take you to where your friend now has his balls sewed in his mouth with barbed wire. Do not lie to me. Where is General Tran Do's headquarters?"

His legs gave way. "Please, please do not hurt me. I tell everything, but please..." His voice faded and he sank all the way down to the ground.

Two Yards lifted him while another one threw water in his face.

"Tell me, where is his headquarters." I kept my voice low but threatening.

"In Tuy Duc," he said so softly that I barely heard him.

"And an ARVN Colonel Pham Ngoc Thao, do you know of him?"

"Yes, I have heard of him."

"What do you know about him?" This time I put my hands on him for the first time. I took him by his neck and gripped my right hand around his thin neck. I squeezed slightly and could easily have strangled him with one hand.

"He is relative of the general," he answered and that was all that I wanted to hear.

Many of our intelligence people in Group had, for a long time, suspected that ARVN Colonel Pham Ngoc Thao was connected with the VC, but they could not get higher headquarters to investigate him.

I had hopes that the additional information I could give our people might just cause them to start an investigation into the colonel's activities. The man was placed in a perfect position to know about our Army's operations.

Sadly, nothing like that took place. That colonel was too popular with the high command, and there were too many gullible Americans who did not want to make waves among the hierarchy of the South Vietnamese government.

I called Tom to me and walked a little way off with him while I scribbled a message concerning that traitorous colonel on my message book. I handed it to Tom and said, "Send this priority and encoded with eyes only for Booby Trap. Give it a Secret classification."

Then I took my time and wrote a long message on all the pertinent information I had obtained. Tom transmitted the information to Booby Trap. I included in the message a statement that the prisoner was killed in action. If I had not done so, I would have been ordered to safeguard him and deliver him to our intelligence unit for further questioning.

Since I now knew where the enemy tanks were, I briefed all our scouts and planned the reconnaissance patrols into that area. I had to be extra careful in the operation against the tanks. Under normal situations, what I had planned would have been unwise, but I did not consider matters to be normal at the time. The distant rumble of a battle in progress against our enemy spurred me on.

When Doc returned to the hootch he could not keep the good news of the North Vietnamese's release to himself. He told Tom in the presence of Cathy.

"Tony surprised me by turning the prisoners loose. I guided one of them out of our area and sent him on his way back to Laos. The others I believe are also on their way back."

Tom said nothing. He knew about the others but must have thought that I had a good reason for letting one go.

Cathy said softly, "I am happy for them. There is enough suffering all around us without harming them. Especially the interpreter. He is such a nice man."

With Cathy believing that I had turned prisoners loose for humane reasons, I seemed to have won her heart and mind for the benefit of our Army. Perhaps for myself, I hoped. It became a plus in a sort of chess game that we were required to play.

A change in her attitude toward me came immediately. Gone was the severe scrutiny she had cast in my direction. It was replaced with a more relaxed and direct acceptance of my nearness to her. No longer did she glue her eyes on me, only to look away quickly when I looked back at her.

Our scouts had brought some fresh meat into our bivouac. It was unnecessary, for we had one full Mermite can in our hut. The Yards were competing among themselves to bring things to Cathy. She had a large barbecued deer steak ready for me when I returned. She served it on a palm leaf.

"Here is your steak. Sorry no lobster or cold fresh milk. And Tony, thank you for letting those men go," she said softly.

I acted thankful for the fresh meat, and was genuinely thankful for the change in her. I forgot the apprehensive feeling I had about the safety of the patrol. Group's moribund display of interest in us gave me reason to believe that we were heading for big trouble.

"Very good," I said, with a mouth full of deer steak that I gladly would have exchanged for what was in the Mermite can. The smell of the spiced rice and chicken that came out of the can made my mouth water. I was hungry.

"These little naked men," she said, referring to my scouts, six of whom where crouched around us. "They brought so much meat and of so many different kinds, that I had to send some of it to the other men."

"I hope you did not ask what kind of meat they brought." I felt relaxed for the first time in many hours.

"Why not?"

"Oh, no real reason. It's just not polite in their society." I had to lie while looking at the snake, lizard, rat, and other delicacies that the Yards had stacked in a dim corner of the hut under large pieces of deer meat.

"I really can't speak to them because they smile so much that I can't tell if they understand me or not. And, Tony, why do so many of them have their front teeth missing? That poor little Mo. His mouth and lips are just too awful for words. I got some salve from Doc and put it on his mouth. What happened to him?"

It sounded pleasantly strange to me to hear her speak my name. I was also glad to know that she was finally adjusting to a situation that she surely must have realized she could not influence.

"Not near as much as what is going to happen to him the next time he hides from me when there may be some fighting. Like when I wanted him to go with Ding on top of Black Face."

I wasn't about to tell her how Mo lost his front teeth, and why. I smiled to myself, thinking how she would have reacted.

"Better you don't know. Eat your meat. Montagnards' customs and habits are not easy for us to understand. We Special Forces study them carefully, and still we get surprises handed to us each day."

I had noticed the absence of hostility, and kept hoping for a measure of forgiveness from her, so I ventured further.

"You're as clean as a Yard who fell into a river. Your hair is beautiful, shining like yellow gold. You are lovely."

She made no reply, but slowly turned away from me and sat down in a dark corner of the hootch.

I heard Tom's voice.

"Look at dis," he sounded disgusted as he handed me a decoded message. "It's de same as de oder one."

I held the message close to the small fire and read. "Operational control of Ba Cat transferred to ARVN - stop - All U.S. personnel extricate GS 10751539 at 0500 — End of message."

"Doc and Mock, deys outside," Tom said, having anticipated what I would do.

"All Yards, you scat!" I ordered. They cleared the hootch. Doc and Mock came in. I had to think fast, for I knew they would keep quiet and expect me to do all the talking. My morale had fallen in ruins.

I was thankful that the hootch remained silent. Cathy had retreated to a dim far corner of the hut from which she kept her eyes on me. I could just barely see her.

A change in her attitude was slightly disturbing. I did not believe it was because I had released the one prisoner. I thought that she actually believed I had released them all. In that case I was able to file away her new attitude toward me for future exploitation.

The small fire inside the hootch was reduced to red embers. Deep in thought, I added a few sticks to the fire. As the small flames grew, to cast their ghoulish shadows around us, I saw that all eyes were on me. I let the message catch fire and held it until the flames completely consumed it. As the last corner turned black, I said, "We three are ordered back to Group." Only silence greeted my words.

I turned to Cathy. "Please give those two some meat. I need a little more time."

She did not answer me. Slowly and quietly she took palm leaves, and using them as plates, handed each a piece of meat. Again she retreated back into the dim corner of the hut.

No one made frivolous comments or gave expressions of disagreement with the command's order. We just seemed resigned to the bitter situation Booby Trap's message had plunged us into.

It was as if someone had sprung a trap door beneath me and I was tumbling into a blank void below. The full impact of the order on the patrol read like a death sentence to each and every Yard around us.

Two Yards brought the creep into the hut, and laid him down on a blanket.

"You're Don, right? Well you have lucked out. Seems as if you are going to live after all."

He gave me a blank look. Perhaps the guy is already dead, I mused.

"Cathy, at 0500 tomorrow, you and this creep will be taken to a spot not far from here. We'll wait for about five minutes, flash a light while Tom transmits a radio signal. We'll hear helicopters. They will be the two Cobra gunships that will suppress ground fire if necessary.

"Then suddenly another helicopter will appear as if from nowhere. It will literally drop from the sky." I stopped for a moment. Cathy had come close to me.

"One of two things will happen. The chopper will actually touch down on the ground, or it will hover at tree top level and drop a sling to lift us up. In either case, we have to get out with the chopper within seconds. Every moment that the helicopter is near the ground it can receive enemy small arms fire."

If Cathy had come any closer to me I would have had to put the fire out. The small flames were slapping playfully around the logs, lighting up the interior of the hootch. I caught Doc's knowing smile. He too was aware that Cathy, seemingly not aware of her own actions, was involuntarily reaching out to hold onto someone. That someone was me.

"If the chopper lands, it will be no problem because the three of us will throw you into the arms of the helicopter crew. You'll be handled roughly, but you'll be okay. If they drop the rope, be prepared for a shock. We'll get you into a sort of harness and put your hands on the rope. All you will have to do is hang on. You'll be unceremoniously jerked into the air with a ter-rible wind-blast hitting your head.

"Before you'll know just what has happened, you will find yourself dangling thousands of feet in the air, swinging crazily below and behind the chopper as it drags you to safety.

"After what will seem like hours, you'll be dumped unceremoniously on the ground, at which time you will get clear of the chopper. You'll either be picked up or left to be taken care of by other friendly elements. That's it," I said. Cathy was sitting tightly against me.

Tom said, "Expect a lot of dust and noise, grass and sticks will fly around when dat chopper come in. Dey be in one hell of a hurry to get back high up away from us ground people. Dem boys, dey been shot at before and dey don't like it."

We all sat around the fire, wrapped in our private thoughts. Cathy asked. "Can these small people find safety after you leave?" She sounded genuinely concerned for the Yards.

You poor misguided, do-gooder, I thought. I did not feel like answering her but I did.

"It will be hard for them, Cathy. You see, they cannot go back to their families at Ba Cat. The NVA have taken that area. We know that it will be but a matter of time before we retake the camp, but then the ARVN will be in charge. And they represent a greater threat to these Yards of ours than does the enemy."

"But why, Tony? Surely they're on the same side in this terrible war?"

Again she used my name and it made me feel good. She had involved herself with us so much that it would have been easy for me to consider her a team member. "Yes and no. I can't explain it all now. However, one over- riding consideration is connected with an incident that took place just prior to our launching this patrol."

"Was it what you mentioned earlier...killing some South Vietnamese soldiers?" She found her words difficult to say. "Yes, eleven South Vietnamese SF. Our counterparts."

"Who killed them and why?"

"Long story, Cathy. One that started thousands of years ago when a very beautiful princess, who lived in these mountains, got herself lost."

I could see Cathy was puzzled. "I... I don't understand."

"Neither do we. Doc and I listened to the story and later we saw the start of another story unfold. The second story is the sequel to the first and is now slowly unfolding before our eyes. I'm trying hard not to make you part of it, since I cannot predict how the story will end. I don't think it will be happily ever after."

Doc spoke up in a light tone. "It would seem, Tony, that at 0500 it will be the end of the story for us."

"And leave de Yards under Mock who ain't gots ten cents of imagina-tion, man! Four hours afta we've left every Yard heah will be dead or cap-tured."

Tom sounded very perturbed and he had reason to be. What he expressed was my belief, too, and I knew that Doc agreed.

They looked at me. "The orders are for you guys to go back tomor-row," I reminded them.

"You guys?" Doc put another piece of wood on the fire. "That sounds as if you are excluding yourself, Tony."

"Well, we all talked and said nothing that we did not already know. How about you two coming up with some answers?"

Tom spoke up immediately, sounding nonchalant. "Easy. We follow Group's orders and go home. On de chopper at 0500, at 0600 we'll be eat-ing steak an eggs for breakfast in a safe American infantry division area. Close by will be a jet airfield wit planes goin back to de real world."

"Be serious, Tom," Doc said softly. "I'm not leaving, you are not leaving and the only way we are going to get Tony to leave our Yards to be destroyed, is to shoot him first. So, there...I've said it."

"And let me also say it. You, all of you. Cathy, you two, and the creep will be on that chopper in the morning if I have to use my scouts. Bullets through the legs and then throw them onto the chopper will be my order to Ding. So, just be ready to board that chopper. Now, you guys, we sleep."

I unrolled my blanket and in a nearby shadow I lay down to rest, but sleep would not come. One could not plan to cross one's personal Rubicon on the next day, then fall pleasantly asleep. I could not even summon my gray veil.

Having made up my mind, away went fear, guilt, reproach, and all my apprehensions about what the Command would have held me accountable for. Again I remembered some words written by a Chinese philosopher — Out of the 39 ways of solving your personal problems, the best is to run away.

Silently I congratulated myself for the guile with which I intended to divert fate's pendulum, and make it swing only on my command, when 0500 hours came.

This time, I whispered to myself, I'll make my own options. The Yards will do as I tell them. Mock and I... A soothing mental state took over. I no longer pondered things. Fate's pendulum had swung.

Dying embers still glowed brightly within the temporary hootch. Crickets tattooed the night-air with their needle-sharp screeches, while weary night owls scared the superstitious.

High within the trees, panicked monkeys noisily swung from branch to branch, while the leopard lay quiet and patient against a tree trunk. It seemed as if it was not only man that lived in disharmony with man. All nature joined in that sorry order.

I wished that I had been given more options, instead of always being washed headlong and pell-mell to wherever the hell I was heading. Then Cathy came to me. She gave her lips to me and the world stood still.

The sweet smell of her clean body took away my thoughts. She was in my arms, where she cam willingly, and she even helped me by wiggling out of her clothes. She gave her body to me to hold, fondle, and to care for with complete, innocent trust.

Ding, with his strange dog-like attention to me, cleared the hut with his boot. Mo hesitated a little but Ding sent him flying headfirst out of the hut.

Alone with the surrendered Cathy in the dimly lit, silent hut, I played my tongue on her breasts and licked her hardened nipples. She cooed softly and held me tightly.

"Please, please," She whispered. "I can't stand it any more, please go inside of me, Tony. I want you."

She seemed to explode with orgasm after orgasm with each thrust I made. She was tight and silky smooth and I felt her wanting to hold me. It was over but she would not let me go.

A silence had settled over the patrol. Overhead, slowly drifting white clouds gazed down on the mountain through a bright moonlit night, while the star-studded heavens rolled on.

All through the night, a determined enemy searched us out. His scouts stealthily slipped among the shadows, and sniffed the cool air for our scent. The soap our clothes were washed in, the cigarettes we smoked, the food we ate, all combined to emit a unique odor, foreign and detectable to the enemy.

My own scouts also guarded the night. They would lie still, untiring and dedicated, to give warning against a surprise attack. They too relied on their senses of smell, hearing, sight and a strange, well-developed and vivid comprehension of their natural surroundings.

After Cathy and I had lain next to each other for some time, I asked softly, "You asleep?"

"No," She cried softly while holding onto me. Tears shone on her cheeks. "What are you doing to me, Tony? You are too strong for me to fight, and if you were not, I would not want to fight you. Everything is so final out here in this strange world of yours, that I have become too weak to fight against what I know to be wrong."

I almost made the mistake of asking her to run that by me again. It sounded too much like double talk, intended to draw out my guilt. I did not in the least feel guilty any more. She was too much of a woman to waste herself on shallow values. To me, life and love were inseparable. And besides, life was too short. Of that, I had daily reminders.

I gathered her into my arms again and if the enemy had decided to attack us, I would not have wanted to fire back. I had become too busy and overwhelmed withthe heavenly feel of her yielding body. Cathy had again given herself totally to me and to the moment.

Later that night I felt two small bodies move close to me. "Ding, Mo, damn you two..." I did not finish what I wanted to say.

Cathy giggled. "There is one next to me too and another is slowly coming closer."

"Yeah," I just gave up. "At least we know that they are on our side. It's like having your guard dogs in bed with you."

"And warmth." She added and cuddled her naked body even tighter into my arms. Her sweet clean smell carried my thoughts to other times and places, well removed from the shadows of Black Face Mountain.

Then I slept. How long I slept I did not know, but as usual, when I was disturbed, I quietly and quickly moved away from where I had lain. Swiftly I slipped my clothing on and, with my pistol at the ready, I crawled out into the open. Behind me came four scouts. All but Mo silently stalked past me and fanned out in front of me. Mo hung onto my belt.

"Ding," I whispered. "You be stay Base Plate and take god-damn Mo with you." I detected a slight shuffle in back of me as Ding pried Mo off me, then the two of them moved back into the hootch.

Mock came up to me and tugged my sleeve. "Enmeny scout they be inside prelemeter defense. Me tink also Yards. Maybe they be Nung Tribe."

"Okay, you be take care. I'm going back to sleep." I peeled the green tape off my watch. The illuminated dials showed it to be 0200 hours.

"What is it?" Cathy asked softly, as I reentered the hootch.

"Nothing much. Just some enemy scouts among us."

"Isn't it dangerous?"

"Not really. They'll just try to get away again. Must have goofed and stumbled past our listening posts. Our scouts will smell them out."

"Smell them out?"

"Yes. The soap they use on their bodies, if they ever do, plus the Turkish tobacco they use and, above all, the oil they cook their food in — all combine to cause a strong odor different from that which we emit. Yes, they'll be smelled out, and if possible to speak with them, they'll be safe. If they belong to any of the tribes we have with us at this time, they will furnish us with valuable information. We may even get them to join us."

"A stranger example of human behavior surely does not exist anywhere else on earth. With all my formal education in sociology, I can't understand all of you. You three, your Montagnards, your enemy, and those who side with you."

"Don't feel lonesome. Neither do we understand, and it is not understanding that makes things a little easier for us."

Before I could drop off to sleep again, Mock called out to me from outside the hootch. "We be gots them enmeny scout. Some be Bru, one he be here wit me. You be know he."

"Okay, bring him in, and Ding, gets be much fire. Base Plate she be boo coo cold."

Ding heaped dry grass and sticks on the dying fire, and flames soon lit the interior of the hootch, casting a pleasant warm glow all around us. Cathy quickly turned her back to us and held her fatigue jacket and trousers around herself. Our primitive surroundings had caused her to forget that she was naked.

A pitifully small, partly naked Montagnard stood before me. Fear and cold had conspired to make him a very miserable, shivering Yard. When I moved him close to the fire I recognized him.

"You be Gia Bac, the Yard we used to call Shylock." He turned toward me and gave me a toothless smile. "Yes be, Sargy. Me be Sylock."

Tom had entered the hootch. "Well, what do you know? Just like old times eh, Shylock?"

Then Tom took him by the neck and lifted him until his small legs kicked violently in thin air. "Where is my cigarette lighta?"

"Me be sell NVA general. Please, be Sargy Tom. Lighta he be cheap. No good."

Tom lowered him back to the ground and turned to me.

"I paid ten dollars for dat lighta and dis sorry excuse fo a Yard scout say it's cheap."

"Leave him to us, Captain Mock. Sit down, Shylock," I said, looking him over. A windfall of needed information had just fallen into my lap. I felt good.

Ding gave Shylock a piece of venison which he had held over the open flames.

"Sargy, you be say kill, please be, I be do job. Sylock, him be damn bad be Yard. Him be take my woman sometime."

"No, you don't," interjected Tom immediately. "Any one do him in, its gonna be me. He used to be ma shadow, until he started to mess wit Ding's woman and had to run for his life. And besides, he stole my cigarette lighta, which is worth more dan his hide."

I heard Cathy giggle in the dark corner. Shylock saw her for the first time. With quick movements he threw himself down in front of her and then made some incoherent noises.

Ding grabbed him and in his own language told him that she wasn't a demon, but Sargy's woman. It took Shylock a few minutes before he would look out from behind me where he had jumped to get away from Ding. His head jerked from Ding to Cathy as if he could not decide who was the greater threat.

He stuck his head out from between my legs and looked Cathy over with quick darting eyes, an action not unlike that of a wild deer looking at a leopard that was about to pounce on it.

"Help, help, Sargy," he begged pathetically, holding on tightly to my legs.

"You poor little thing." Cathy expressed her sympathy.

"Don't worry, Shylock, I'm not going to let anyone do you in. I can use you. You better go back to Sargy Tom. You be try run away again, Sargy Tom be kick hell out of you."

I tried to get him to let go of me, but he held on tightly to my legs and pointed at Cathy.

"Hair bad...hair be bad." He pointed at her long blond hair. I realized that his fears were all centered on Cathy's hair. He may have seen such hair at one time and it reminded him of evil.

"Ding, you be tell him, Base Plate okay. She blong me."

Again I heard Cathy snicker, then she mixed her words with laughter, "Base Plate... Blong...I no be gots... Oh boy, wait till I tell my friends back home."

In a few minutes, after Ding spoke to Shylock in his own language, he settled down to eat the piece of meat he had hung onto even though he was scared. He was very hungry.

"And Ding, check out the other enemy scouts we captured before Captain Mock kills them. Find out if we can use them."

Tom took Shylock by the ear and steered him to where he could see his face clearly in the fire's light.

"You be stay all time six feet from me...not seven...not more...just six. Dis long." Tom drew a line with his foot about six feet long on the dirt so that Shylock understood just how far he was authorized to be away.

"You be understand, dumbbell?"

"Yes be unstand, Sargy Tom. Me no be leave you till be go Ba Cat." He smiled, now that Ding had left.

As soon as Tom left with Shylock, I chased the rest of the scouts out into the night. Cathy and I were then left alone with the friendly, brightly burning fire. Lively flames were slapping and crackling around the glowing logs.

"I don't want to go back to sleep, Tony. Only a few short hours remain before we leave this unreal world of your Lilliputians."

She sounded resigned and quite contented, with her head resting snugly against my chest. To me, she had become a tender-hearted, incurable romantic. I liked it.

I smiled. "What a pity there are no words with which I can explain to the Yards, just what their Base Plate called them. What was it? Lilli...What are they?"

"In a wonderfully kind and gentle world much different from the one we know, a children's story gave birth to little people who lived in a make-believe world. Lilliputians were story people and where they lived was also a story world. Everything about the story took place in a strange and unreal world, as if it was all a dream.

"Just like what is happening now. Soon I'll wake up and find that all of this was but a dream." Then she reached and took my face between both her hands and said. "I don't want you to be but a dream. You have torn my heart from me and I am now spinning in uncertainty. I need you. Hold me tight."

With that she again held onto me and I could feel that she wanted me to make love to her. Afterward I smiled with the thought of what I was doing out there on a combat patrol. I thought like she did for a while.

I told myself it was a dream, perhaps. But I would not allow myself to slip from reality into a dream world at will. I softly cussed myself under my breath. It was not what I had bargained for. I never could find comfort in a woman's love, for it bound and disturbed my freedom. How uncomplicated and satisfying a night out with a paid prostitute had invariably been. When it suited me, I could always walk away, whistling a happy tune, and she waved an equally happy goodbye from her upstairs window, fondling the money I had paid her. Both of us quite satisfied by the knowledge that we would not see each other again.

Now this. I had to change the situation. I feared that the next thing Cathy might say would be "I love you." A few, direct enemy mortar hits on my patrol would have less impact on my morale than those three words would have.

She dropped the bomb. "Tony, I love you. Hold me tight and never let me go."

Oh my God, I thought. I did not know how to cope. I was aware that she was a virgin when I first took her. And I had heard many stories about a woman's uncontrollable romantic sentiments toward the man who took her maidenhead. I wondered if it was a permanent affliction. I did not think that it was fatal. I wondered if there was a cure for it.

I thought of clinging vines. There were sure as hell enough of them stuck to the trees close by, and I marveled at the trees' ability to cope with them. After a few minutes of silence, while I stroked her smooth, warm body, I turned the conversation to safer grounds.

"I have a problem to solve regarding our Yards," I said with feeling.

"What a shame that we cannot take them with us tomorrow, back to their home." Her mind had shifted to the Yards and I relaxed.

"They have no home left. Remember, the NVA has the camp and their hamlet. And as to their continuing to live in these mountains the way they did before we came, well, that too is denied them. The introduction of the helicopter, sophisticated long-range artillery, and war planes has made their jungle unsafe."

I was also sure that if such a large armed force of Montagnards were to roam in those mountains uncontrolled, both the NVA and the ARVN would want them destroyed. I did not tell Cathy that. It would have further complicated matters.

"Tony, it is up to you to fight for their cause for them when you get back. I'll help you," she said seriously.

I found that humorous and verging on the ludicrous. I would have my own problems with the command if and when I did get back.

"It will be a losing battle, little girl, for the sad and bitter truth is that the Yards on this patrol were the ones with weapons in their hands at the time the eleven ARVN SF were done in. The ARVN investigators must have concluded that."

I placed another log on the fire. Cathy sat cross-legged like an Indian maiden opposite me. The atmosphere inside the hootch was reminiscent of a painting I once saw. An Indian maiden, hopelessly consumed by love, prayed to the fire to warm her lover's heart.

"We can be sure that the ARVN will not let this patrol live, whether they return to the camp or remain in these mountains. The ARVN will demand that they die, all of them."

"Tony, it cannot be. Surely, in a civilized world..." She reached out for me as if she could, with my strength, halt the deterioration of her own faith in humans.

"Yes, perhaps in a civilized world. Do you see one here?"

"How can we help them? Maybe the World Coun..." She stopped herself, evincing some embarrassment. It had come to dawn on her that most of her prior convictions needed some modification. The thought of the World Council of Churches to her at that time must have had an empty and disconcerting ring.

"I just do not know, Cathy." I chose to ignore her slip and subsequent discomfort. What I did not tell her was what I had planned to do about the matter. I instinctively knew that she would have been dead set against my plan, and I wanted those moments to pass in pleasant misunderstanding. I also dared not fully dwell on my impending action for fear that its dire consequences could not be justified.

I stepped outside the hootch to await the dawn. It was not long in coming. The gray-black of the eastern sky slowly gave way to a russet glow that spread its singular beauty around us.

As I stood musing outside the hut, Cathy came out to stand beside me. "You will miss this hostile land once you leave," she said sweetly while I folded her into my arms. "And I'll remember it always. In many ways it is so beautiful that I wonder at God letting all these horrible things spoil it."

"The way you put it makes me feel guilty," I answered her while a red smear spread across the early morning sky to the north and east of us. There, a fast crescendo of the night's gunfire gave proof that the battle still raged, and was going to continue well into the new day.

"You need not feel guilty. Yours is but to do or...."

I interrupted her. "Yes, I know, but that threadbare cliche always sounded hollow to me. It does nothing to dispel guilt. I have a better way to cope with unpleasant events."

"How is that?" she turned to look me in the eyes.

"A private gray mental veil, through which nothing can be seen as it really is." I did not want to talk about my own cowardly way of dealing with nasty things.

A large volume of small-arms fire crackled not far from us. It was not my men in contact with the enemy. Hundreds of illumination flares kept the lingering night sky lit up where I believed our Americal Division to be in action against the NVA.

Every muscle of my body tightened and I felt like screaming for time to pass quickly. I wanted to finish the air evacuation and then move against the enemy's rear, for I still commanded a well-supplied and powerful combat patrol. Any positive action against the enemy in the area, I felt, would help our men who had been battling the enemy all through the long night.

"I am so glad that we had these moments together. So different, so memorable, that surely it must have been specially created as a foundation on which some understanding between my world and yours could develop," Cathy said, seemingly unaware of where my thoughts were at the time. Her innocent mind was floating through a friendly and kindly romantic make-believe world.

"You are not listening to me, but I have to talk to you, Tony. All my life I have been lonely. I was so afraid of men and what they did to women. My mother taught me to hate men because of the way my father treated her. He used to beat her when he had had a few drinks, which was often. He would then make love to her, sometimes in front of me, but he was mean to her, not kind like you.

"When you took me against my will, I hated you because I saw in you what I saw in my father — a beast. Then later I wanted so much to feel your arms around me for protection. First, because I was afraid of what was taking place around us. The enemy and the terrible explosions all around us would have driven me crazy had I not found solace in your strength.

"You made me love you. My mother was wrong. All men are not beasts with women. And, Tony, when you released those prisoners I knew then that you are a very kind person."

I looked at her.

"Woman, you sure talk a lot." I felt uncomfortable with what she was saying.

"I have to talk to you, Tony. If I don't, I will lose my mind. So please listen and let me speak. Once, a long time ago it seems now, I wanted to change the world so that men and women of all nations could live together in harmony. The World Council of Churches sounded just the right organization. I joined them."

"Enough, Cathy." I ordered sternly as if she were a trooper in my command. "You keep this up and I'll forget where we are. This is not the place or time to try and get my mind to float with yours through a make-believe romantic dream world."

The earth beneath our feet trembled slightly as increased air strikes and artillery-supporting fires were poured in to soften the tenacious enemy.

"Hold on, boys," I whispered to myself. "We'll help you soon."

"What did you say?" she asked. "You did not listen to me."

"Oh, yes, I listened," I answered, not knowing all that she had said. "You are an incurably romantic optimist."

That caused her to hold me even tighter.

Only minutes remained before I was to cross my Rubicon. I moved with Cathy to the designated helicopter landing sight. Tom and Doc half-dragged, half-carried the American creep between them. Captain Mock, with a rifle squad behind him, followed close by. I knew that they would stop any Yard who came close to the chopper when it landed. I also knew that the helicopter pilots were aware of the problem that faced us on the ground, and would do all in their power to minimize the danger to us. They would make a fast extrication, down and up again, before any panicky Yard could grab hold of struts to go out with the chopper.

Chapter 7

Laos,
Here We Come

It was 0500 hours. I heard two Cobra gunships high overhead. They came closer and started to circle. As if out of nowhere, a Huey appeared. It skipped over a nearby mountain peak and slapped treetops as it approached.

I flashed my light with the prearranged signal at the pilots, while Tom talked to them over his radio. In seconds the Huey descended close to us and engulfed us in billowing clouds of dust, dirt, flying sticks, and stones. It came all the way down to hover noisily inches off the ground.

I grabbed Cathy and ran to the chopper where I lifted her and deposited her unceremoniously in the waiting arms of a surprised crewmember. The helicopter had already started to lift off again when I saw the creep fly past me and onto the floor of the chopper where Tom threw him.

Tom grabbed me, and I grabbed him. He landed inside the helicopter first, and then I seemed to fly right through the two open doors. I found myself under the propeller blast and sailing twenty feet through the air to have the wind knocked out of me as I hit the ground.

The helicopter canted to the right and under full power veered out of sight, first down the mountain and then upward into the clouds. Below it swooped the two Cobras, one behind the other, with mini-guns and rockets at the ready to blast any enemy interfering with the operation.

For a split second I saw one of the Cobra pilots jerk his head toward me, surprised to see me still on the ground as he flew past to leave silence all around me.

I moved my limbs to determine if I had broken any bones. Thanks to my airborne training, agility, and excellent physical condition, I was still in one piece.

When the full realization came to me that I had finally taken the first step along that long and lonely road of no return, I gave vent to my pent-up emotions with loud laughter. I remained on hands and knees in the dirt where the momentum had carried me. The sound of my laughter rang dull, against the mountainside.

My laughter stopped. Beside me I heard a familiar voice.

"He finally flipped."

"Not finally. He was always this way," came from another familiar voice.

I looked up to see Doc and Tom standing over me with big grins spread generously over their smudged faces.

"You two bastards!" was all I could say. We looked at each other for what seemed minutes, then all three of us broke into mad laughter and threw each other with playful wrestling into the dirt.

Out of breath, we remained sitting on the ground.

"What next?" I asked.

"Nothing new," answered Doc. "All that happened to us was that we slipped on banana peels, and before you knew it, we were on the ground."

"Remind me to tell Booby Trap about banning banana-eating helicopter crew members, and also remind me to file court-martial charges against you two for disobeying orders."

I fumbled with shaking hands for my message book, then wrote a message to be sent to Booby Trap. "In direct contact with enemy unit — Stop — Impossible to effect extrication — Stop — Will."

I handed the message to Tom. "Tom, send this. I want him to think that the enemy caused you not to be able to get the entire message out.

"We might just as well have something to fall back on if and when we get out of this mess. It will be a damn sight better than to just say...ah...ah...ah, when asked why the hell we did not obey orders to get on that chopper. All we have to say is that we heard small-arms fire among our Yards and had to control things before the chopper came under either friendly or enemy fire.

"Who knows, we might even get decorated for having saved the helicopter from being shot down." I said, while fighting to control a nervous laugh. The body of that message caused another ulcer for Booby Trap. I knew that he would not believe me, but then, we all had problems, and he was paid more, so I did not feel any sorrier for him than I did for myself.

Mock was standing a few feet from us. Tears rolled down his dirty cheeks. He made no effort to hide his emotions. I pretended not to have noticed it. "Captain Mock!" I called. "We have a patrol to run. Warning orders! We move against the NVA tanks in 30 minutes." He saluted smartly and swung around, heading to the main body.

"Did you see...?" I cut Doc off.

"Yes, I saw, Doc. And it is the first time that I have ever seen tears in Mock's eyes." I had always thought of Mock as a person devoid of sentiment. Then I was handed another first, this time by Doc.

"Tony, you and Tom, please listen to me." Tom and I noticed something new in Doc's bearing and voice.

"Now I have the same feeling that Tom expressed about getting killed on this patrol, but unlike Tom, I feel good about it. Not about getting killed but about what we are now doing. Saving, or at least trying to save our Yards, wipes the slate clean for me."

He approached Tom and me and put a hand on each of our shoulders. With a smile and a look of serenity and contentment on his face, he continued.

"You are really a bastard, Tony, but a lovable bastard. You and Tom —"

"Doc," I wanted to interrupt but he would not let me.

"Listen, you two. I am going to speak if I have to whip both of you first," he said smilingly.

"Tony, you and Tom are perhaps the two biggest cheats I've ever known. Only, instead of cheating the world or other people, you cheat yourselves. You cheat yourselves out of receiving love and kindness from those who care for you and then unselfishly give your all to others. That's what you are doing now."

"Cut it out, Doc." I had become uncomfortable.

Tom acted as if he did not understand what Doc had said and perhaps he didn't, but he didn't like it either. "You're one nut, Doc. You talk like you been on de bottle, Babe." It was the first time Tom ever called Doc, Babe. A change in their attitude towards each other had taken place. I detected embarrassment in Tom.

I had to put a stop to the theatrics Doc had injected into our serious situation. We were damn near surrounded by a determined and dauntless enemy, and we were three well-trained SF soldiers.

I turned to Tom and sternly ordered, "Tom, unplug your damn transmitter. Only monitor Group's transmissions. Let them think what they will, only don't answer them."

"Gotcha, Boss." He sounded optimistic. Then he added, "Laos, here we come... wine and women."

"What happened to the 'song,' Babe?" Doc asked. It was the first time I had paid much attention to the use of the term Babe. That morning quite a few firsts were being thrown at me in quick succession, by Mock, by Tom, and now by Doc. I had had enough of firsts for one day, and the sun had not yet had a chance to scoot across the nearest mountaintop.

I could not have seen the sun anyway, for we were sweating in the damp heat under a triple-canopy jungle. The jungle growth hid the sky from us so that all we could see when we looked up was darkness. It was a maze of entanglements, webbed closely together by a mass of clinging vines. Many moss-covered branches seemed to have wiggled themselves with great difficulty upwards to catch a ray of sunshine.

Some plants, the ones close to the ground, had given up and just spread their branches and leaves outwards as the first canopy. Others that did not give up quite so easily fought their way further upwards before they too gave up the fight, forming the second canopy. The most determined ones reached the clear sky and with the help of the sunshine further blanketed their weaker brethren below.

"Song, song? Who tinks about songs? I gots oder tinks on my mind, Babe." Tom smiled.

I wanted to smile at the change of attitude between the two of them. They were so much unlike each other that I did not expect the newly found tolerance of each other to last.

A cold shiver ran down my back when I thought of what Doc said about getting killed. What the hell is going on with those two, I wondered. Soldiers don't function well with stupid thoughts like that sloshing through their peanut brains. What could I do about it? Nothing. It was something Fort Benning's leadership school had not prepared me for.

I knew that the people of that area had gold. Like the Indian women of India, they carried their wealth wherever they went. I was right to think that it was gold that Tom had on his mind.

I remembered that I still wanted to speak to him about the American money Mock and my scouts had. Tom was not aware that I knew about his privately recruited squad, who gathered valuables for him.

Just prior to the attack on Black Face I had seen Tom speak to the 3rd and 2nd Platoon leaders to make the swap with his squad, so as to reward that squad by not letting them lead the attack. He had goofed, for he did not anticipate my last minute change, that caused me to commit the 3rd Platoon. His entire squad was killed in that action.

When the platoon leaders joined me, I went through the patrol order for the attack on the tanks and the military village that was located a few miles east of Attapue. I kept it simple since there were still too many unknowns. I did, however, make them understand the reason I decided to move back into Laos.

They showed approval when they were told that we were doing it to save their hamlet, Ba Cat. I was glad that no one asked me to explain how I came to that reasoning.

"We be attack NVA rear, NVA be get boo coo pissed off we. They no be go Ba Cat they be come afta us."

They smiled and thought me a great tactician and wise leader.

The village that I wanted to attack was not recorded on our military maps. We called it Attapue after the other village not far from it. The intelligence I had received about that village made me believe that it was a military establishment of approximately 1,000 people, mostly support personnel. I was puzzled about the tanks being away from other combat units.

I categorized the village as an enemy supply depot, and thus a legal target, not that legality played much of a role in our operations in Vietnam. We had not initiated the barbaric rules of engagement, the enemy did.

Thoughts of World War II and Korea flashed through my mind. The mass bombings of German cities, the complete destruction of Korean towns by both the Communists and us as we destroyed each other on that mountainous peninsula. Wars were where non-combatants were killed.

With those thoughts, I bitterly wondered why my conscience should be pricked, and why it was expected of the American soldiers who fought in Vietnam to sanitize warfare.

Damn, damn, I muttered to myself. Was I going crazy? Never before had I let those thoughts muddle up my mind. It started to dawn on me that Cathy could have injected some measure of her innocent kindness into me. I did not like it. I cleared my mind, and again turned to the business at hand.

The terrain surrounding the village was flat, and exposed on all sides for excellent fields of fire. My scouts reported that there were no cultivated fields near the village, no shops, no markets, not even the usual hustle and bustle of a normal village.

What I had received from the NVA officer became of importance to me. He had stated that a large amount of military supplies were stockpiled about a mile north of the village.

"The tanks, then the supplies," I told Captain Mock.

Early in the afternoon we halted the patrol. We were still inside South Vietnam. Our progress had been slow because I avoided the slate-covered creek. It was just as well that I had, for the enemy was waiting for us in that creek.

While we were working our way through the heavy growth of monkey vines, bamboo, and creepers and their air plants, one of my scouts reported that he had seen an enemy rifle company dug into defensive positions at the creek's upper end. If I had used that creek, as Mock wanted me to do, we would have gotten involved in a battle not of my own seeking. The close call made me skittish, and caused me to swing further south inside South Vietnam. We were puzzled about the information we had received about the village. I called for Shylock.

"Shylock," I asked, "Have you been inside that village this side of Attapue, and Shylock, that village, he be gots a name?" I had to let him know that I was not speaking about Attapue.

"Yessi, Sargy. Me be go village much, much time." He smiled happily. We knew that we could believe half of what he said. The Yards' desire to please us often caused them to say what they thought we would like to hear.

"You be hungry, where you be eat that village?"

"No can be eat Attapue. No stay long time Attapue. Attapue he no blong Laos. He blong NVA. Also, Sargy Tony, Attapue no gots name."

"That explains it,' I said to Doc and Tom, "It is a North Vietnamese Army depot of sorts with mess halls and a general logistical support system for the workers.

"Also," I stressed the next, "remember what that NVA officer told us. Mostly unarmed personnel in the village, so it should be a pushover. Noncombatants working the area."

Doc agreed.

"Could be. Another consideration is what that other NVA POW came out with — NVA withdrawal from Cambodia. Attapue is not far from the

Cambodian border. In the event of a U.S. invasion of Cambodia, a supply dump where Attapue is would be right handy for the enemy."

"I agree. Also, studying the terrain between Attapue and our most-likely avenue of approach into Cambodia, supplies and reinforcements could easily be moved by trucks to NVA combat units remaining in Cambodia. And do not forget enemy Camp-102, inside Cambodia. It's close to the Laotian border."

Tom thought of something that also worried me.

"What about de five NVA tanks? Why no rubber-tired vehicles, no fuel trucks, no infantry with APCs to protect de tanks."

"I don't know, Tom." I said, thinking things out. "All I am sure of at this time is that there are five Rusky-built T-54s, and what appears to be a sleeping village of approximately 1,000 people in a NVA controlled complex. No infantry...that beats the hell out of me, unless the NVA has committed every unit they could muster against our forces."

We could hear a ground battle going on about 20 miles to our north and east. An uncomfortable gap remained in intelligence on our objective. I pursued the question further with Shylock.

"Shylock, you be want woman, where you be go Attapue?"

I saw a smart-ass look and a shit-eating Montagnard grin spread generously over his face.

"Me be want woman me no be go Attapue. Me be go Ba Cat."

If I had not acted fast and jumped between them, Ding would have stuck his bayonet into Shylock. Tom grabbed Shylock from behind while I shook Ding's bayonet-wielding arm violently until he let go of the bayonet.

"Me be kill damn Sylock!" Ding screamed then let out a string of Montagnard cuss words.

"Hold it, you two! All I want to know is if there are prostitutes in Attapue."

"Attapue be gots boo coo woman. All blong VC. Gots black, white scarf. All same all VC woman be gots scarf," Shylock said, relieved that Tom and I had saved his life.

"Interesting," I thought. If those fanatics had weapons, they would have to be taken into consideration.

"And weapons, Shylock. What weapons you see with VC woman?"

"VC village, me no be see much, much weapon. Many gots stick only," said Shylock from behind Tom, where he kept an eye on Ding.

"Thanks, and you two behave yourselves. Any killing to be done, Sargy, Tom, and me, we be do. Understand?"

Tom, Doc and I were hard pressed not to laugh at the two Yards' antics.

"You guys, do you see it the way I see it? Enemy supply unit. No weapons since they do not expect an attack from across the border. I am still just a little worried about the absence of infantry. Where is the support for the tanks? Unless the tanks are merely in transit at this time. But then, the prisoners said they were there a few days ago, too."

Tom looked over my shoulder at the map that was spread out in front of us. "I tink de infantry units could be somewhere near, wit APCs. But we could get de job done and retreat back across de border before dey come at us. And if dey do come afta us like dey did at de guns, we could again set a ambush."

"Sounds good. I'm going to take the chance and attack the tanks and the village. It will take time to destroy the supplies so we must hope for luck, too." I walked away from the two of them. I needed time to prepare myself mentally and to formulate an attack plan. I needed the mental picture of how the attack should go against the tanks.

During the late afternoon, a number of reliable reports came in from our reconnaissance patrols. They confirmed the exact location of the five tanks. They were dug to hull defilade. No troops with infantry weapons were sighted. They also reported large stacks of rice and ammunition under canvas cover near the village. One scout section reported having seen women wearing black-and-white-checkered VC scarves.

A support unit, I thought. My casualties should be light.

Then my mind turned to what I was once told by men who fought against those VC women. "Be careful, they are part of that communist indoctrinated mass, and act as if they have little to lose. And, for God's sake, don't fall into their hands alive."

With the information I had received, I became enthusiastic about the mission. I especially wanted to destroy the storage area. If I had any doubts about the prudence of attacking an NVA armored unit that far from friendly indirect fire support, the distant rumbling sound of battle, where U.S. soldiers were engaging the enemy, would have driven me on anyway.

"Mock," I said. "Tonight we move close to the tanks. At daybreak we'll hit them. Then into the village, where we'll stay after we have won their hearts and minds. There we'll wait and see what the NVA will do. I no want a hit and run. I want the NVA to get boo coo worried about us." I let that sink in. Tom and Doc also listened attentively. "The NVA is getting the hell beaten out of them by our boys." I pointed in the direction from which we could hear an air strike taking place. It sounded as if it was centered ten miles northeast of Black Face.

"An attack in their rear will further play hell with their morale and I am going to stick around to see what they intend to do about it."

"I like it," said Tom.

"Same here," echoed Doc.

"Tom," I drew his attention. "I know you to be the best radio operator in the Army."

"Tanks. You want de quarter now?"

"I say this, Babe, because I want you to prove to us just how good you really are." They waited for me to explain.

"We have agreed that to hit the enemy in their rear would help our side. But none of our actions will have an immediate effect unless enemy units, those in direct contact with our boys know about what is going on."

"You is right der, boss," said Tom with a frown on his face. "The snag is that if we tell Group, they'll order us out of Laos. But Tom, you can play games with Group. Make believe you can't get their transmissions clearly."

"I see." The frown on Tom's face disappeared. "I can do it. It will drive de radio operators at Group and at a few udder places, like MACV, up de wall. Dey will later want to hang me, but dats okay, fo I tells dem dat you is in charge, and I tells you to go home, but no, you is one stubborn honkey. Also de NVA will get de word."

"You sure as hell are one talking nigger, Babe," I said.

"Tom, I've changed my mind. I'm not going to vote for George Wallace." Doc's smile and remark earned him a finger from Tom.

"Mock, old buddy, get the word out to the Yards that we hit the tanks and the village to draw the NVA and VC out of Ba Cat." The entire patrol had heard that the enemy was in their hamlet.

"Much good. Yards dey be sad. Now dey be happy NVA leave Ba Cat. Dey be fight like hell, tanks be blow up, Attapue he be burn big flame. Yards no be say 'Nui Coto kill,' dey be say 'Ba Cat kill, Ba Cat kill, kill.' You be like, Sargy?"

"Yes, I be like, Captain. Ba Cat, kill, kill. Yes, I be like. You be tell Yards."Poor bastards. I could not tell them that the NVA was not the real reason why I could not lead them back to their families.

For the rest of the afternoon we lay hidden in the thick jungle growth. Heat and humidity combined to make our hours miserable. Most of us stayed bathed in our own sweat and demanded a large amount of drinking water. Luckily Booby Trap had ordered plenty of water to be delivered at the last air drop.

Nothing indicated that the enemy knew where we were. I had some apprehensions that our side, with our sophisticated electronic equipment, would locate us, mistake us for an enemy unit, and plaster us with air and artillery fire.

Being left alone with my thoughts, I went over the operations plan to see if there were any real blank spots. One dark area was the absence of information on enemy infantry.

I centered my mind on the terrain. Over and over I went through the exercise of tracing the map's contour lines as I had studied them. The terrain did offer all the cover and concealment necessary for the safe approach.

This was important, for should our presence become known prior to having moved into 3.5-inch rocket launcher range, the tanks would become more than we could handle. How I wished for the more accurate 90mm anti-tank recoilless rifles, or even a few LAWs. On the last ammo resupply Booby Trap had not included the LAWs. Those low angle rockets were more accurate.

The reason we did not have the standard infantry's anti-tank 90mm recoilless rifle with us was because of their weight. The weight of the 3.5 was peanuts compared to the 90mm rifle, which was too heavy for our Yards to carry.

"Tom," I said. "I want you to take charge of the attack on the village." He didn't like it.

I explained. "Those tanks are in hull defilade, or should be. I can't see a tanker leave his tank vulnerable to direct fire weapons for any length of time, and all indications are that they have been in that area for some time. That makes it necessary for me to move the 3.5s to almost on top of them, or maybe even to inside the parapets to destroy them.

"They will have guards outside the parapets. These guards will be part of the tank crews. I take it they will sleep far enough from the tanks to warn of danger, and near enough for control.

At your attack on the village, the tanks will kick over their engines. The out-guards, being part of the tank crews, will make all haste back to their tanks. At that time I move in with the rocket launchers.

That would do away with one dangerous uncertainty, that of whether they are so deeply dug in that they present too small a target. And also whether the guards could give warning and the tanks button up and use their machine guns on us."

"Sounds okay to me," Tom answered.

"The timing will have to be just right." Doc did not seem to like the idea. "Tony, the large body of men that Tom will move against the village may trip an alarm before you are in place, and if that happens, you and your men will not have a chance. You will be caught in the open, on flat terrain, with the tanks safe from attack by your 3.5s. It will take but one tank to get alerted and you will not get close to them."

"Good thought, Doc. You hear it right, Tom? Your men goof, I get it and then you. I have to get all the tanks and you must not alert the village until the right time. Timing will be 90 percent of the plan. Any screw-ups, and we'd better hope for a miracle. I'll take the six launchers, two men per launcher, all the scouts, and one full squad from the 4th Platoon. Each of us will carry one HE round. I think we can get the five tanks."

I turned to Tom. "Your watch, buddy. Let's set our watches."

"At exactly 0500, I don't care how far you are from the village at that time, you open up on the village. Not before. Understand Tom, not prior to 0500 hours, even if you are spotted and fired on. Of course, ideally, you move to within 200 yards of the village undetected, wait until 0500 hours, and then win their hearts and minds.

"After that, you move to the storage areas. I'll join you there. We'll set up perimeter security on the western edge of the village. It will be from that direction that I expect the enemy to send reconnaissance patrols."

Shortly after dark we entered Laos. We went slowly to save energy and also because I had ordered stealth. Ding and two other scouts stalked in front of me. Mo followed close behind. Behind him came the six 3.5-inch rocket launcher crews. My contingent became the point for the patrol.

I had to push Mo away because he kept bumping into me each time we stopped to listen for unfamiliar sounds.

"Mo, damn you," I whispered. "Next time you stay home." Then I cussed myself in bitterness. "Home? Where is home, you miserable Yard? And why do I care what happens to you?"I could not see his dirty sweat-smeared face, but I knew that he was scared and puzzled by my words.

Just a little further behind Mo, the twelve launcher men were gingerly placing their feet through the dead-fall to make as little noise as possible.

On each of their backs was strapped an additional HE round. They were all well camouflaged with green branches and leaves, as were the rest of the command.

My watch read 0340. We were a half mile from the tanks. Tom and the main body had veered away to approach the village at a 40-degree angle away from me. The stars stood out bright and clear through the trees. We had moved almost out of the dense jungle growth to flat clear areas that lay exposed under the moonlight.

A lovely, silent night for lovers. My mind inadvertently drifted to Cathy's sad blue eyes and long silken blond hair. I wondered if I would ever see her again.

We pressed on, closer and closer to the five steel monsters which had become an obsession to me. Where possible, we crept close to the ground, and stayed in the moon shadows cast by the numerous whitewashed sepulchers under which the dead slept for eternity.

My watch read 0450 hours, and I became nervous. I stumbled into Ding. He whispered, and pointed to a dark spot about 50 to 60 yards from us.

"Enmeny guard. Tank he be no far. Me be smell tank."

"Good," I whispered back, while I motioned for all to lie down flat on the ground.

Another look at my watch. It read 0455 hours. "Not bad," I thought. The first unknown had been solved. The tanks were still in place. That was, unless Ding's sense of smell had played tricks on him. I did not think that it had.

I signaled for all of us to continue crawling forward. It no longer mattered if the guards spotted us. They would immediately be shot and we could then storm the tanks. My men were well briefed on the danger if but one tank could button down and cut loose with their 12.7mm machine gun.

I wiggled my body forward, close to the ground, with my rifle cradled in my arms. My eyes searched the ground ahead. The men around me were so silent that I had to glance around to make sure that I was not alone.

During those critical moments prior to the attack some strange thoughts flashed through my mind. I felt honored to be where I was, and honored to be trusted by my country to face her enemy in decisive battle. I forgot that I would later have to lie to others, and to myself, to retain some vestige of the honor, even though I was prepared to sacrifice all for honor's sake.

A bright glow was just beginning to spread across the eastern sky when I heard the distant crackle of small-arms fire. Tom and the patrol had opened up on the sleeping village.

"What a way for the villagers to wake up," I thought.

Things moved fast. One barely discernable enemy guard jumped up and ran for the nearest tank. Two others jumped up not far from us. They surprised me. I did not see them even though they were sleeping only ten yards from us. The scouts killed them with silent arrows before they reached the edge of the parapets. Initially no rifles were fired, which turned out to be a plus for us. The crewmembers close to the tanks did not consider themselves in immediate danger. They had their attention drawn by the distant gunfire.

As I ran to the first tank I stumbled over three enemy soldiers who were still wrapped inside their blankets and close to the huge black hulk of the Russian built T-54 tank. I fired point-blank into the three of them. For a split second I wondered at the configuration of the tank. Something about it looked familiar. I did not dwell on it.

I felt the back-blast of a 3.5 rocket launcher as the first shell exploded against the hull of a tank. The hot blast singed my eyebrows. Without looking at that tank, I knew that it was completely destroyed. Flames shot out from its commander's hatch. Its fuel tank exploded to add carnage to its surroundings.

With that tank went my first two-man launcher crew. The crew was too close when they fired. It was something that I had foreseen, and chose not to talk about. The tanks had to go and the best way was to go inside the parapets. I knew that our Yards would do just that, and the dangerous back-blasts would deflect off the edge of the parapet and kill the launcher's crew. I regretted this, but knew it went with the job.

My scouts were running from tank to tank pitching Thermit grenades into open tank hatches. The grenades lit the targets for my men and also exposed the crews who were desperately trying to get either inside the tanks or run away. One terrible explosion rocked the ground around us. The tank in the furthest parapet disappeared in a flash of fire, smoke, and dirt. Its ammunition had caught fire and exploded. So great was the destructive power of that explosion that it took away the dividing earth between itself and two adjacent parapets.

That blast threw me down on the ground and covered me with dirt. Pieces of tank tracks, bogie wheels, and half of the tank's turret flew past me and hit the ground hundreds of feet away.

Blast after blast followed as the launcher men destroyed the tanks. All but one of the launcher crews was killed by their own back-blasts. After five long minutes I assembled what was left of my men. Mission accomplished!

Four enemy tanks were burning hulks, and the fifth tank had been blown into "tank Valhalla," for only a hole remained where it had been. The crews were dead. Only one 3.5 rocket launcher and two high-explosive rounds were left to me. I had exchanged a total of ten of my men for twenty enemy tankers and five tanks. I considered it worthwhile.

When the job was done, I gathered those who were left and we set off at a brisk trot towards where the main body of the patrol seemed to have run into trouble. Something had gone wrong, for too heavy a volume of small arms fire was still heard.

I detected the sound of long bursts of fire that could only come from a water-cooled heavy machine gun. It was a World War II type of .30-caliber machine gun usually associated with static defensive warfare. The Chinese captured many of those machine guns from us during the Korean conflict.

Tom met me a mile from where we had destroyed the tanks. The main body was retreating toward us.

"Enemy infantry!" he screamed at me, his loud voice only barely audible through the sound of incoming enemy mortar rounds which started to explode some distance from us. I realized that whoever was firing those mortars did not know his business.

"Hold on! Hold on! Forward to the village!" I ordered loudly and clearly.

Tom looked at me as if I had lost my mind. "We can't take de village. Enemy regulars dug in all around de damn ting."

"We can't make it to the mountains and sure as hell can't stay here. Captain Mock!" I called. "Fourth Platoon! Fourth Platoon! Hold the line!"

My first efforts to stop the confused retreat came to no avail. Our formation was too far gone in disorganization, with individuals panicked to a point that each man was about to fend for himself. They could not and would not follow orders.

"Scouts to me! Scouts to me!" I screamed at Ding, knowing that if I could give an outward appearance of a command post, I would be able to regain command of the patrol. I hoped for a last minute miracle.

"Tank!" I heard Doc's voice close to me and I saw an enemy tank spout an orange flame ahead of itself as its first shell plowed a long furrow not far from me.

I immediately recognized the tank as a U.S.-built M-41, light recon-naissance tank. I had had enough dealings with those tanks during WW II and Korea. My mind flashed back to the five destroyed tanks in the para-pets. They too were not Russian T-54s as I had thought, but U.S. M-41s. Captured from us in Korea.

"You did not get dem all," Tom accused me.

"I did get them all." No sooner had I said it than I realized how dumb it sounded, especially as another tank shell exploded in the middle of four of our Yards who were desperately trying to dig in near a small puddle of water.

My intelligence analysis as it pertained to the number of tanks that were in the area was in error. I was told by one POW that there were seven tanks in the locality but other reports I received gave me five. All of the reports were correct. Five in the parapets, and two somewhere else. It was a mistake that looked as if it was going to cost me the entire patrol.

It did not solve the dilemma to know that the tank I saw was from the headquarters section that would not have been located with the tank pla-toon. There should be another tank somewhere, I knew. Headquarters had two tanks. At that time our intelligence on NVA order of battle in reference to their armor was skimpy.

From my right came a hot blast of a 3.5 rocket launcher, our last and only hope against that tank. It missed. The tank's machine gun returned the fire and the rocket launcher crew was cut into minced meat.

"Fourth Platoon. Lay down base of fire!" I hollered while running among the Yards with scouts around me.

Mock also helped to stop the retreat. Within a short time we had most of the 4th Platoon in a skirmish line. Their sustained fire quickly caused the enemy to take cover. The withdrawal was partially halted and the enemy's fire temporarily subsided.

Even though the 3.5 missed the tank, it did cause the tank commander to reconsider getting himself involved. He probably had decided to wait until he could better assess the situation. His tank was too valuable for him to expose it to rocket fire in flat terrain. It gave me the chance to reor-ganize. I got my miracle.

Many of the scouts were gathered around Mock and me giving the appearance of a headquarters section. The men rallied on their platoon lead-ers. We were again ready to fight as a unit. I could fire and maneuver, either against the enemy or toward defendable positions from which to inflict damage to the enemy.

To move toward the mountains was out. As long as a tank was out there somewhere, maybe even two tanks, it would be suicide to attempt it. The best plan was to get as quickly as possible into the parapets where the still smoldering enemy tanks were causing confusion for the attacking enemy. They ceased firing mortars, and for that matter, they just ceased firing when we came close to the tank hulks.

I ordered Mock to the rear to have the 1st Platoon hold the line further back. I had to give the 4th platoon a chance to withdraw. We were fighting a well-organized delayed-action tactic as our Yards were trained to do. I regretted not having that 3rd Platoon.

"Back to the burning tanks!" went my orders to the runners. They quickly got the word out to the platoon leaders.

Our 60mm mortars were laying accurate fire on the enemy, who did not seem to be fully organized. That would come later, I knew. Our mortars were hidden near the downward slope in the heavy brush where I wished my entire patrol to be.

Over my radio I ordered smoke rounds to be fired between us and the enemy. This helped tremendously to effect our final withdrawal into the holes where the four enemy tanks hulks were.

We were now in a perfectly defendable position. Nothing could have been more ideal except that we were stuck there, and that we were outnumbered by the enemy. I knew that before it ended, it was going to get worse. My losses were lighter than they would have been had we not caught the enemy off guard. By the time they had correctly assessed the situation, they had lost the chance to destroy us completely.

I reorganized the command. Firing positions were assigned, machine guns emplaced, ammunition redistributed, and a first-aid station set up. Mock and I went among the men to motivate them.

Here and there I patted a man on the shoulder, telling him that I had seen how well he behaved under fire. Many an encouraging smile and proud bearing reappeared after Mock and I had spoken with our men. It brought morale back to an acceptable level.

Captain Mock also seemed to have regained his former composure, although he had been very upset with the men because of their poor behavior.

Fire control was established before our Yards could shoot up all available ammunition. This had been a constant leadership problem since the advent of fully automatic rifles. A 30-round clip could be used up within about three seconds.

A lull had settled over the battlefield. I knew that it would take the enemy time to determine the status of their tanks, among which we had established ourselves. I told Mock to get our mortar men to us. I gave a silent prayer that the tank, or tanks would not spot them while they were in the open.

"Tom, message, in the clear on all the main frequencies. Say Attapue destroyed — Stop — My regiment advancing north — Stop — Destroying all enemy logistical supplies — End of message."

Tom smiled and tattooed the message out. Doc also had a smile on his face, having heard my misleading message.

"Tony, that message is going to cause one hell of a confusion up and down the chain of command. From Eighth Army, MACV to Booby Trap," said Doc.

"That's what I want it to do, but mostly to the NVA. A pity we cannot tell our side what we are up to. But what the hell do I care. We have things to do here."

I was disgusted with myself for talking so much. I had the patrol in a dangerous position, and it was up to me to put into action all the combat training I had received. "This was the final pay-off. Now I would do my thing. This is what the United States trusted me for." I was in my element.

I figured that I had some minutes of respite. I expected the enemy to establish what had happened to their five tanks before they started to pour their 75mm shells into us from the remaining M-41 tanks. They needed to find out who was in charge of the tanks and if any of the five tanks could still fire. At least I knew the capabilities of those tank guns, and also of their .30-caliber machine guns. They were not as great a danger to us as the Russian T-54s would have been.

"Tom, a coded message to Booby Trap. Request air and artillery strike on grid square 106159 — Stop — Fire for effect — End of message. And do not acknowledge any of his or any other friendly traffic. I do not want them to think that we can still receive their messages. Just ask for the support. After that request, send another message in the clear. All enemy resistance neutralized — Stop — Continuing our advance northward along Ho Chi Minh Trail network."

"That ought to stir up the NVA," Doc said laughingly.

And our own people. I muttered to myself. I had a guilty feeling, not only about the messages, but also about what I had gotten the patrol into. I had blundered one final time. My impulsive nature was to blame. I caught Mock's eye.

"Captain, redistribute ammo and tell the men we be kick much ass they no stop waste ammo. We be stay here long time. Not much ammo."

"Okay, Sargy. Me be tell me be kick boo coo ass."

Doc stood close to me awaiting orders.

"Doc, set up your aid station near that first tank and for a little while gather some of the scouts around you so that the command gets the impression of an organized headquarters."

"Will do, Babe," he answered, and quickly moved his wounded and the scouts to the designated area. I felt a closeness to Doc which I had not had before.

I saw him order some scouts to go inside the tank and move the gun barrel. That was a good idea. From a distance the enemy must have flipped, believing that their own tanks were still operative. The other three tank barrels were also showing movement. The Yards were struggling with their manual traversing and elevation mechanisms.

I hoped that from a distance the enemy would be shocked to see their own tanks threatening them. The sun had cleared the distant mountains and was brightly shining from behind us directly toward the enemy. It hampered their visibility of us, but I believed that they could see the tank barrels move. They held back. I knew that we could not keep the ruse up indefinitely, and I expected them to attack us soon, even if it was but a light probe to determine our true status.

Although we could not fire the tank guns, the four burned out hulks were perfect pillboxes from which my men could deal out death to an attacking force with relative safety. In evaluation of my defensive position, I could not have wished for a better one. Four large steel bunkers, great grazing fields of fire, and the parapets themselves made it possible for my men to stay dispersed and covered against direct enemy fire. Even the enemy's indirect fire could not cause us much damage.

"Captain Mock, please get our 60mm mortars to me."

I had an idea. The outside diameter of the 60mm mortar tube was about 73 milliyards. The inside diameter of the M-41's gun barrel was exactly 75 millimeters.

As it turned out, it worked another miracle. It was simple. I showed the mortar men how to put a round into the mortar barrel, let the round slide to the rear of the tube, maneuver the front of the barrel into the tank gun from the breech side, push the tube into the gun barrel as far as it would go, hold it tight, close their eyes, and trip the firing pin.

The mortar round cleared out of the gun barrel and flew in the general direction of the enemy. That trick was done on two tanks only, because the other two remaining tanks were too badly damaged. It must have scared the hell out of the enemy. It held them back for more than two hours, the time it took for us to run out of 60mm mortar ammunition.

Mock was elated at how things were going. He was satisfied with himself and the way we had managed to turn a completely chaotic withdrawal into an organized defense. We knew that it was going to be our last stand unless Tom could get us the necessary supporting fire.

About two miles away, I saw the enemy getting ready for us. They had drawn up in a wide skirmish line. I estimated a 1,000-man regular NVA battalion, reenforced by two tanks and some mortars. I later found out that I was wrong. There were no NVA regulars involved. It was just as well, for we were not strong enough at that time to hold back NVA infantry regulars.

My own strength had dwindled to 110 men on the line and 35 wounded, some of whom were still capable of handling a weapon. The rest lay dead or dying between us and the enemy.

I considered my options. Disregarding any friendly help, I saw but two. One — we would hold out until dark and then fight our way to the mountains and the deep jungle. Two — we could stay where we were and fight to the end taking as many of the bastards with us as possible. As usual, I had no real choices. Neither option was anything to rejoice over. Things were going to happen without my being able to influence the situation much.

We were going to need another miracle if any of us were to make it back to the mountains and safety. Before I turned my attention back to the situation at hand, I took a short moment to say goodbye to the world. The air was so sweet that I wanted to breathe in forever.

Then it started. All around us mortar shells exploded. The damage they did was minimal since most of the shells landed outside the parapets. Again I wondered at the inaccuracy of the enemy's fire. Even though they could not see to direct their fire, trained mortar men should have been able to do better. We took cover wherever we could, and remained there, since we could do nothing until the enemy came to within rifle and machine gun range. That was when I wanted to inflict damage on them. I wanted their first assault on us to give them second thoughts about frontal attacks and cause them to withdraw and act with greater caution. That way, we could buy time until dark.

I called Mock and the platoon leaders to me and explained our situation the way I saw it. They readily agreed with me. They were to hold their fire until the last possible moment and use the rifles on full automatic and to fire only short bursts.

As always, it was necessary to remind our Yards of the importance of short bursts of fire. They should graze the bullets over the ground and not allow their rifles to climb up, which happens with long bursts.

"Remember the killing zone of the M-16 rifle. The bullets must fly between two feet and four feet above the ground," I said with much emphasis to the platoon leaders.

We were ready. My M-60 machine guns were in perfect position to graze their fire over the flat terrain. I knew the enemy was going to walk into a blanket of steel when they came to within 240 yards, the battle sights set on our rifles.

"Tom," I called.

He came close. "Keep sending messages in the clear. This time tell them that an enemy regimental-size unit is in disorganized retreat and we are destroying more enemy supplies and reinforcements heading east."

"On de way, Babe. But you should heah de messages I'm receiving from Booby Trap. He is shitting himself."

We laughed.

On they came. Small, black, Russian-built shoulder-fire A-7 Strelas rocket launchers were fired, but their projectiles exploded against the front of our defenses. Some flew harmlessly over our heads.

A few enemy mortar rounds exploded inside the defiladed position, killing some of our Yards, but most of their shells did not come close.

Among the attacking enemy force I could see hundreds of soldiers that had sunrays bouncing off shiny white-and-black-checkered scarfs. They were shamefully bunched up as if they were morally supporting each other.

"What a motley excuse for soldiers. Hopefully they can do better in bed," I said to myself, very much elated that they were poorly trained.

They were 300 yards away. I could have put every round I fired between the eyes of anyone I aimed at, but we waited. At 250 yards, over a thousand crazed and frenzied screams all but drowned out the mass volume of SKS carbines and their drum-fed RPD light machine gun fire. I was correct in my analysis of the enemy's proficiency. They were poorly trained.

With their supporting fire having been lifted, they poured massed unaimed fire from their rifles harmlessly against the forward slope of the parapets, and I saw streams of tracers fly over our heads into the clear sky each time they fired too long a burst of automatic fire.

To make things even worse for them they sadly failed to keep a steady volume of fire hitting our positions, thereby keeping us pinned down as they advanced toward us. Masses of bullets would slam all around us and then there would be lulls, some as long as two seconds.

For each ten yards that they advanced during the assault phase, the enemy soldiers used up at least one full clip of ammunition.

When their forward element came to where we opened up on them, most of them were out of ammunition. The losses I took came mostly from airburst mortars and from bullets ricocheting off the tank hulks.

At 200 yards, the tumbling lead slugs of our M-16 rifles swept the oncoming enemy as a scythe of death. The M-16 rifle and its type of ammunition were especially designed to wound, not to kill. A wounded soldier needs people to take care of him, and he becomes a burden.

Our M-60 machine guns carried their longer killing range deeper into the dwindling mass. Their 7.62mm bullets ripped through bodies. It was a slaughter. At point-blank range the crazed and maddened screams of the enemy were cut short and the ground became covered with blood-splattered bodies. Some of them had managed to stagger to within ten yards of my men. Most of those who managed to penetrate our blanket of steel wore the checkered scarfs. Pathetic wails could be heard, mingled with the loud orders from my lieutenants and sergeants to cease fire.

I called out to Tom again, "Still with us, Tom?"

"Always!" He answered back. "Another message?" he asked.

"Yeah, send a message. Also in the clear. Enemy suffered heavy losses — My regiment destroyed all North Vietnamese units north of Attapue — End of message."

"On the way," answered Tom. He, like myself, was satisfied with the way our action was going.

A third and a fourth assault on us were beaten off before the afternoon shadows started to lengthen. To our front lay hundreds of enemy dead and wounded. The air was filled with the pitiful cries of the wounded. The mournful hum that came from them penetrated deeper and deeper into my nerves. I wanted to scream back at them.

"Shut up, damn you! Someone please shut them up!" But the sorrowful wails continued.

Twice, U.S. Air Force F-105 fighters swooped low over the battle area but they did not release the napalm and the bombs that I could plainly see below their fuselages. Neither did they fire their deadly rockets.

"Why?" I asked myself. "Could it be that those pilots had received orders not to?" I smiled bitterly. Perhaps it was because Laos was a country at peace with the world, and did not let North Vietnam use it in its war against South Vietnam.

As the wails of the wounded became weaker, we could again make out the distant rumble of the battle that was still going on across the border in South Vietnam.

"Tom," I called. "You still with us, Babe?"

"All in one piece," came his answer. "You want me to keep the air confused?"

"Yeah, send this message, also in the clear. Enemy suffered heavy losses — Stop — My regiment completed the destruction of all North Vietnamese units north of Attapue — End of message."

"On the way."

Tom was still in high spirits. Like me, he must have felt that we were in so much trouble with the Army that anything else we did didn't matter.

I noticed one of our reconnaissance aircraft circling up high. They were photographing us and relaying intelligence back to Eighth Army Headquarters.

"Damn!" I said out loud. It was something I had not taken into consideration when I made the decision to move into Laos. I should have known that Group could keep tabs on whatever the patrol was doing.

I was proud of the way our Yards had responded to our fire control orders. They had waited, as they were ordered, before firing. With methodic crescendo the slaughter had covered the ground with bodies. Some were wounded crawling, some were too weak to crawl, some were ripped apart, and then there were the lucky dead ones.

Their wailing and screams became drowned out by the enemy mortars that took over after their assault force had failed. Within a few minutes after they had started to fire, the mortars again fell silent, to leave only the heart-wrenching pleas of the wounded to attest to man's inhumanity to man.

The muffled steady moans traveled through the midday air to string nerves so taut that one wanted to cry out to heaven for help. But the world rolled on, impotent, uncaring, and unaffected, while blood soaked the dirt and pain ran rampant. The sound of the wounded, both ours and theirs, and the dead bodies of both sides mingled. No one cared for those that ceased to function as killers. The able-bodied were the only ones of importance. Let the wounded and the dead care for each other. Let them lie where they are.

One vital prerequisite for success in an infantry operation is fire control. It requires the attacking force to keep up a steady volume of fire without running out of ammunition. It was that failure on the enemy's part that gave us respite between assaults.

Fully automatic weapons in the hands of irregulars or poorly trained soldiers during close contacts left the bayonet as the only remaining option.

It was of some consolation to me to see that the enemy showed a disgraceful lack of fire control. Their use of automatic weapons was appalling. Not only were they burning up barrels, they were wasting ammunition.

Something was not right with the enemy's behavior. With all the formal training I had, I should have been able to take better advantage of the situation, and effect a disengagement from them early in the action.

There were no trained enemy combat units near — no NVA infantry, armor, or indirect fire units in place to move against us. We had engaged a supply depot where the majority of enemy personnel were not armed or trained for close combat. The fire they brought against us and the ground assaults were hastily organized by rear echelon leaders with whatever weapons they could get.

We could easily have continued through the village had we not overestimated the enemy's strength. If I were Booby Trap, I would have blamed Tom for what took place, but that sound military axiom, "You can delegate authority, not responsibility" held. I became another Monday-morning quarterback, and added yet another sore to my overloaded conscience.

Inside our own positions, the dead lay where they fell. The wounded were scattered unattended. All wounded that could still handle a rifle were placed in firing positions and encouraged to hold their positions while they could.

A few times an enemy loudspeaker, which was located in a hastily dug foxhole about 300 yards from us, offered us safe-conduct back across the border. The only answer I gave them was carefully aimed rifle shots on that foxhole.

Doc had ceased to amputate limbs, for he had run out of morphine. Tourniquets were about the only medical aid he could administer. I had ordered him to stop the bleeding where possible and to get as many of the wounded as he could on line.

Here and there, a wounded Yard had killed himself with his own grenade when he had become delirious and thought that the enemy was about to take him prisoner. Luckily the men were so spread out that only a few unnecessary casualties were inflicted by those suicide grenades.

"Two more hours, men!" I hollered to my Yards. "Two more hours we be fight to the mountains. Save ammunition for good kills. Remember all training." I motioned for Mock to come to me.

"Mock, old buddy, we are about out of ammo. Go among the Yards and tell them I want bayonets with the next assault. We be wait till they be ten yards from us next time. No fire until I give the word and then go with bayonets. If they fall back we make for the mountains. It is our last chance."

"Me be know, Sargy. We be finis. All Yards dey be know we be finis, but we be take boo coo NVA wif us."

Doc and Tom had also crawled toward me. There was no need for us to express our feelings. Each knew that it was the end. Doc had blood dripping from a nasty wound above his right ear.

Tom's left arm had been all but blown off. Doc had tied a tourniquet around it to stop the bleeding. I could see that Tom was about done in. The luster had left his eyes, and I wondered if he was not hit somewhere else, for he could not use his legs.

"On this final stand, Doc, are you going to fight with us?" I asked.

"No, Tony, I do not kill," he answered shaking his head.

"Will you do yourself in?" I knew what his answer would be.

"No, Tony. Not that either. Let the enemy do it."

Tom made an effort to get up.

"I'm not...going to let dem bastards take you," he said with difficulty. A thin trickle of blood dripped out of Tom's mouth.

"That's up to you Tom, old buddy." Doc tried to smile but could not. His words conveyed finality. He knew that he was going to die.

"Nort Viets come!" screamed Mock, and dashed to a machine gun whose crew seemed to have been blasted into small pieces. A rocket had exploded right above their heads.

"Ding, Mo, you stay close to me! We fight this one out together," I said loud enough for them to hear. They moved close to me. Mo trembled so much that he could hardly hold on to his rifle. I placed my arm around him.

"You be stay Sargy." I said with a moment's kindness that I truly felt. I hated myself for being responsible for causing his death at his tender age.

You poor innocent little Yard, I thought. How can I protect you when I myself am about to join the dead?

All I could promise him was that he would go with me when the time came for me to pull the pin on the grenade strapped against my chest.

Ding had a smile on his face. He seemed to have enjoyed himself all through the action. Either he was not capable of understanding the danger, or he had an impenetrable gray veil, one better than mine, to hide behind.

A few more rockets exploded harmlessly around us. The enemy seemed not to have gotten any smarter in the use of their rockets. It also seemed that they had run short of indirect fire support ammunition. I took some comfort from that, but it was immediately dispelled when Mock yelled out to me.

"Tanks!"

And there they were, slowly grinding their tracks, coming straight at us.

"The fools," I thought. Just as well that they were fools, for had they used those two tanks to do what they were capable of and barreled directly into us with their 30-caliber machine gun and 75mm gun blazing, we would have been done for.

The tanks stayed 20 yards apart, and I saw strings of soldiers crouching low behind them. All came with fixed bayonets, and from the distance I noted the contrasting colors of white-and-black-checkered neck scarves.

"More damn fanatical VC women!" I called out. Finally, more women than I can handle, I muttered bitterly to myself. I did not find it humorous.

Slowly they advanced in a methodical and determined manner. Their rifle fire was of minimal volume, indicative of a shortage of small arms ammunition.

Tom grabbed his transmitter microphone as if he only then thought that just maybe there was still hope.

"Black Bird, fire mission...fire mission...tanks in open. Infantry in open...please you bastards give us fire support...we out of ammo... please... plea...." His voice faded as he fell forward into Doc's arms. At the same time, a rocket round exploded close by, and Doc was killed instantly. Most of his head was blown completely away. When Tom released his microphone, there came an American voice, loud and clear, over the air.

"This is Thunder Bird. Black Bird in receipt of your transmission. You're under surveillance. I'll adjust fires, I say again, I'll adjust fires. We're all with you. Heavy artillery battery volleys on the way. I say again. Battery volleys on the way. Hang in there. Over."

Another voice came in, also strong and clear. "We're coming in on the tanks..."

The wording was lost as a hot blast of air from two U.S. Air Force jets streaked low over us, directly in line with the tanks. When they pulled up to disappear into the clouds, the ground shook behind them in a blinding bright flash with chunks of steel from the tanks flying for hundreds of feet into the air. When the smoke and fire cleared, all I could see were two holes where the tanks had been.

Hundreds of enemy soldiers were then frantically running toward us. Most of them had discarded their weapons and headed straight for us, where they believed the only safe area to be. There were no enemy soldiers alive who did not know about, and who did not fear, the massive firepower that the U.S. Armed Forces could bring to bear when the time came, and they believed that time was about to come.

It happened. In front of us, the entire world lifted into the air as if a volcano had erupted. The ground trembled and shook before the deafening explosions reached us. From more than 20 miles away, our U.S. Army artillery poured a steady stream of eight-inch, high-explosive shells, with some set for air-burst, into the then totally demoralized enemy.

When I was sure that the enemy was completely destroyed, there came the sound of increased explosions. I looked over the impact area just in time to see the entire enemy supply and staging area disappear in a dense cloud of fire and smoke, as dozens of heavy bombs rained down on them. The only possible safe area left for the enemy was inside the parapets with us. On they came, no longer aggressive, as only a few had retained their bayonet-fixed rifles. There were no frenzied screams, just fear and confusion written on their faces.

Many of them knew about the devastation that Spooky, a modified C-47 aircraft, could wreck on humans, and it must have been on their minds that the next weapon the U.S. would turn loose on them would be that much-feared aircraft. That weapon system could saturate an area the size of a football field, placing a 7.62mm bullet within every half-inch square. The aircraft had a number of mini-guns, each of which fired at a rate of 6,000 rounds per minute.

If the knowledge of Spooky's devastating power was not enough for the enemy, the thought of napalm would have been. The latter was perhaps the most dreaded weapon ever devised by man.

For a fleeting second, relief and hope had flashed before my eyes, to vanish in the blood-curdling screams of my own men, mixed with screams of fear from the enemy who had sought safety inside our parapets.

During the mad melee, I had a feeling that almost none of my men remained alive to continue the defense of our area. The enemy, too, made me question my assessment of the situation. They did not show any outward desire to continue the offensive. I did see some of my Yards use their bayonets, but the battle was over for the enemy, as it was for us.

I saw Tom pull Doc's dead and mutilated body close to him, and with great difficulty he said "Don't die please, Babe...I'm sorry I told...you join girl...Camp...I is...."

"He is dead, Tom. Let's move back to the mountains. We have a chance now." I reached for him but he pushed me away.

"Tony, please...de ninet grave...Maggie and ma boys. Please go...you promised me....money fo dem..." Then he fumbled for the grenade tied to his load bearing harness.

Shylock clung to Tom. "Me be good damn Yard you, Sargy Tom. No be leave... you Sylock. Please be, Sargy... me be go you." He too had blood dripping from his mouth and I saw a large cut across his back where a piece of shrapnel was sticking out. Tears flew freely down his cheeks.

About ten yards from us came six enemy soldiers. All had white-and-black-checkered scarfs flying in the wind as they ran toward us. They had retained their bayonet fixed rifles.

"Go, Tony...go...Maggie and de boys...please," were the last words Tom spoke.

With Ding and Mo close to me I ran from dead body to dead body, searching for ammunition for my rifle. I looked toward Tom. I saw checkered scarves and bodies scatter in a terrible blast as Tom and Shylock must have pulled their grenade pins together.

The enemy had seen the American and had vied among themselves to get at him. They were motivated for the kill, not only because of hatred for the Green Berets, but also because of the $40,000 to $50,000 prize money each of us had on our head.

I saw Mock being overwhelmed by bayonets. He nevertheless took four with him when his grenade exploded. Mock went to meet his ancestors in a fiery blast of glory. I was not aware that he also had a Thermit grenade to back up his concussion grenade. I saw a VC woman on fire and with a hole blown clear through her. She staggered a few feet, then collapsed.

Those of us still capable of moving were soon among the underbrush that led away from the carnage. We ran toward the relative safety of the mountainous jungle east of Attapue, and did not stop until we were deep inside the jungle's flourishing entanglement. Ahead of me were 15 Yards. They pushed and pulled the vines apart so that I could follow them. Ding and Mo stayed close to me.

When I decided that we were far enough away from possible pursuit, I called a halt.

"Tell the Yards we rest here," I told Ding. As soon as we stopped I sank down against some foliage.

"What happened?" I asked myself. I did not feel remorse, pain, heat, fatigue, thirst, hunger, or fear. That sweet gray veil was there to protect me. Later I would feel the pain of failure. For a failure I was. I had failed to die out there among the many mutilated bodies of the men that I had trained and motivated to fight. They were men who looked up to me for sound tactical decisions. There was no one to blame but myself for not having recognized that I did not have to stay pinned down.

When it became evident to me that we were facing a disorganized and untrained enemy element, I should have gone on the offensive. Booby Trap would have a ball with what had happened. For once he could justifiably place the blame on someone else.

The static defense I had ordered was unnecessary, and for that error we paid dearly. Any fool would have realized that there was no way for my patrol to conduct that type of combat in the absence of indirect fire support. The only reason we lasted as long as we did was because we were fighting off an untrained, unprepared, rear echelon unit.

It was a good thing that I had my convenient veil behind which I could hide. I could be thankful for the strange fact that a person's mind, in the heat of battle, seldom feels the pain and anguish normally associated with the loss of comrades.

I took stock of where we were. The slate creek tht I knew so well was about two miles from us. That would make us six miles from the peak of Black Face and four miles from the border. The dull rumble of that distant battle, which was still raging, guided me as to direction. I decided we should get a good rest before we moved on.

"Mo," I called. "Make space for us. We stay here tonight. Ding, you be tell Yards we want meat."

Ding babbled something to Mo and then gathered the Yards around him. He seemed to have adopted an overbearing attitude with the 15 men that had escaped with us. He had quickly assessed the situation and decided to take Mock's place. I smiled at the thought of calling him Captain Ding.

Mo stood there looking at me as if I were his mother. I often forgot that he could not understand a word I said, especially when I wanted him to work or to put himself into harm's way.

Ding stood in front of me, much as Captain Mock used to, with what he took to be a military bearing.

"Sargy, we damn scout all be left patrol." He showed me three fingers of his right hand.

"You be dumb scout. No can count to two." Then as an after thought I added, "Unless you count me as scout, too." He looked puzzled, the way he always did when I spoke too fast.

"Scat." That they both understood. I knew that we would have meat before dark and also that we would have a warm fire. No NVA or VC would have the guts, or could have retained the will to follow us that deep into the jungle, not after what they had gone through that day.

There were 18 of us who walked away from that direct encounter with the enemy. Eighteen, out of more than 250. It was all that remained of a patrol that 72 hours earlier I had considered too powerful a unit to be allowed to roam at will. Its strength had allowed three Americans to disobey orders from Booby Trap.

I started to reflect on what had taken place. Silently and with justification, I gained a measure of satisfaction from what had happened. The many enemy soldiers that we sent to hell seemed to vindicate me of some blame. What bothered me most was that I had disobeyed orders. For that, I knew, the Army would send me to Leavenworth.

Two clearings were cut for us within which we would spend the night. Our headquarters area was about ten yards removed from the 15 common Yards. Ding saw that the lower class Yards did not mix too freely with what he considered to be upper class headquarters personnel.

Reluctantly, I went along with him, especially since the 15 riflemen were the only ones with blankets still strapped across their backs. It was going to be a cold, cold night.

I counted ten M-16 rifles and three crossbows. I had two rounds of ammunition for my rifle. It was all that I could find before leaving the parapets. None of the Yards had ammunition left. I was surprised that they held onto their weapons, although this was a result of training. Most well-trained soldiers would rather throw away their clothes in the middle of winter than discard their weapons, even when the tactical situation has deteriorated to where each man has to fend for himself.

The long day's sweeping events seemed like a distant vague occurrence, but the veil that obscured the unpleasant memories was slowly being penetrated. The full realization of what had taken place, and the true situation I found myself in, wanted to become clear.

Tom, Doc, and Mock were all dead. With them had gone more than 200 of our Yards. The Yards, I reasoned, were not really dead, but were only on their way to join their ancestors. It bothered me that I had to leave the dead, while I walked along my own dead man's path. I felt that Doc, Tom, and I were already dead in our world.

I wanted to return to that field of battle to lie down among my Yards, unwept, unhonored, and unburied. How sweet a thought, to be safely dead. It was not to be. I was cursed to walk a little longer along that lonely, uncertain, and bitterly confusing road, seeking respite like a coward behind my flimsy gray veil.

I saw tears in Mo's eyes while he looked at me. He reached out with a hand full of grass and tenderly wiped the tears from my cheeks. I held him close to me.

"Oh my God, how lonely I am," I said aloud.

Mo showed his battered and blood-smeared toothless gums in that familiar and unique Montagnard expression of silent understanding. He knew who I was and just how lonely I was. He too felt swept headlong down fate's shadowed, narrow path. He had been robbed of his childhood and forced to blunder recklessly into manhood. Perhaps he thought of death as a safe corner, free of VC and NVA bullets, rockets, bayonets, and the long, cold, mountain nights.

In asinine nostalgia, my thoughts drifted to a biblical passage I had once heard Tom refer to. To the bewilderment of the two scouts I quoted Tom. "Yeah, though I walk through the valley of death, I'll fear no evil, for I am the evilist son-of-a-bitch in the valley." I smiled in kind remembrance of my fallen comrade-in-arms. The Yards joined me in laughing, not understanding a word. We were still very much aware of how close we had come to failing to escape the tank parapets.

Our small fire cast ghoulish images flickering among the thick bamboo and vines. The twilight slowly descended like dying embers all around us. The darkness surrounded our small, black world and left us with but a small circle around our fire.

Two snakes, a monkey, and an owl were held silently over the flames. I wondered where Ding got the nocturnal owl. Usually the owl sat high up in the trees during daylight hours. One of the snakes was large enough to have swallowed the owl... I changed my mind. I was not going to have Ding explain to me how he managed to get the owl. I was hungry.

Ground breadplant, mixed with a strange yellow root that tasted salty, was spread generously over the slowly frying meat, giving it all the flavor that was needed.

During the night, the three of us huddled together. It was cold and too many thoughts were drifting through my mind for me to settle down.

Sometime during the night, a Yard came and offered his blanket to me, but Ding sent him and his blanket back to where he came from. To Ding, it would not have been right for us exalted headquarters personnel to share a blanket with common soldiers. I could have kicked Ding for having turned into such a snob. But who was I to take away that which he cherished so much in his otherwise barren life.

I found it difficult to resign myself to the fact that I no longer had the means to strike at the enemy and had to seek safety instead.

The guilt was mine. It only remained for me to pay the piper. I had found myself guilty, not of misconduct, but of being in the wrong place at the wrong time. It could very well have been another master sergeant in the U.S. Army.

Toward midnight, I dozed off into a troubled slumber. All around us the jungle's disharmony reflected my own anxiety. No creature in the jungle was safe from attack by some predator, as we humans were not safe from each other.

Huddled close together for warmth, the three of us shivered the night away. Our small fire was kept alive. It burned our dirty bodies on one side while the other side was exposed to the damp cold of the mountain's night air. We constantly shifted our bodies to seek warmth.

As soon as the first sign of daylight filtered through the multi-canopied labyrinth, we slowly headed eastward down the mountainside. I knew it would be about six hours before we would break out of the maze and enter the large stretches of open areas where Agent Orange had done its work.

While in those areas, I expected air observers to spot us. When they did, one of two things would happen. We might immediately come under deadly fire, or be recognized as friendly and receive the necessary support.

The easier the going became, with less and less vegetation to hamper our progress, the more and more uncomfortable I became. I had one most unpleasant matter to settle before we were spotted by our aircraft or detected by electronic heat-seeker devices. At last I could not postpone it any longer.

"Ding," I called. "You and Mo. You be come me and call the Yards. Tell them come close. I gots something to tell them." They came silently, wondering what they had done wrong. Very slowly and deliberately I explained, with Ding as interpreter, the problem which they would encounter once under the control of the Army of the Republic of Vietnam.

"The camp is no more. South Viets they be kill you for killing the eleven SF you be kill," I explained.

I made it plain to them that their only hope was to disappear into the mountains and fend for themselves. I told them that even if it were not for the present danger with the ARVN, as soon as we Americans left South Vietnam, they would again be hunted down by the Viets or chased back into the mountains as had been done before we came to help them.

"Me be stay, Sargy. Mo, him be say him also be stay, Sargy. Other damn Yards they be scat now. Me speak they scat," Ding said with a command bearing that he must have thought appropriate for the occasion, and as the late Captain Mock would have done.

Ding turned to the Yards and babbled something to them. They slowly shuffled away from us, confusion written on all their dirty little faces. I felt as if my heart was being torn out of me. I cursed the fate that made me live when better men than I lay dismembered on the last battlefield.

Fate's heartless blundering had left some human feelings within me. To care for others and to feel kindness toward others caused more pain — and pain I had had enough of.

"No, Ding. No good. I want you all to scat. I order you. You understand? Scat! You and Mo. I don't want to see you again. All you have been to me was... Can't you see I don't want you?"

The two of them just stood there looking at me with their small black eyes shining as tear drops began to show.

"Please be, Sargy..." Ding started to say something but could not. He seemed overwhelmed with emotions.

"I go now. You go now," I said roughly, and started to walk away from them. After a few steps I stopped and looked back. They were still standing where they had been before, dejected, making no signs of leaving.

"Go! Go, you two damn scouts!" Still they stood, their eyes lowered to the ground. I walked off at a brisk pace, but the further I walked from them the heavier became my heart. Without looking back I knew that they were following my every step with their tear-filled eyes. I could not continue. My steps became slower and heavier until I could no longer endure it.

I stopped and looked back. Two pairs of small black eyes, full of tears, looked at me in pathetic silence. They could not understand the reason for my sending them away. All they knew was that the only person in all their short lives who had shown them kindness was now rejecting them openly.

"Come!" I hollered at them. Toothless smiles immediately spread across tear-and dirt-streaked faces, as they ran as fast as their short little legs could carry them into my open arms. They clung to me tightly, and would have stayed there forever, but I pushed them roughly away.

"You two much boo coo dumb Yards. You be go wit me Viets they be kill you."

"We be okay. Sargy be take care we dumb scouts. Me an Mo," smiled Ding. He did not even try to wipe his tears away.

You are a fool, I kept telling myself. I knew that as soon as we arrived among United States forces, I would be ordered to report directly to Group Headquarters, and the two Yards would be handed over to the ARVN.

Knowing the ARVN's way of dealing with Montagnards without provocation, what they would do because of the eleven murdered ARVN SF could well be imagined. It did little for my morale to know that Ding and Mo would be the only survivors of the patrol which the ARVN would get their hands on. The NVA collaborated unwittingly with the ARVN by overrunning the A-Camp and the hamlet of Ba Cat. The slaughter that took place there was probably cheered on by the South Vietnamese. It was something that the ARVN would have wanted to do themselves, but they had to consider the U.S. Army's reaction.

Once free of the mountains, we descended into gentler terrain. We crossed a number of clear spots where Agent Orange had done its job. Within these areas one could see the sky, for all leaves had withered and the winds had carried them away. All plants underfoot were dead, and I was especially thankful for the absence of pesky crawling creeping insects and flying bloodsuckers that the Agent Orange had also taken care of.

After we had walked three days, we started to come to places where isolated hamlets littered the green fields, and the jungle gave way to trees that grew free of clinging vines. We kept well away from the populated areas, for I had no desire to come into contact with either North or South Vietnamese people.

Each hamlet and village had its own Indigenous Civilian Defense Force. Usually this force was under the control of a few ARVN soldiers with American Advisors, and I assumed correctly that the information pertaining to the killing of the ARVN SF had been well disseminated.

As we followed a narrow winding footpath in single file, I let my eyes wander toward the distant mountains from whence we had come. Again, a great sense of wonder filled my tired mind. The marvel of nature... to create such beauty and then with dastardly abandon, bathe it in blood. Surely, I thought, some reason must exist, perhaps in the beyond where all of us were yet to go. There it lay for centuries embalmed in its own breathless beauty, undisturbed and unaffected by good or evil.

I snapped out of my day dreaming and reentered the world around me. Mo and Ding sat tightly against me, their eyes searching my face for guidance.

The Huey's crew chief handed me an intercom head set.

"Welcome aboard, Sergeant. We heard some of the radio transmissions concerning you. Did the three of you actually walk all the way from the Laotian border?" asked the pilot.

"Yes, Sir, we would loved to have taken a taxi but we were broke." Some giggles followed my humorous answer.

"We heard that you three are all that walked out of Laos, is that right?"

"Yes, Sir," I answered wishing that they would not ask so many questions.

"Well, I'll be damned." Then over the radio I heard the pilot receive orders to transport us directly to MACV Headquarters in Saigon. Thereafter there was silence on the intercommunication system. Both pilots turned to look at me over their shoulders. They acted slightly embarrassed. Perhaps they had become uncomfortable at having asked questions of me.

We sat down at Tan Son Nhut airfield. In three hours, the helicopter had transported me and my two Yards from their world into mine. All around us there were U.S. soldiers and civilians surrounded by stacks of luggage. They stared in open disbelief as Ding, Mo, and I walked through the main terminal toward an exit sign over a far door.

The three of us clashed with the rest of the crowd inside the terminal. What the people saw were two five-foot-tall, childlike black persons wearing only deerskin loincloths, and carrying crossbows across their backs. They were carelessly hanging on to their bayonet-fixed, M-16 rifles, while walking close to a six-foot, strongly built Green Beret whose dirty and disheveled appearance could only have inspired sympathy or outright disgust.

The strong smell and sight of dried blood on all three of us, plus the stink of our unwashed bodies, mingled with the sweet perfume of the gentler sex as we pushed our way through them.

Mo hung onto my belt, trailing his M-16 rifle as if it was a stick he had played with and then lost interest in. Ding acted as if he was uncertain as to what was expected of him. Should he clear the area ahead of me with his bayonet, or run for his life. Both Yards' eyes were darting from side to side.

The passengers inside the terminal were businessmen, tourists, soldiers, students, or merely bored rich travelers who were curious about the war. Saigon was so pacified at that time that it had become a tourist center. A place of joy, with flourishing nightclubs and brothels that catered to every kink in human desires.

Ding grabbed my arm and pointed to two SF men approaching us. He had spotted the first thing in my world that was familiar to him. It was the Green Berets that Group had ordered to meet us. The two men came to us with broad smiles. I recognized them as old friends of mine. The burly sergeant first class was the first to speak.

"Tony, geez man, what happened to you? You look like hell."

"Hi, Bill, Frenchy,"

I greeted them while receiving warm and enthusiastic handshakes.

I realized what I must look like. A stubby beard, days old, my uniform, blood-smeared in places, with a few tears completed an appalling sight.

"How about something to eat, you guys? We're starved." I pointed to a nearby sign that read "Snack Bar. "

"Sure, Babe. Anything you want." They led the way through the gaping crowd that followed us with their eyes.

I knew that most people had never seen one of our tiny dark Montagnards, let alone two with crossbows and arrows tied to their backs. My two SF escorts had relieved them of their M-16 rifles. We were all fortunate that Ding and Mo did not have ammunition.

The line at the snack bar cleared quickly for us. Soon each of us had a glass of cold fresh milk and a hamburger in front of him on the table. It was the first time Mo and Ding had ever sat on a chair and eaten at a table. The table even had a white tablecloth spread over it.

At first, they had backed away from the chairs and crowded closer to me. Frenchy and Bill understood, and with smiles helped them to sit down. Our Yards then reverted back to themselves. One quick glance at me for approval, and they disregarded the strange surroundings and turned their full attention to the hamburgers.

One sympathetic American girl, a college student standing close by, expressed wonder and said with moisture in her eyes, "The poor little darlings are starved."

"What a pity they can't understand you. Especially this one." I pointed at Ding. "No one has ever, not even remotely, dreamed of calling him a darling," I said to the girl. She looked puzzled. Frenchy, Bill and I exchanged knowing looks.

All of a sudden Mo spat out a mouthful of milk and hamburger and pointed behind me saying loudly, "Base Plate!"

I twisted around expecting Cathy. Ding cussed Mo out in a fast clatter of Montagnard for being so dumb as to think that every blond woman was Base Plate. Maybe to Mo, all round-eyed, blue-eyed women with blond hair looked the same.

"Mo him be boo coo fuck be dumb Yard," said Ding loud enough for many of the bystanders to hear. The many giggles that followed confused Ding so much he wanted to reach for his M-16 rifle. Just as well that Frenchy had taken it from him.

Poor Yards, I thought. They were completely confused by our western intrusion into their culture. The confusion it created in their minds was something that, to them, a crossbow or an M-16 would have fixed.

An American woman, one who had fought a losing battle with middle-age spread, pushed her way through the circle that surrounded us. As soon as my attention was drawn to her I sensed trouble. She came to stand close to me and said.

"You should be ashamed of yourself taking advantage of these innocent people. I have heard of your type..." She got no further. A number of young girls got between her and me and pushed her away.

"You want to be a bitch, be it someplace else and not where I am, one said." A few other people made strong stinging remarks to her. There were many who wanted to usher her out of my sight.

Another Green Beret sergeant showed up. He had to push his way through the many giggling-age females.

"Transportation for you, Sergeant. I've orders to take you to San Loo for a rest and whatever you need. Pretty nice small SF compound about two miles from here."

He was happy to carry out his orders.

Among many sweet smiles and good wishes we were escorted to the waiting jeep. One girl hugged me and told me that she was proud of the Green Berets. Even Mo got a hug, but no one could get near Ding. He had reached for his crossbow, and Frenchy had to relieve him of it.

San Loo was located within sprawling, congested Saigon. It was a city of motor scooters, bars, night clubs, traffic jams, and prostitutes. It was a veritable jungle of disorganization, especially noticeable to the military mind. A number of high-ranking officers had showed up when we entered the compound, but they remained at a distance from us. Among them was my Commanding Officer, Lieutenant Colonel Becket, aka Booby Trap. He and a full colonel approached me. I saluted the highest rank and smartly reported to him as was dictated by military courtesy and orders.

"Sir, Master Sergeant Blondell reporting to the Colonel."

"Welcome back, Sergeant." He returned my salute and then gave me a warm handshake.

"I have given orders to have all that you need made available to you immediately. First you clean up, have some food and a long rest. You sleep as long as you wish and then we will talk. Again I say, Sergeant, welcome back, and anything, I stress, anything you need, just ask for it. We'll see that you get it."

"Thank you, Sir," I answered while remaining at strict attention, then added, "Sir, these two Yards are also in need of care. They must be protected from the ARVN. They are..."

Booby Trap interrupted.

"I'll take care of them, Sergeant. They are my responsibility now."

He sounded as if he would love to have had the military police around instead of that full colonel, to whom he gave a quick glance for approval.

Hopeless anguish permeated my mind because of the plight of our two Yards. As an enlisted man in the presence of two field-grade infantry officers, I felt the burden of subordination restrict me, as if I had been forcibly locked into a steel strait-jacket. My position precluded me from speaking further to the officers concerning the danger to Mo and Ding.

Booby Trap knew what would happen to them if they should fall into the hands of the ARVN, and the bastard, with great pleasure, read my mind. I just knew that he could not wait to turn the two of them over to the ARVN.

He knew nothing about Mo, but he must have heard about the close relationship that existed between Ding and me. Finally the bastard had found my Achilles heel, and the pleasure it gave him to see me squirm was written clearly on his face. Bitterly, I had to pay for disregarding another sound axiom of an infantry command: Do not get emotionally involved with your men.

As I faced the officers the atmosphere caused a foreboding awareness that rang a loud, clear warning bell in my head. The full colonel, whose nametag read Wallace, did not seem perturbed with me. Instead, I detected a measure of sympathy from him. Even though I was very tired, my mind was working well, for I had many things to fend against if I wanted to stay out of prison.

I was on the alert for any direction from which help might be offered, and was ready to reach out for it. Colonel Wallace seemed the first hope that shone through the clouds.

I could not look Ding and Mo in the eyes as the jeep pulled away with them in the back seat and Booby Trap in the front seat. The two of them turned and kept their eyes on me where I stood, much dejected.

Colonel Wallace touched me on the shoulder and said kindly, "You have done for them what you could, Sergeant, now let us find a way to take care of you." With those few words Colonel Wallace declared himself to me. It again gave me proof that the Army had a heart for those they believed had screwed up in the performance of their duties. That is, as long as the screw-up was not connected with personal gain.

I conveniently stuffed the plight of Ding and Mo behind my mental gray veil, where it would be temporarily smothered among past miseries and hardships that I had caused others and myself.

After a hot shower, shave, clean underwear, fatigues, and a big steak dinner with all the cold fresh milk I could drink, I walked straight to the hut that was assigned to me. I kicked off my fatigues, and crawled between two clean white sheets. Within seconds I was fast asleep. For the first time in many days I felt safe. I was tucked securely within the protection of our powerful U.S. Regular Army.

While I slept the hours away, two class-A uniforms, complete with all my war ribbons, service and rank insignias, were made ready for me. My debriefing was scheduled at MACV Headquarters. No one up the chain of command had objected to the delay that gave me the necessary time to recuperate.

The report from the helicopter pilots who rescued me stated that I was in a condition of utter exhaustion and that my outward appearance attested to that. It must have shocked them all into temporarily granting me forgiveness for my many transgressions, and therefore I was rewarded with enough kindness to be allowed to rest. It was not the reception that I had expected. If I had been met by a firing squad or a hangman, I would not have complained.

My return to U.S. control caused consternation to ripple up and down the U.S. Army Command structure, with SF Headquarters at Nha Trang being the epicenter. When the remainder of the SF A-Team at Ba Cat was extricated, some hope had surfaced that light would be thrown on just exactly what had happened to the eleven ARVN SF A-Team. To the dismay of Group, they all conveniently remembered that they were deep inside their own bunker and could not possibly have had any knowledge of the killing, or for that matter what led up to the killing of the ARVN SF. This bit of information was music to my ears and I believed that the information was being given me for a purpose.

It left but two people to worry about before I faced the debriefing at MACV Headquarters. They were Cathy and the American creep. I did not know what they had told the command. A fleeting thought turned to the Yards, who might have told the command things, but I discarded that.

I wanted to laugh, for no Yard could damage me. A South Vietnamese would not lower himself to ask questions of a Montagnard, or believe anything a Yard might tell him.

By that period of my life I had long since lost the talent to gain solace from prayers, but in sheer desperation, I gave it a try. What a surprise it was to me to immediately hear a knock on my door.

A lieutenant walked in. "Sorry to disturb you, Sergeant," he said so amiably that I took him to be solidly in my corner. "I was just passing by (I knew he was lying), and thought I should stop and tell you that you need not worry about the two Americans you saved. They're at Group.

"The lady spoke well of you and had nothing detrimental to voice against the military. For that matter she just flatly refused to hear bad things about you. You made a friend there."

He smiled, obviously relieved that he had gotten that bit of information out to me as he probably had been ordered to do.

"How about the cree...I mean the man, Sir?" I asked.

"Not so good. I'm afraid he was not quite up to the ordeal he was exposed to. He arrived here a basket case. Stayed in the fetal position most of the time. I don't think anyone will ask him questions, and even if they did I don't think he would be able to give a convincing answer.

"You see Sergeant," he gave me a knowing smile. "that B-52 strike did some good, after all." The lieutenant then turned to leave. He had done his job. Before he closed the door behind him he gave me a last look. We looked each other in the eye and there was no need for further words. I got the message and I could not let him leave without giving him a reward to carry back to the high brass.

"Sir, it's perhaps just as well that Captain Mock got himself killed. The ARVN would have hanged him for what he did."

The lieutenant was well satisfied with what I said. He would take that information back to the colonel responsible for the debriefing. How convenient it was going to be to blame the late Captain Mock.

On the jeep ride through Saigon's traffic, I was accompanied by the same Colonel Wallace who had met me at the gate of San-Loo. Only a few words passed between us during the ride.

"Remember Sergeant, no matter what transpires during the debriefing, I am on your side."

"Thank you, Sir. I'll remember it."

As we wound our way through the morning traffic, I thought about another philosophical axiom that had often stood me in good stead. I don't know what sage thought of it, but it often worked well for me: You cheat, you get caught, then lie. How sad and asinine a situation when it is necessary, in the course of serving the best interests of our country, to lie. How true it also is that the first casualty of war is always truth.

At MACV Headquarters, a colonel by the name of Brooks met us in the parking lot. Both Colonel Brooks and Colonel Wallace wore infantry division patches on their right sleeves. Their decorations showed battle stars on campaign ribbons from WWII and Korea. In the briefing room, Colonel Brooks introduced me in an informal manner to the other officers in the room. Each officer in turn gave me a friendly, firm handshake. When I came to greet Lieutenant Colonel Booby Trap, I looked him straight in the eye and he me. There was no friendliness there. The man was not going to forgive me. The room became silent after the introductions. All eyes were on Colonel Brooks. He shuffled some papers in front of him, as if he wanted to prolong the time before he had to begin.

"Gentlemen, I want this debriefing to remain informal." Then he looked at me. "I have explained to all the officers that whatever transpires here is classified, so I am also informing you of that now. What is said here is classified information, Sergeant."

"Yes, Sir. I understand."

"We want answers on a number of questions pertaining to the operations of the United States Army Special Forces Camp 106."

While Colonel Brooks spoke, he kept his eyes on me, and I had the feeling that he was trying to assess my character. I felt sorry for him, because my character had stumbled, fallen and been dragged through the mud too often to present any clear pretty picture for the officers.

"I'll be frank with you, Sergeant, I do not derive pleasure from sitting in this chair at this time. However, I, too, carry out orders. So now, the questions." Some preliminary questions and statements were covered to satisfy the requirements of an official military report. With that out of the way, it started.

"What led to the killing of the eleven ARVN soldiers?"

"Sir, it is a long story."

"Go ahead, Sergeant. We have time. Just tell it the way you saw it happen. Take your time." The colonel leaned back in his chair and waited for me to speak.

"Sir, Captain Van Trang was not a good officer, Sir. He and his men, during the last four weeks, especially, did everything they could to sabotage the turning over of the camp to the ARVN. They stole rice, meat, ammo, and weapons, selling them to the VC, then blamed our Yards.

"I know of five M-16 rifles and two 60mm mortars with ammunition that were sold to a VC unit that once operated near us. My captain and I reported it to our C.O."

I looked Booby Trap straight in the eyes. He must have sensed my hatred for him because of letting Ding and Mo fall into the hands of the ARVNs. He returned my hostile stare. Immediately, I felt that Colonel Wallace was aware of the feeling that existed between Booby Trap and me. I was aware of knowing looks being exchanged between Colonel Wallace and another officer each time Colonel Becket and I looked at each other.

"It was explained to us that Captain Van Trang had too much power in Saigon for us to do anything about him, and we should just forget it. Then another thing, Sir, something that I knew was going to get Van Trang killed one day. It was his telling our Yards a story which made them out to be the offspring of a dog and a woman." That last bit of information made all the officers sit up in their chairs.

"Also, Sir, once I heard one of his sergeants tell our Yards that the way a Yard gets a woman to screw is for the Yard's mother to tell her son to go around one side of a mountain and the first woman he meets on the other side, he beds immediately. "When the son takes off to go around the mountain, the mother takes off to go around from the other side."

"My God," said a colonel by the name of Wakefield. "Within such hostile surroundings, one would have thought talk like that suicidal."

"Yes, Sir," I came back immediately believing that I had all the officers, except Booby Trap, on my side.

"And one other thing, Sir, on two occasions, I was told that the ARVN SF took Montagnard girls into their bunker and raped them, and those things, Sir, were what led up to him and his men being done in."

A lengthy silence settled around the table. None of the officers looked at me. After a while they exchanged looks among each other as if seeking answers. I was wondering why the wall clock did not go tick. Finally they remembered me.

"Who killed Captain Van Trang?" asked Colonel Brooks.

"Captain Mock and his men, Sir. They just shot the ARVN soldiers to pieces. Those ARVN soldiers above the ground were riddled with bullets and the ones in the bunker were done in with grenades."

"How did it start? I am referring to the actual killing."

"Well, Sir, it started because we could not bring in the weekly meat supply because of the cloud cover over the camp. With clouds over the nearby mountains, enemy snipers sometimes hit the chopper. My colonel's chopper has seven holes in it, at least it did the last time I saw it."

The officers around the table looked at Booby Trap and smiled. Booby Trap was not unhappy with the attention. I thought I had temporarily scored perhaps half a point with him.

"Please continue, Sergeant."

"Sir, I merely asked the chopper pilot to drop the meat anyhow. I did not want to upset Captain Van Trang by not letting him have the meat. Only he took it wrong. He was not the type of man to appreciate a good deed.

"In short, Sir, he cursed me aloud in front of our Yards, and that was something he should have known not to do. But he did it to my captain once, and thought he could get away with it, so I guess he felt like he was God." I thought I did well explaining a ticklish situation to the officers.

"Go on, Sergeant," said Colonel Brooks after a few seconds of silence.

"Nothing more, Sir. Captain Mock's men did them all in."

"What about someone killing Captain Van Trang with a knife?"

"It could be, Sir. Many Yards have knives."

"Sergeant, what about Sergeant Tom Morsby throwing a knife?"

"Sir, I only saw Tom take his knife out..." I stopped, somewhat disappointed at myself for having said too much.

"Go ahead, Sergeant." Colonel Brooks did not look at me. He had become interested in the papers in front of him.

"Sir, Tom died for our country. You should have seen how he went. He took a number of gooks with him. And besides, Sir, I really was so afraid at the time I could not truthfully tell just what took place. All I can swear to, Sir, is that Captain Mock was then the ranking officer in the camp. He was responsible for everything that took place in the camp." I saw all the officers around the table relax a little and Colonel Brooks stood up.

"Gentlemen, let's take a break. There is a snack bar down the hall, Sergeant. See you in 15 minutes."

I knew the officers wanted me out of the way to hash over the new development of my blaming Mock for everything. It did have its merits. The lucky Captain Mock was then happily basking in glory among his many ancestors, none of whom would understand or give a hoot about what was taking place in my complicated world.

Down the polished hallway, I encountered more people than I expected. Many were just sauntering aimlessly around. Perhaps I looked like some kind of weirdo, the way I did when I came out of the mountains with Ding and Mo. That thought I dispelled quickly when I saw my own reflection in a window. I looked smart in my green beret and wearing my newly pressed Class A uniform, adorned with an enviable array of decorations.

I knew that the questioning had not really begun. Many serious things had taken place that had put the Army in the awkward position of having to defend itself without having a clear understanding of just what really happened. I warned myself to be on guard. Those people could hurt me, especially if they found out what happened to the missing World Council of Churches' people and the disappearances of a number of POWs.

"Yes," I thought, "there are things that I'd better consider carefully."

At the coin-operated coffee machine, a blond woman with a lovely figure touched me affectionately on the chest and said sweetly, "Let me treat you to a coffee, Sergeant." She gave me a coy look that conveyed a promise.

"The warrior, back from a victorious battlefield." She brought her body close to mine and looked into my eyes.

"Tony, I'm Penny. I work for the J-3 here at MACV." She handed my coffee to me. I think that I blushed. However, her lovely eyes showed no humor, just sincerity. Also I was aware that the many uniformed and civilian people in the snack bar had become quiet, and they evinced a friendliness I could not mistake.

"You are lovely, but lady, this is the twentieth century, and I'm all you see — an American soldier." I did not make a good show of my smile.

"Many of us know about you, Sergeant. We are all proud of you."

Having handed me the coffee, she took my arm and led me to a table that was quickly vacated. Just then Booby Trap came in.

"Sergeant, come with me." He looked with disfavor at the woman, who in turn gave him a sour look. She did not strike me as being a woman who could be easily intimidated, even though she showed all the necessary refinement and feminine qualities that I looked for and appreciated in a woman. In the hallway Booby Trap said to me, "You were told not to discuss the debriefing with anyone."

"I did not..." was all I could say before he cut me off.

"Never mind, just get back to the debriefing room," he said curtly. In the debriefing room, Colonel Brooks spoke first.

"Sergeant, for now we will skip over the demise of Captain Van Trang and his men, and center our attention on the patrol. Before you tell us, first give us a run down on your Order of Battle."

I gave them a comprehensive breakdown. Within the command structure I repeatedly mentioned Captain Mock as the commander and me as a mere advisor. It was an escape route for me and also for the Army.

It did not prick my conscience to blame the late Captain Mock. I felt that he was looking down on me with great compassion, his only regret being that I could not be with him to share his bliss among his ancestors away from the damp, cold, long mountain nights, bullets, and people who asked too many questions.

When I was through reporting the strength of the patrol, I mentioned also that the Yards were well trained and many of them were veterans of that abortive action on Nui Coto.

"Sir, we left the camp with more than 250 men and I walked out of Laos with 18. Two of those brave Yards are at this time being tortured by the ARVN."

The sadness with which I expressed the latter was not faked. I felt that the officers around the table knew it.

For the moment no one spoke. Then Colonel Wallace asked, "Who in MACV can best see to the matter of the two Montagnards?" Colonel Brooks looked at the lieutenant who stood near the door. The lieutenant immediately jerked to attention. He looked as if he had just swallowed an M-1 rifle ramrod. All the time that he had been standing near the door he had become so involved with us that he had completely forgotten where he was until the colonel called on him.

"Lieutenant, see to it," he ordered the lieutenant.

"Now, Sergeant, we are going to ask questions. And while we do, you may as well forget Captain Mock to whom you seem to have assigned all responsibilities. I can understand that you could possibly make some people believe that you followed the vague concept spelled out in Special Forces Operations. We know you personally, and like just about all Green Beret A-Team sergeants, you are aggressive.

"You are a well trained veteran of other wars, so Sergeant, you are not going to make us believe that you took orders from an irregular. Remember, you and your captain appointed Captain Mock to that nebulous position. Do you understand what I am saying, Sergeant?" His tone of voice had changed. I understood that I had better not rub that colonel wrong. The man had a glint in his eyes that conveyed a warning.

"Yes Sir, I understand. But, Sir, it is not fair to blame me for everything that went wrong, when Captain Mock..." I was cut off by Colonel Brooks.

"Who said anything went wrong? And who is blaming you?" he said with a smile.

"Your mission was to occupy the mountain summit which is generally known as Black Face. Is that correct, Sergeant?"

"Yes, Sir."

"We are aware that you accomplished your mission, but why did you first go into Laos?"

"Sir, at first I was not aware that we went into Laos. We were attacked by the NVA. We did what is taught at the Fort Benning Infantry Training Center: Close with and destroy the enemy. We had to, lest we be wiped out and not be able to accomplish our mission."

"You refer to the artillery which fired on you?"

"Yes, Sir."

"Were they zeroed in on you? And did you give a thought to the possibility that perhaps they were not firing on your patrol, but were engaging another target?"

"No, Sir. I wasn't thinking about that. When their rounds exploded close to us all I wanted was to give them no chance to zero in on us."

"Their fire was ineffective since their visibility of you was just about negative, right?"

"At the time yes, Sir, but I did not want them to get the chance, so, Captain... well... we moved against them, to stop them." When I wanted to mention Mock, the colonel's eyebrows raised. I got the message.

"And what about the village of Go Dia? The small village in the close proximity of the guns?"

"They were the worst, Sir. They attacked us first. I guess they took a dim view of us doing their guns in." A few snickers, which puzzled me, followed my remark. I did not find anything humorous about that damn Go Dia, for it was there that we got involved with civilians. I expected it to be brought up next. It was.

"At Go Dia you took prisoners, right?"

"No, Sir. I ordered no...I mean Captain Mock did." I said in a positive manner after a near slip up. No way in hell was I going to get trapped by getting blamed for taking those civilians prisoner.

"You knew about it, though?"

"Yes, Sir, much later I did. Only after we accomplished our mission."

"We'll return to the prisoners and also the two Americans you took out of Laos. For now, tell us briefly why you went into Laos the second time?"

The way the questioning went, and the ease with which my answers were received gave me the feeling that everything pertaining to the patrol was already known. I guessed that I was being analyzed, so that an acceptable report could be finalized. One that would exonerate me and consequently the Army.

"Sir, it fell in with why we three Americans could not get out with the evac chopper as Colonel Booby — Colonel Becket."

I turned red in the face and I felt the sweat run down my back. My palms became clammy. I did not dare look at Booby Trap. "Ordered," I finished finally. "We were pinned in. The only direction which lay open to us was to the west. And Sir, the terrain out there made it impossible to determine if we were in Laos or Vietnam. Also, Sir, we did want to get to where we could call in for tactical support. Something else, Sir, I wrongly thought at the time that it was our 23rd Division engaging the enemy some miles north of us, and us getting close to NVA's logistical supplies would play hell with the enemy's morale."

Colonel Brooks looked at Booby Trap for some clarification. "Yes," Booby Trap said reluctantly. "A large operation involving the ARVN 23rd Infantry Division did take place at that time north of Black Face. The operation is still a matter of grave concern to us, and classified."

"Continue, Sergeant." The colonel's demeanor was friendly.

"Sir, they had a sanctuary in Laos. I thought that the NVA and VC were having trouble with our 23rd. It was foremost in our minds that we were in a perfect position to create one hell of a headache for the enemy.

"In the past, the bastards always fought us with a clear avenue of escape to safety. We wanted to let them find out what it felt like to have no place to run."

The officers looked at each other as if they had not expected me to sum things up quite like that. Neither did I, for it was somewhat corny, but the best I could do on short notice.

"Would that account for the strange, to say the least, radio procedures your radio operator followed after your attack on the tanks, Sergeant?"

"Yes, Sir. I did order my radio operator to transmit messages in the clear."

"What about the radio messages that I had transmitted to you ordering you to disengage and pull back for extrication?" asked Colonel Becket. He received hostile looks from Colonel Brooks and from Colonel Wallace.

"What messages, Sir?" I asked. I saw Colonel Brooks and Colonel Wallace smile.

"You must know about the messages I am referring to, Sergeant. There were enough of them transmitted to you. Our communications specialists claim that you must have received at least 90 percent of them."

None of the other officers said a thing. They sat back and waited to see how the conversation between Booby Trap and me was going to go.

"Sir, those specialists can say what they want. Under fire, things present themselves just a little unpredictably — different from what they teach those specialists in Fort Gordon."

Colonel Brooks waved Colonel Becket to silence. "Sergeant, did you receive the messages sent to you by Colonel Becket? I am referring to the messages that were transmitted within minutes after every tactical radio receiver in Southeast Asia started to get dozens of messages, in the clear, about a great big battle, involving a regiment or was it a division," he smiled, "in action inside Laos?"

Good old Tom.

"No, Sir," I lied. "I did not receive the messages." I had a strong feeling that all the officers around the table, except Colonels Wakefield and Wallace, were unhappy with my answers. If Booby Trap could have commented on it, he would have said, "See, I told you. The sergeant is a born liar. You cannot believe a word he says."

I was not about to complicate matters for those Army officers who would step forward in the end and defend every action of mine, as long as all my actions were honest mistakes connected with the destruction of the enemy, and not a violation of military discipline because of cowardly actions or personal gain. That truth has often manifested itself throughout our United States military history. At that time I had judged correctly by having singled out the two infantry officers, Colonels Wallace and Wakefield, as being there to look after the interests of the service, which of necessity included me. Colonel Brooks looked up from his papers.

"What about the infantry? Surely you must have known that the enemy would have infantry elements in the close proximity of tanks."

"No, Sir, I did not know about their infantry. The reports I received from my recon patrols gave no information on infantry.

"They reported support personnel which consisted of a large number of VC women. Sir, the women were the assault element. Those untrained fanatics scared me. I don't think that there were trained soldiers among the mass that attacked us."

"Interesting. Let us forget the debriefing for a few minutes while you qualify the observation of yours in reference to the VC women."

Colonel Brooks pushed his papers further away from him and sat back waiting for me.

"Sir, they came at us with complete disregard for fire and maneuver. Their sustained fire on our positions, and where they delivered their fire was disgraceful. Most of their bullets flew into the air over our heads.

"They also disregarded the terrain. By the time they came close enough to us, where even their blundering would not have mattered, Sir, they were out of ammunition. But, Sir, in the end there were just a few more women than my men could handle."

All the officers at the table laughed. It took me a few moments to understand why they did.

"Thank you, Sergeant. Your observations are interesting and informative. Tell me, Sergeant, do you people in A-Camps often start an offensive against the enemy with such a lack of intelligence on your objectives?"

"Yes, Sir."

"Sergeant," Brooks sounded tired. "Let us get back to your A-Camp. Just prior to leaving on your patrol, tell us again what took place in reference to the ARVN soldiers."

"Like I said before, Sir. Captain Mock, with me as advisor, took over the command of the camp and I followed orders that were given to me by my commander, Colonel Becket. The mission was to occupy Black Face. We accomplished that mission."

Again, I went through what happened up to the killing of the eleven ARVN soldiers. No one interrupted me. I took my time and every so often I mentioned the late Captain Mock's name. When I thought that I had satisfied them all, I stopped. Colonel Brooks nodded his head. He seemed satisfied.

"Sergeant, we have not been able to get a very clear picture as to just what happened during the few hours prior to your departure from the camp. The little information we have thus far pieced together has not been corroborated by any substantial proof. To the contrary, much confusion developed as we delved into the investigation. One stumbling block in our quest for the truth came because of the reluctance of all involved to blame you for anything. That is, nearly all." He looked at Booby Trap. He may as well had said, "all but Colonel Becket."

"You are either an outstanding combat leader or you are a master at winning hearts and minds, or both."

Colonel Brooks changed his tone of voice. He became very curt. "Who stuck the knife into Captain Van Trang's neck?"

Immediately all my defenses were up. That infernal mental gray veil descended over my mind to blot out nearly all memories of the killing of Van Trang, but not before I caught a fleeting glimpse in my mind of Van Trang sprawling on the ground in front of me trying to crawl in two directions at the same time with blood spouting out of his mouth.

"I...I don't know, Sir." I stammered, then shook off some of the gray veil.

"What knife, Sir? What...Van Tr..." It dawned on me that I could not very well deny having known Captain Van Trang, even though the thought was tempting. I saw smiles cross the faces of Wallace and Wakefield. Booby Trap again looked as if he was going to burst, and with a red face poured out words in quick succession.

"See, I told you. The sergeant has convenient memory lapses. He almost denied even having known Van Trang." His face turned redder. All eyes were on him. It was a few minutes before Colonel Brooks continued.

"The knife, Sergeant, well?"

"Yes, Sir, the knife. I know, Sir. But I did not stick the knife into Van Trang."

"I know, Sergeant." He sounded tired. "I know that it was not you who stuck the knife into Captain Van Trang. I asked you who it was that did. Now that should not be too difficult for you to understand and give us an answer."

"Yes, Sir...well, it did not really matter who stuck the knife into the bastard's neck for he was dead long before he was struck with the knife. Just plain full of holes, Sir. Whoever threw that knife did not kill the captain."

"Sergeant, will you listen to me, please. I asked you who stuck the knife into Van Trang." His tone of voice had become soft but dangerous.

"Sir, I did not see Tom throw the knife." I put into practice my act of playing dumb before Colonel Brooks became violent and slapped some insubordination charges on me.

"Ah, you admit it was Morsby, your communication sergeant!" He acted as if he had scored a major victory. He was smiling, but that smile did not last. "No, Sir, all I said was that it was not Tom."

"Oh, my God, what have we here?" Colonel Brooks looked me over carefully, trying to make up his mind what to do about me.

"Tom took the knife out of Van Trang's neck. That is all I saw, Sir. I was determined not to have anything mar Tom's record with the Army. I was uncertain as to what the Army could do if they knew that it was Tom who killed Van Trang. I have heard of the military using a fall guy if it would serve to appease civilians or if politically expedient, which is usually the same thing.

"All right, Sergeant. We'll let it stand for now, that is, in reference to the knife.

"You took some prisoners in Laos. Reports have it that you gained some valuable information from them, some you forwarded to Group. Correct, Sergeant?"

"Yes, Sir."

"What happened to those prisoners?"

I was ready for that question. "They were killed, Sir. Killed in action against the enemy. Well...our enemy."

I heard an aircraft take off from the nearby airfield. I wished that I were on that airplane going home, or anywhere else, just as long as it was away from people that ask questions and then listen to my answers.

"Two French nationals, one North Vietnamese civilian, and yes, two other NVA officers, were your prisoners when you came back into South Vietnam. Am I correct, Sergeant?"

For some reason I was glad they did not mention the VC female. Sitting at that clean shiny table, with all those smart and organized men around me, the thought of the final disposition of that damn VC woman left a sour taste in my mouth.

"Yes, Sir. The two Frenchmen I sent back to Laos, and also the North Vietnamese civilian. My men made a mistake taking them. The two NVA officers, Sir, I guarded them well. Just like the Geneva Convention demands." I was warming up to the subject, feeling on safe ground. No matter what I told them they would have to believe me. There were no witnesses.

"So, you guarded them well. Then tell me. Where are they?"

"I don't know, Sir, other than that they're dead. Killed by the enemy." I still felt that I was on safe ground.

"Explain."

"I had them in the rear, where they should have been safe. The enemy attacked me from the rear and there they were. Directly under fire." What I said made me blush slightly. Damn, I thought. How corny. They're not going to buy it. Everyone was looking at me. The silence dragged on until I felt that I had better amplify some.

"Sir, I had more than 250 men under me, and during the patrol we must have killed more than 800 of the enemy. I just did not have the time to nursemaid anyone." I was thinking fast. What information did they have regarding the POWs? Ding or Mo? No, they were too dumb, and besides the ARVN had them.

Cathy? Perhaps. Of course I realized that she would have little choice but to tell the truth, but then, what did she know? She did not see any of the unaccounted for being done in. Her word against mine was the worst that I would have to cope with.

"Sergeant, it will be better if you simply answer the questions," said Colonel Brooks. He did not seem upset anymore.

"Now back to my question. The two Americans. Were they, too, in the rear, safely taken care of?" I noted a slight sarcastic touch to the colonel's words.

"No, Sir. I kept them close to me. To me they were special." He seemed to have become quite satisfied with the way I was answering him.

"After the POWs were killed, you buried them?"

"Yes, Sir. Properly. With prayers and all." I had no sooner said that than I knew that I had rubbed it in a little too deep.

"That's not what I heard!" Colonel Brooks almost screamed at me. The sudden switch in his tone shook all of us at the table.

"What did you..." was all I could say before Colonel Brooks interrupted me.

"I'm asking the questions," he cut me off. "What are you taking us for?"

There ensued a long silence while I could hear the street noises of Saigon many hundreds of yards away. That wall clock. It seemed to hold its breath. Oh, boy, I thought. I had that colonel really pissed off at me, but of one thing I was sure. I was not about to tell them what really happened to the missing prisoners.

"Let us continue. We'll pass over the last question. Tell us about the two villages you fired on."

"Yes, sir. I'm not denying that we returned the fire we received from the two villages."

I was not worried about the questions in regard to the villages.

"If this line of questioning and your answers continue, you will get us to believe that the villages were in South Vietnam and that they fired on you first. Did you attack the village of Go Dia?"

"Yes and no, Sir. Well...I did not get the chance to attack the village. We merely defended ourselves against them. They attacked us with heavy artillery. I was telling the truth and the whole truth for the first time and it scared me, while at the same time it made Colonel Brooks mad.

"You're innocent then of killing civilians in Go Dia?"

"I'm innocent, yes, Sir. But we killed many villagers. They fired on us and we returned their fire. I hope we killed them all."

The atmosphere in the room had taken a hostile turn. I could not believe that anyone expected me to deny that I ordered my men to fire on the village of Go Dia and the other village. Brooks seemed to consider it a breakthrough because I admitted it.

I was aware that in the presence of the six Army officers, I was safe from self-incrimination. The Army had had enough of stupid My Lais, and would not freely invite another fiasco for our hostile news media to wallow in. No matter what I said, none of it would later be used in the unlikely event the Army would prefer court-martial charges.

I was tired, and wanted to get out of the debriefing room, out to where I could get a cold beer and enjoy some moments quietly where no one knew me, in a place where I could say whatever came to mind without someone analyzing each word.

"We were informed that you had the two North Vietnamese POWs killed after you interrogated them. Tell us about it, Sergeant."

"Sir, my interest in all POWs ceases after I gain combat information. What happens to them after I am through with them is a matter dictated by the tactical situation. If possible, I transport them back to headquarters, if not, we guard them real good. We surely would not turn them loose."

"Very good so far, but what happened to them?"

"I'm sorry, Sir. I thought I answered that. The NVA killed them, Sir."

The room was too quiet, so I thought I had better cover my ass a little more. "And also, Sir, you should see what they do to our men when they take one of them prisoner. They use barbed wire to sew their balls up inside their mouths while they are still alive. I buried four of my men who were treated that way only a few days ago."

"I think a recess is in order, gentlemen," was all the response I received. However, I felt that I was not alone in my hatred of the Vietcong and the NVA.

I walked once more down that same hallway with the brightly polished floor. It was strange to see that most of the office doors were standing open on both sides of the hallway. The office air conditioners had cooled the hallway. Many eyes turned on me as I passed. Again there were quite a few people around the vending machines. It was not a mere coincidence. It had become obvious that I was the attraction.

Wherever my eyes roamed they were met with friendly smiles. I started to feel that I was receiving warm approval from fellow Americans, but too much was at stake for me to bathe comfortably in such popularity.

Whispers spread through the hallway. Once I heard someone say, "That's the Green Beret sergeant who is the sole survivor of that Laos patrol." I detected no condemnations, just approval and proud feelings for the uniform I wore. I was among our own.

"Sergeant, again may I buy your coffee?"

There she was once more, with that same lovely smile conveying a promise. This time I felt like hiding from Booby Trap. The woman, about 35, presented a sophisticated elegant appearance. Under the tight, silky-smooth outfit she wore, her sensual curves must have been the envy of many a younger female. Like Cathy, she too had that special low-slung ass.

"Please, all I have with me is hundred dollar greenbacks." Again I told the truth and no one believed me, but how could they know about the ninth grave and the stack of money Mock had handed me. My remark was greeted with smiles.

"Nice to have you safely with us. In J-3, where I work, we have followed your patrol with interest through the many radio messages..." She was interrupted by Booby Trap.

"Sergeant," Booby Trap called.

"Thanks for the coffee and your lovely smile," was all I could say before Booby Trap came between us. He behaved as if I had no right to speak with anyone. Those who were close to the woman and me backed off. She stood her ground, and there was no misunderstanding her resentment of Booby Trap. Before she stepped back she handed me a note and made no attempt to hide it from Colonel Becket.

Word had spread fast among our side, as it had among the ARVN, about my return. There was little that I could do about it.

I looked at the slender, beautiful Penny, and gave her my stamp of silent approval. A quick glance at her hips showed seductive curves where her tight slacks and thin blouse spread over the nicest figure that I had encountered in many a year. She walked past me, and gave me another coy look. I patted her note in my pocket.

"Mail for you, Sergeant." Booby Trap handed me two letters. A quick glance showed one to be from a female who for years had retained hopes of buying me with her fat bank account. That one I normally would have thrown away but my problems with the Army made me re-evaluate all options. I put it in my pocket. It could turn out to be a meal ticket if the Army kicked me out.

The other I opened. It was from the Army library in Fort Carson, Colorado. It read, Subject: Book overdue: *The Pleasures Of Bird Watching.* Return book immediately, or mail money order for $2.15. If you fail to comply, your Commanding Officer will be notified for disciplinary action.

"Damn," I said out loud, "Bird watching, where the hell..." I did not finish what I wanted to say. I handed the letter to Colonel Becket to save myself the cost of a postage stamp and $2.15.

"It is for you, Sir." I said seriously.

He read the letter, gave me a dirty look, crumbled the paper into a ball and threw it into the nearby wastepaper basket. I could tell by his look that he was not amused.

"You are not to discuss matters with the people out here. The proceedings are classified, as you were told." He seemed worried. He pulled me to the side and spoke in a low voice.

"The shelling of Black Face will come up soon. I'm not telling you what to say, however, it would not help matters for you to talk about a non-existing ARVN or VC hospital. You have absolutely no intelligence that there ever was a hospital on that mountain. You understand, Sergeant?"

"Yes, Sir, I understand." And I sure as hell did understand that any information about an enemy hospital anywhere near an attack of mine would open a Pandora's box.

I was thankful to him for bringing up the subject. I would have goofed and brought the entire Army down on me. We Americans do not shell hospitals, at least not knowingly. Nothing indicated that the command had expected an enemy hospital to have been inside that mountain.

Since Booby Trap spoke about the hospital with me, I thought it possible that he would answer a question for me.

"Sir, what did Miss Friem and Don Gates say about me?"

He smiled. "I should ask you why you are asking me that, but I won't. Miss Friem refused to say anything derogatory about the Army or for that matter, about you. It makes me wonder just what transpired between the two of you. Mr. Gates, well that is something else. He is a mental case. You need not concern yourself about whatever he could have reported."

We were motioned to return to the briefing room. Quickly I ran through my mind where trouble for me could develop. Now I knew that I need not worry about the World Council of Churches screaming for my blood. I was ready for round three.

Back in the spacious office with the shining mahogany table, we were all seated once more. It seemed that the stacks of paper in front of each officer had increased considerably.

"Sergeant, some additional information has come to our attention." Colonel Brooks shuffled his stack of papers, not looking at me.

All other eyes were on me. My chair became uncomfortable, even though I did not feel any hostility toward me. After agonizing moments, Brooks spoke. "The South Vietnamese Army is demanding that we show them reason why we should not charge you with the murder of their eleven soldiers."

Silence hung heavy all around us.

"Murder?" I asked.

"Yes, they chose to use that word. And indications are that they are serious about it. But we do not..."

Colonel Wallace interrupted. "Sergeant, the United States Army does not, I say again, does not take orders from the South Vietnamese Army. We are not here to infer guilt or recommend further actions. The debriefing will now continue."

Colonel Wallace's last five words came out as an order, and left no doubt in anyone's mind as to who was in charge.

Brooks relaxed and settled himself back in his chair. It seemed that he welcomed the curt order from Wallace.

"Sergeant, we had a few matters under discussion. I do not hesitate to state that for some matters we received far from satisfactory answers. However, be that as it may. We have now arrived at the stage where I am asking you to start from the time you received the patrol order from Colonel Becket. Then report step by step the conduct of the patrol, ending where you disengaged from the enemy. It is your patrol Tactical Report."

Brooks sounded so sincere and amiable that I wondered if he was for real or just a good actor. He seemed to vacillate too easily between being perturbed with me and then being fatherly. He looked at the officers around the table.

"Gentlemen, feel free to stop the sergeant at any time for clarification, although where possible, let the sergeant continue at his own speed and in the manner that he may see fit."

He nodded for me to start. I had no trouble, since all patrol debriefings took the same route, and I was well trained in that phase of the operation.

Many questions were asked, most pertaining directly to combat tactics. I even detected approval and some expression of exultation. The latter became most evident when I mentioned how I anticipated the NVA charging headlong toward us on APCs, and the resulting combat loss to the enemy.

No one said a word after that about any miscalculation of mine. Colonel Becket made a feeble attempt to retreat from his earlier stance by saying, "Now I understand your actions."

Through the day the questioning continued. All in all I did not fare badly. The only items which became of major significance were going into Laos, two Frenchmen and one North Vietnamese civilian not properly accounted for.

Some resentment was voiced against me about the disposition of enemy and friendly wounded on top of Black Face. I blamed all on the

NVA. It was obvious that the matter would not be pursued outside the briefing room.

I had an opportunity to blame Booby Trap for the shelling of Black Face, as Tom and I once jokingly decided to do. But was just as well that I didn't, for too many follow-up questions would have been asked. Also, I had by that time effectively and conveniently jammed that incident with the rest of the worrisome items behind my gray veil. The one thing and perhaps the only thing that saved me much grief was my answer to Colonel Brooks.

"Why did you direct artillery and air strikes on the mountain you call Black Face? I am referring to the fire mission a few days before you received your orders to occupy the mountain."

Instead of denying that I requested and directed the fire on the mountain, and blaming Group for it, I answered, "Sir, I do not try to imagine what the NVA use a mountain for. The fact that he was on that mountain made it a target. We spend 99 percent of our time looking for the bastards and, any time we think we know where they are, like on top of Black Face, we try to do them in. Maybe I goofed."

There was no doubt in my mind that every officer around the table knew who was responsible for the pounding of Black Face. I judged rightly that they wanted to find out if I was going to blabber out my innocence. It would have been most embarrassing if I had blamed Group.

Group could help me get out of any trouble, but no one could help Group, if they were to assume the blame for the shelling of an enemy hospital. A smart soldier reasons that way.

I thought I detected confusion written on Booby Traps's face. To him it was inconceivable that someone would accept blame when they weren't guilty. He believed and lived by the motto, "Cover your ass." I heard later that he expected me to swear that no one knew of a hospital on Black Face.

All eyes then turned to Booby Trap. At first he must have mistaken it for approval of something he did, for he just sat there looking dumb. Then it dawned on him.

"Sergeant, you're not to discuss these proceedings without specific permission of the command, and then only with representative council appointed by appropriate authority, which in this case would be your immediate commander, me. "I further order you to confine your physical activities to the military compound in which you are now billeted, that being SF Compound San-Loo."

"Yes, Sir,"" was all I could say to the Restriction to Quarters order.

"May I contact Miss Friem, Sir?" I dared to ask. "No. I have been informed that Miss Friem is in a state of shock, so I order you not to contact her."

"Sir, about the two scouts. Unless we interfere, the ARVN will kill them."

The officers looked at each other in a manner indicative of embarrassment. A major named Blake, spoke up.

"The South Vietnamese Army has jurisdiction over them. We did, however, request leniency since the records of one revealed outstanding service to his country. You can be assured, Sergeant, that we did all that could be done under the circumstances."

Yeah, I thought. I bet you did. If either Wallace or Wakefield had said that I would have believed it.

Chapter 8

Honor

Whcn I thought of Ding and Mo, I felt a bitter hatred for all that
I saw. The only sanity came from the thought of revenge. That
the South Vietnamese Army would torture the two Yards to
death I did not doubt.

When I walked away from the debriefing room, I was no longer an
American soldier but a person possessed with but one thought. My entire
energy, mental and physical, was focused toward helping my two Yards. If
I was too late to save them, then one hell of a revenge would be mine. I
swore this to myself.

I squashed my anger, since anger without power is folly. Like the fox being
chased by a pack of hungry hounds, I started to lean heavily on cunning.

From MACV Headquarters I returned to the SF compound at San-Loo.
During the jeep ride, I opened the note from Penny. "You can reach me by
calling the J-3 duty officer. Ask for Penny. I would love to hear from you."

I promised myself I would call her, but first things first. Ding and Mo
would have to be taken care of. Even though my mind had jumped from
Booby Trap, my restriction, and that lovely ass at the coffee machine, a
plan was nevertheless taking shape.

I approached the problem of getting Ding and Mo out of the hands of
the ARVN like a tactical plan. At the dinner table I let my mind wander to

a number of my SF friends who could help. One man came to mind. It was Sergeant First Class Jim Filbert.

I smiled when I remembered old Jim. Surely he would help. Just a few months earlier I had saved his hide. Some years ago Jim had caught an enemy bullet in his right knee. It disqualified him from jumping and he lost his jump pay.

The assignment he ended up with was coordinator for an intelligence unit. His duties consisted mainly of liaison work between U.S. units and ARVN units. As such, I reasoned, he would have access to the Palace Guard and thus to Colonel Van Trang, the brother of the late Captain Van Trang of Ba Cat fame.

While sipping my after dinner coffee, I remembered how worried Jim was when our finance officer found out that he had been drawing jump pay for at least two years after being disqualified from jumping. The officer had told him that all the money would have to be paid back, unless he could prove that he had actually performed the minimum required jumps, which was at least one jump each three months.

When I heard about it, I took three men with me, broke into the personnel records branch office, where we worked all night altering flight manifests. By sunrise Jim was in the clear.

Yes, I knew Jim would help me. The position he held as Intelligence Coordinator could open many doors, and I guessed correctly that he had a key to Colonel Van Trang's door. I also guessed correctly that at the Palace Guard Headquarters Ding and Mo were being held.

I briefed myself thoroughly. The stakes were just as high as they would have been in an operation against the enemy. Two men's lives were at stake.

I did not dare bungle. I knew I had but one chance at saving them. The many problems I had caused myself throughout my life because of my impulsiveness, and the many years that I had walked in harm's way, had sharpened my mind. When I was satisfied that my plan was good, I put my coffee cup down and walked out of the mess hall.

Having stolen many jeeps during my 30 years in the service, I was soon driving down Saigon's main street toward the Intelligence Compound in yet another one.

A smile crossed my face as I mentally reviewed each step along the way toward freeing Ding and Mo. I did not allow myself to think that I might already be too late.

I knew that Jim, as coordinator, was issued extra ration cards with which to procure black market items: cigarettes, alcoholic beverages, jewelry, radios etc. These rationed items were the keys that opened all doors in South Vietnam.

The corruption within the military and political structures of South Vietnam was so well established and accepted that every signature of approval had to be purchased.

Inside the U.S. Army Intelligence Compound I asked for directions to Jim's quarters. I found him stepping out of the shower. There were three other sergeants in the wash area.

"What do you know, my old buddy from Fort Bragg! How are you, Babe?" Jim sounded elated to see me. "Tonight we party. You guys, know who this is? Well, let me tell you. You're in VIP company..."

I interrupted him. As usual Jim was overly talkative. "Hold it, Babe. Not so fast. Get yourself dressed, then we'll go for the drinks."

"Sure, sure. But let me tell these desk jockeys who you are so they can put a little reverence in their speech when they address you. This is that famo..." He did not finish.

"Not that?" one sergeant asked.

"Yeah, that sergeant, you guys. The one and only trooper who can fall into a bucket of shit and come out smelling like a rose. Good to see you, Babe."

"Welcome, partner," another sergeant said while giving me a warm handshake. "You took a beating on that patrol. Where I work we monitored just about all your radio messages. I work in J-3 at MACV. Glad to meet you, and also to know that you are now safely back among us. I would like to buy you a drink."

"Thanks, but not tonight. I have some important matters to talk to Jim about. But you said you worked in J-3. Know a woman by the name of Penny?"

"Oh yes. She is a lovely one. Looks like a million dollars, and I heard that she is one rich woman. Money pouring out of her ears. You should see the diamonds she wears. She, too, cannot talk about anything else but you and your patrol.

"You see, J-3, the place where she works, mans the War Room. Nothing happens in Vietnam that does not go through the War Room. From what I picked up, they were at first real pissed off with what took place, and later seemed to condone what you Special Forces got yourselves into with that mountain, Black Face."

"Interesting. I would like to speak with you some more on that. Will you join Jim and me later?" I asked.

A new and interesting piece of information had dropped into my lap. I promised myself to draw more information out of that sergeant. But first things first.

"Be right with you, Babe," said Jim as he got dressed. Within a few minutes he and I were alone in the parking lot.

Jim knew that I wanted something from him.

"Okay, Babe, lay it on me. To what do I owe this pleasant visit of yours? What can I do for you?"

"First off, Babe, I want you to trust me."

"Okay, I trust you." He answered without hesitation.

"I came back with two Yards. Scouts of mine. I want to get them away from the ARVN."

"How in hell are you going to do that, Tony? The ARVN Ranger Battalion of the Palace Guard has them. I heard that today. They have them right here in Saigon, ready to hang them in public. As a matter of fact, only a few hours ago, the commanding o fficer of the Rangers made a public statement that he and he alone will put the noose around their necks and then personally kick the trap door from under them.

"And Tony, do you know who he is? Well, let me tell you. He is none other than the brother of that ARVN SF captain you guys did in at Ba Cat. Oh, boy, you sure wiped some ARVN faces in the shit with that one."

"Are you going to let me talk? Seems like I'm going to have to belt you in the mouth before you are going to listen to me."

"Okay, okay, I'm listening, Babe, but only one thing more. That same ARVN Colonel, Van Trang's his name, of course it would be the same as the..."

"Damn you, Jim."

"Just a minute, Tony. That colonel threatened to do you in. Said that publicly, as soon as they heard that you were in Saigon and..."

"Shut up, damn you, Jim. Just listen to me. Okay? Okay?"

"I've..." I held my finger on his lips.

"I have a plan that will work. All I need is for you first to shut up, and then to help me."

Jim became attentive.

"Okay, Babe, lay it on me." He stepped closer to me to preclude anyone overhearing us.

"Like I said, Jim, just listen for now and don't ask questions."

"I'm listening."

I felt like belting him as I had threatened to do. He must have expected me to, because he finally shut up.

"When we attacked the NVA guns in Laos, Tom found over a quarter million American dollars in a village. Money that the NVA and VC used to buy arms and ammunition from the ARVN."

Jim said nothing. He looked me in the eyes to try and see if I was lying to him or merely relating a story manufactured especially for the ruse that I had planned to use on the ARVN.

"Tom's slicky boys stripped the NVA and VC villagers of valuables. In the village there must have been at least 1,000 inhabitants, so you see, we are speaking of a large amount of loot. Remember that. A large amount of loot. I estimate it to have a monetary value of over a quarter million dollars, jewelry and money put together.

"Tom and I buried the money and the valuables in among those mountains near Black Face. We are the only ones who knew about the cache and roughly where it is. Tom is dead, which leaves only me.

"But, I have a problem. That is the reason I am speaking to you. Follow me, partner?"

"Yeah, I follow you. You want me to go with you..."

"No, Jim." I took out the roll of hundred dollar bills and handed it to him.

"Give this to that Colonel Van Trang. Tell him it is payment for having the two scouts draw a map overlay of the escape route we took after we destroyed the guns."

Jim turned pale as he looked at the large amount of American money.

"Tony, you're crazy. That colonel will grab the money and then demand the real reason why I came to him."

"Right, Jim. Then you tell him that I, and you mention my name, have to submit the patrol overlay to Group and have forgotten the exact route I took. That is why I want the two scouts' information."

"Jesus, Tony! Have you flipped? That man will know that we are lying. First off, who the hell heard of a Montagnard being able to read a map, let alone draw an overlay, and besides, partner, all these greenbacks?

"Man, are you crazy? It is worth a thousand times more on the black market. That colonel will never let us get away without telling him the entire story as to where you got it and..."

"Shut up, Jim." Jim was getting excited and talking too loudly and too much.

"You have the drift, Jim boy. You are functioning now." To me, things were taking shape as I had hoped they would.

Jim was puzzled, so I explained further.

"You see, partner, I want that son of a bitch to disbelieve you. I want him to demand that you tell him the truth. Only you say you do not know the truth, which you don't, and besides, I want you to pretend at that stage.

"Many Vietnamese officers judge intelligence on a graduation scale commensurate with the military rank structure. He is a full colonel, even though he is but 22 years old, and you are only a sergeant first class. You are therefore just one rung above a donkey in intelligence."

"The bastard, wait till..." Jim made a fist and pulled his arm back as if he was about to smash someone's face in.

"Damn you, Jim. You listening to me?"

"Oh, yeah, Tony. I'm listening to you but you're not making sense. That colonel..."

"Just listen, Jim." I cut him short. "He'll pressure you for additional information. You then act dumb enough to want to confide in him. Tell him, but reluctantly at first, tell him that you have heard that I buried a large amount of loot, but can't find the place without the map overlay from the two scouts.

"Tell him you heard from someone else also that I had buried some money and other things out there in the jungle. Make him promise you that he will not tell anyone that you told him. Tell him that you are afraid that I'll kill you if I find out that you told him." Jim was quiet for a few moments. I could tell his mind was acting on what Colonel Van Trang would do as soon as he was informed about the cache.

"Tony, he is going to demand that I take him to you. If he does not believe us about the money cache, he will still demand to see you so he can put a bullet into you. If he believes you about the money and jewels, he will want it all.

"Oh, he'll promise you all the help and most of the loot, but he will wind up with all of it, and you will wind up dead. You see, that way he can really brag to the world. His face will have been saved and you will be dead."

"You have it, partner. Just the way I have it worked out."

"Yeah, I don't see what good that would do the two scouts or for that matter, you."

"Just leave it like that, partner. Don't think any more about it. Just get your ass into this jeep and guide me to where that son of a bitch is. You are going to see him right now, and do what I told you."

Reluctantly, Jim stepped into the jeep and sat down next to me.

"I'm heading for trouble," he muttered to himself so softly that I could hardly hear him. Then he said to me, "Every time things start to get peaceful with me, some former SF buddy shows up and I get right back behind the eight ball. Won't be a bit surprised if this jeep is stolen."

"It is," I said with sadistic pleasure.

"Oh, my God. The same old story. Before this night is over, we'll probably have so much trouble, a stolen jeep charge will seem like pissing on the wrong side of the street."

"Don't sound so sad, Jim Boy. Just think of it. Ding will be one hell of a happy Yard, not to find himself dancing in the air at the wrong end of a rope."

"Ding one of the two? I should have known. That dumb Yard is about as indestructible as you are, Tony. Surprised that they managed to get him. One would think that he would have made for the mountains instead."

"Long story, but they got him, and the other one is a twelve year old. Also no front teeth, so he is worth saving."

"I grant you that, but how you are going to save them is still a mystery to me."

"Just keep it that way, Babe. Like I told you. Don't think. Just do as I asked you to do. This way to the Palace Guards?"

"Yeah. Turn right at the next traffic jam."

It took us some time to wiggle the jeep though the congested streets of Saigon. It was about the time when most workers were heading home. As usual, each Honda driver had but one thing in mind — to scare the hell out of pedestrians as the driver barreled full speed into the masses.

At each red traffic light the road in the direction that you were traveling got filled up from curb to curb. When the light turned green those on your left shot across in front of you to miss the oncoming traffic. It was one of the modern miracles of Saigon traffic that they did not collide head-on in the center of the intersection, for from the other direction the same thing was happening.

Soon we were close to one of the heavily guarded steel gates leading into the palace grounds. I pulled to a stop near a small but noisy bar, jumped out of the jeep and motioned for Jim to get behind the wheel.

"I'll be inside that bar if the colonel wants to talk to me. I'll be expecting him, Jim. You bring him."

"Hope you know what you are doing, Tony. You're armed and so am I. If it comes to a shoot out, count me in. May just as well go out fighting a South Viet as a North Viet." With that, he let out the clutch and screeched towards the nearest palace gate.

It was a dimly lit bar. Only three customers were at the bar. They were dressed in the uniform of the palace guards, with decorations adorning their immaculately fitted and pressed jungle fatigues. Their dress was in glaring contrast to mine, which fit me okay, but was free of unauthorized alterations.

When they saw me, I was greeted with outstretched arms.

"Green Beret, Sergeant. Come drink. We be good friends. We be gets boo coo good mama san fo you."

I joined in the jovial atmosphere of the bar while acting partly drunk. I tossed two U.S. $20 greenbacks on the bar counter.

"Drinks on me," I said happily.

When they saw the greenbacks, three barmaids jockeyed amongst themselves for a position next to me.

"You be my sargy, you be good sargy, I be love you boo coo too much..."

No doubt about it. I had established myself among them. As far as they were concerned, I was just another dumb, half-drunk American with too much money.

So be it, I thought. If shooting started, I wanted to catch them by surprise.

The soldiers were all armed with .45-caliber service pistols the same as I was. None of them had rifles. Mine was loosely slung over my right shoulder. I had a clip rammed home and the selector was on full automatic. The safety was off with a round in the chamber. With one split-second flip of my arm I could have the weapon at the ready. Years of living with my rifle had made it a part of me.

The place had become rowdy with the juke box blaring, "Why, why, why, Delilah..." The three palace guards tried to get me to join them in the chorus of *She'll be Coming 'Round the Mountain.* A skimpily dressed, sweet-smelling barmaid was blowing in my ear.

No one but me saw the two ARVN full colonels enter the bar. They came directly to me. I had my eyes on them through the mirror behind the bar and my .45-caliber pistol was in my hand, but hidden from them.

"What the hell, Jim? I told you not to..." I turned slowly while I held my pistol behind my back.

"That's all right, Sergeant. Jim be good friend us," said the colonel, whom I immediately recognized as the late Captain Van Trang's brother.

The strangeness of the human mind once more acted in defiance of reason and a quick mental picture flashed before me. It was that inquisitive proboscis monkey, which I had once compared with Colonel Van Trang. Quickly it dawned on me that I need not fear that colonel for the time being.

The bar had suddenly gone quiet. Even the noisy jukebox was quickly unplugged. An electrified silence had taken the place of what had been just another bar seconds earlier.

"You be join us," said Van Trang and he motioned me to a nearby table that was swiftly vacated. Without their seeing it, I slipped my .45 back into the holster. I walked slowly and with a faked show of reluctance to the table with them. The bar's madam, accompanied by her perfume, shuffled toward us from behind a curtain to show us her best, but nervous smile, and offered us her personal attention.

Jim spoke first, "This is Colonel Van Trang, and Colonel Ngoc Thao."

I made the necessary acknowledgment nods. My mind flipped to the name, Pham Ngoc Thao, a colonel. Somehow I knew that it was the same colonel who had been reported to me by that NVA prisoner we interrogated. Small world, I thought.

"Why did you bring these gentlemen out here when all I asked you to do was a simple little thing and nothing to bother the colonels with." I spoke harshly to convey my displeasure with Jim.

"No bother, Sergeant. Me want talk to you. Please sit down." He ordered the madam, "Drinks for all. Whisky?" he asked.

I nodded but again turned my attention to Jim.

"You talked too much as usual," I accused him.

"I had to tell, Tony. The colonel..." Van Trang cut him off.

"Everything is okay, Sergeant. You no be angry with Jim. He good friend us. Everything he say okay us."

Colonel Van Trang's voice was amiable and he placed his arm on my shoulder to convey a friendliness toward me that I knew was faked.

The madam placed the drinks on the table, then made a respectful retreat, giving us her final smile and bow as she subserviently shuffled backward out of sight. The atmosphere in the bar had taken on a feeling of respect upon the entrance of the two feared colonels.

If I were to return to the bar after the two colonels had left, I would most certainly get back all the money that the barmaids had stolen from me in the short period that I been sitting at the bar.

They were so completely impressed by my importance, being singled out and invited into the company of those illustrious colonels, that I would also have qualified for the normal price of 50 cents per PX black market beer instead of the $1.50.

Van Trang and Ngoc Thao were both in their twenties. They were probably about 28, and the usual rear-echelon officers who owed their ranks to relatives in high offices. The saying those days was, "We promote them, the Yankee suckers pay them."

It was not uncommon to see a 21-one-year-old two-star general, hanging around the U.S. Embassy as liaison officer between AID officials and the black market recipients of U.S. goods to South Vietnam.

My total attention was focused on Colonel Van Trang.

He seemed the more aggressive of the two. With my military training I could grasp the tactical situation around me, and my analysis made me feel confident that no matter how things turned out, I could walk out of the bar without a scratch.

Colonel Van Trang was dressed in his full splendor. His chest displayed such an enviable array of decorative campaign and service ribbons that he outflaunted the late Hermann Goering.

The most conspicuous of the decorations was the French *fourragère,* a colorful braided shoulder lanyard award given to each member of a combat unit that had performed in an exemplary manner against severe odds.

With the close correlation of Van Trang's age and the date of the last French battle in which he could have won the award, the battle at Dien Bien Phu, 17 May 1954, I concluded that he was at the tender age of ten when the French bestowed the great honor on him.

My disrespect for him and my disgust for such dishonor grew.

Yes, Van Trang, I thought, you are going to be easy to manipulate. We did your brother in, and you may be next.

"The money and the jewelry?" Van Trang whispered to me as soon as the madam was out of earshot.

"What money and what jewelry are you talking about?" I asked and at the same time put a look of disgust on my face while staring daggers at Jim.

"You, Jim. You talked too much." Then I looked appealingly at Van Trang.

"Sir, all I asked Jim to get for me was a map overlay of the patrol route. Nothing more."

Colonel Van Trang gave me a fatherly condescending smile, and showed a parental patience. I would gladly have knocked his teeth down his throat.

Colonel Thao showed approval. After all, they were colonels, and my being a mere master sergeant placed a trying gap between their intelligence and mine. I felt like slapping those better-than-thou smirks off both their faces, but I had Mo and Ding's welfare at stake.

Damn you two, I thought.

Van Trang looked at me with such kindness that I believed he actually pitied me for believing him such a fool.

"No, Sergeant. You do not can get overlay. Montagnards cannot read and he be big fool that think they can make overlay. "No, Sergeant. You be pay money for nothing. And patrol debriefing no be need overlay anyway."

He then sat back in his chair to enjoy my squirming.

His English was fluent, but heavily accented and often incorrect. The overuse of be was typical of the Vietnamese and Montagnards.

I did not disappoint him. One of my parents must have been a Hollywood actor, for I certainly gave a commendable performance.

"Jim, goodbye. I don't want to see you again. Just give me back the money I gave you."

Jim looked hurt. "I don't have the money...I..."

"I have the money, Sergeant. I don't want you to be mad at Jim. He be good friend to you. He come to the right man for to help you."

Somehow Jim must have gotten the cue, for he stood up and prepared to leave.

"I'll take the jeep and I don't care how you get back. I tried to help you, and then you start talking shit."

Van Trang wanted to interfere, but I waved him off.

"Let him go."

A faint smile crossed Jim's countenance. We understood each other.

Alone with the two colonels, the conversation soon centered on the money and jewelry.

"Okay, Sir. You guessed it right. I don't need the overlay for a debriefing. I need it for something else." I made sure that they thought me gullible.

"Now you be speaking good, Sergeant. I and Colonel Thao, we be help you get all money and jewels you be buried. Like Jim he say to us. We help you for sure. First you tell us how much money you be buried."

They were both attentive and leaned close to me.

"I...I..."

I stammered, pretending I was confused and at a lost for words.

"I need help to find the place where I hid the jewels and money. I was afraid at first, but now I think I can trust you, Sirs."

They looked at each other, hardly believing their good fortune for having run into such a dumb sergeant.

"How much money?" asked Thao. "You be take us to money now."

"How can I, Sir? I cannot find the place without..."

He interrupted me.

"God damn Montagnards too dumb for to make overlay. They no can tell, they no can read map, God damn stupid Montagnards."

Thao was getting red in the face with frustration.

"How much money?" he asked again.

"Adding the jewelry, about a half-million dollars. All in 20 and 100 dollar bills.

I think it is money the World Council of Churches gave the NVA to buy things for the VC here in South Vietnam. We got the money when we attacked a village in Laos. If I get an overlay..."

Van Trang interrupted me. "How much is jewelry?"

"I don't know, Sir. We got into two villages. Bangles, necklaces of gold and also some diamonds." I laid it on thick for them. Their eyes shone with glee.

"We be work together," said Van Trang. "We be split four ways."

"Four ways?" I asked, showing just enough surprise to draw an explanation from them.

"Yes, four ways. We three, and General Mhin..."

He caught himself before giving the general's full name. He might just as well have said it, for it was common knowledge that General Mhin Duc Lap was the black market king of Saigon.

And he might just as well have left me out, for I would have indeed been a dummy if, for one moment, I believed that they would split it with a dead U.S. master sergeant.

"You win, Sir." I put on my best act of looking dejected. I wanted them to get the impression that I had given in, and was ready to agree to whatever they wanted. It paid off beautifully. Van Trang took charge, just the way I had hoped that he would.

"Okay, now I take charge," Colonel Van Trang said. "I know you got the money and the jewels hidden, but you no can find the place by yourself. A G.I. no can move in the jungle without he be get lost."

He leaned back in his chair, obviously satisfied with the way things were turning out for him. He took out a pack of cigarettes. Slowly, with deliberate moves, he started the same ritual that his late brother had used. The cigarette took a number of detours before it finally wound up in his mouth. Only then did he continue.

"You be in much trouble, Sergeant. My brother you kill in Ba Cat. You no know he be my brother? He be, but I no be mad you. You gets money and jewels, we share. I gets Montagnards out and you be go on helicopter. Montagnards show place, you bring back. Okay?"

I almost fell into disaster, but quickly recovered before he assumed that Ding and Mo knew where the cache was.

"No, Sir. The Yards do not know where I buried the money. They must just show me where we bivouacked one night. I can find the place from there."

"Oh," was all he said.

I thought it a good idea to make him feel even better.

"Sir, will you help me with the Army? They are mad at me for going into Laos."

"I take care all. But Sergeant, I think U.S. Army they gots a few other things they be mad at you for," he said with a shit-eating grin on his face.

You sarcastic bastard, I thought, but I let it slide. I had gone far enough, and I wanted to close the deal.

"How am I going to get away from the Army? They have me on restriction."

"I take care all. You be come TDY my Ranger battalion. One day, maybe two. Tomorrow I see orders cut. You just wait. Do nothing, but wait for order."

They stood up ready to leave.

"Colonel, the money I gave Jim was all I had from the money that is buried. I want to stay here for a few drinks. Can I have some of it back?"

"No need, Sergeant." He looked at the madam, and shook her up by calling her over. He told her to let me have all I wanted and he would pay the bill. He also ordered one of his Rangers at the bar to see that I got a jeep ride back to my compound.

I thanked them, and sauntered over to the bar as the two of them walked out. As I expected, the event had crowned me an instant hero. By way of rewarding them for their reverence and awe of me I ordered drinks for the house.

Quite an eventful night ensued. Within an hour the bar was packed, for they had found a live one. As fast as I ordered the drinks the barmaids would set them up. The madam in the background had some apprehensions about the astronomical bill I was creating for Van Trang, but did not dare refuse my orders. I had two sweet-smelling professionals on my lap and one hanging onto me from behind, when in walked, or rather fell, Jim, as if drunk.

"Whee, you bastard! You have all the fun without your old buddy. Move over and make room for a good man."

He picked up a girl and threw her up in the air, then caught her neatly. She weighed all of 80 pounds, the usual weight of those sweet-smelling, well-powdered ladies of the night.

"Good to have you back, partner. All the drinks are on me. Just holler your pleasure." I hugged Jim and slapped him on the back.

"All is A-okay. My scouts will walk," I whispered to him. He said nothing, but nodded. He was not drunk as he wanted all to believe. He was ready and able to help me when and if I needed help. I found out later that Jim had stood outside the bar prepared to get involved if things went wrong.

It was early morning when we finally crawled out of the bar. A shiny ARVN ranger jeep and driver were waiting for us outside. Our stolen jeep had long since been stolen again.

I slipped back into the compound where I was billeted. Whether I was missed or not, I did not care to know. Before I was through, I was going to be in so much trouble that a little thing like breaking restriction would seem like sticking out my tongue to a passing truck full of U.S. Marines.

That night I slept badly. Two sets of tear-filled black eyes kept drifting through my mind as I lay in my dark room. The overhead electric fan made a noise like a miniature helicopter, but it was not loud enough to drown out the distant, outgoing artillery rounds that kept up a dull rumble throughout the night.

Neither did it drown out the Saigon vehicular noises. Honda horns beeped between the clinking and clacking of bullock cart wheels. Farmers were moving their produce to the bustling open markets which were scattered throughout the hungry city.

Shortly after sunrise came a knock on my door.

"Come in," I called, not caring who it was. When I looked up I was surprised to see a U.S. Army major enter my room.

"Sorry to disturb you this early, Sergeant." He had not shaved. A black stubble spread like a shadow on his tired face, giving his swarthy complexion a dirty look.

"It's okay, Sir. I was awake." I made a move to get up and show the proper military respect to an officer, but he waved me to remain where I was. He took the only chair in the room and moved it closer to me where I lay propped up on my pillow.

"I'll come straight to the point, Sergeant. You lucked out, but we need your cooperation."

He then settled comfortably back in the chair.

Here it comes, I thought. I did not believe his opening statement. Just when I thought things were straightening out for me, something else always came along to mess everything up.

"If only the world would stand still for a little while and let... damn it! I could not very well get off."

"The ARVN officers who conducted the investigation on the deaths of their eleven soldiers made us an offer. Your cooperation, and all charges against you will be dropped. As a matter of fact, the U.S. Army will be absolved of any possible suspicion of neglect pertaining to the loss of the A-Camp, and the killing of non-combatants. We cannot have another My Lai on our hands.

"The death of the ARVN soldiers and the whereabouts of the World Council of Churches representatives would be explained."

"It sounds good, Sir," I said without enthusiasm, for I knew there was some payment to be made and I was going to be at the giving end.

"It is good, Sergeant. And all you have to do is recognize the truth of the entire situation and then openly admit it."

"I don't understand, Sir."

"Sure you do, Sergeant. After all, what and who is really responsible for what happened? Not you. Not the United States Army and not the ARVN. It was the Montagnard command.

"Captain Mock and his company. Right from the start, as soon as they killed the eleven ARVN soldiers, they took charge of the camp, including the scheduled patrol.

"No one could possibly expect you and your few men to have held back the entire Montagnard tribe.

"You see, even our Army was helpless to intervene. It became a thing of diminishing guilt, the more helpless the situation became. Remember at one stage you were ordered out, and the ARVNs were taking over the patrol?"

"Yes, Sir. I remember."

"Good. So, let them rightfully assume the blame, since in reality it matters little now for hardly any of them are alive. As a by-product of bringing the truth to light, the ARVN will look kindlier on the fact that they lost eleven men at the hands of the Montagnards, for we also suffered losses."

Yeah, I thought. That was so they could save face.

"Yes, Sir. I see. It makes no difference to me. Only thing that bothers me is that they are holding two Yards who served us honorably. What about them?"

"Sergeant, they are part of the Montagnard command that killed the eleven ARVN soldiers, and also the ones that moved into Laos. What are we supposed to do? Coddle crime? After all, Sergeant, let us be honest with each other. You did wrong and should be thankful to walk away with your stripes. As it is, we may still find it necessary to bring charges against you, but that is not why I came here to speak to you.

"I want you to agree with me now that the blame rightfully lies with the Montagnards. That has been established. All that remains is for you to do what you are ordered. And I may add that orders should not be necessary, if you follow proper military procedures and conduct yourself as an American Soldier."

"Yes, Sir," I answered. I was not going to get the major upset with me. He sounded sincere and was right about things.

"Sergeant, now we understand each other. This is what I want you to do. Just remain here in this compound until we can get an order cut for you

to report for TDY to an ARVN unit here in Saigon. It will be of short dura-
tion. Just long enough for some ARVN investigators to ask you some rou-
tine questions. All of which you must answer as truthfully as possible.

"It will be a mere formality to establish that the U.S. Army and the
ARVN hold no animosity towards each other and that we can resolve
misunderstandings in a civilized manner."

"TDY to an ARVN unit, Sir?"

"That is how the order will read. However, you will be quartered at the
military attachè billets and an officer from the attachè staff will be in charge
of you for the two or three days that you will be there.

"It is also understood by me that an officer will be your counselor and
represent you at all times while being questioned."

I was then sure that Colonel Van Trang had power. It scared me to find
myself a pawn in a chess game played by the Army of South Vietnam, even
though I had invited that chess game.

Another frightening thought within that game of chess played by the
South Vietnamese, which piece was the United States?

The major was pleased with me after the rather ticklish situation he
had to smooth over. It was not a pleasant thing for a major to walk into a
sergeant's hootch and explain protocol and the Army's subservient status
in political power plays.

When he opened the door to leave, he turned to me once more.
"Sergeant, just as an additional piece of information. The ARVN officer in
charge of the investigation is the brother of that Captain Van Trang that the
Montagnards killed. You need not worry about him, though. I spoke to him
on the phone a while ago. He holds no animosity toward you."

I gave that some thought. It was clear to me who he would not hold
animosity toward me for the time being, but later he was going to hate me,
himself, and the world in general.

After the major left, I remained propped up on my pillow for a long
time. My thoughts drifted through the many possible directions my plan
to free Ding and Mo might take. My plan was sound.

The danger to myself I understood and accepted. The danger to Ding
and Mo did not matter, for if I did nothing they would be worse off. If they
died with me, so be it. After all, we had been living on borrowed time for
awhile. Things were falling so nicely into place that I felt like rewarding
myself, so I headed for the nearest telephone and called MACV, J-3. I got
Penny on the line.

"I have the day free, can you develop a headache and join me?" I asked.

"Of course I can. But where is your hospital?" She answered sweetly.

"The SF compound San-Loo."

"No problem, Sergeant. And I also know that you are on restriction, and you like your scotch with a dab of ice water. The scotch and I will see you within the hour. Don't go away."

"You know, Penny, I'm going to love you boo coo too much and I don't care about the PX." She laughed and hung up.

Among the reasons our soldiers were popular with the women of Vietnam was our soldiers' access to the well-stocked post exchanges. A woman that could win a soldier over so that he would buy her items from the PX would have most of her financial problems solved.

The women's skimpy knowledge of our language and customs usually caused them to make a direct approach towards solving their monetary difficulties with something like, "I boo coo love you too much, GI, what time PX open."

I made good use of the hour. After a welcome shower and clean clothing, I called outside to a passing private. I asked him to be nice to me and get me two glasses and a bucket of ice. He smiled and gave me a friendly salute.

"On the way, Sergeant," he answered good naturedly.

He must have heard of the famous SF master sergeant under guard and waiting to be placed in front of a firing squad.

Within minutes I had a two glasses and a bucket of ice.

"Anything else, Sergeant, just holler. I live next door and will hear you," he said sincerely.

When I heard a knock on the door, I called "It's open. Just enter and give me one of those lovely smiles of yours,"

Luckily for me, it wasn't some soldier at the door.

Penny stepped into the room. At first we just stood there looking at each other. It seemed such a natural meeting. No coy make-believe, hard-to-get, or faked embarrassment. Just two free people, over 21, and wanting to get to know each other. I opened my arms and she fitted in just right.

I felt a slight trembling of her full body under the thin silken outfit she wore. She did not wear a bra, and I soon found out why. It would have been a sin to have restricted the two hard nipples.

"Penny, you are the best thing that has happened to me since I lost Ba Cat," I said, looking into her clear blue eyes.

"Liar. What about that small World Council of Churches female you stole out of Laos?"

"Damn, what all do you know about me?"

"Just about everything, Soldier. I work for J-3, remember."

"Yeah, I guess you are on the receiving end of what takes place."

She pulled me to the bed, sat down, and held my hands.

"From the time you left Ba Cat until today, I've kept track of this famous Green Beret master sergeant's unorthodox compliance to orders."

She shook her head.

"I can hardly believe that I am sitting next to you. You should be dead, killed by the enemy or hanged by our side. You live a charmed life, and for the next few hours I want to share that life with you."

She slowly slipped her blouse over her shoulders and with her eyes looking into mine, wiggled herself out of her tightly fitting, silky garment to reveal her perfect sensuous body. The slacks she wore at work did not do her body justice. When she lay back without a stitch of clothing on, she was beautiful and had all the right curves.

I held her face between my palms and said softly to her, "Such a woman as you should not be wasted in a J-3 office, but should always be waiting for the warrior returning from the battlefield. Somehow, somewhere, someone has seen it fit to reward me for something I must have done right along the way by sending you, Penny. I am now being paid in full."

"What a wonderful thing to say to a woman. I am going to cherish those words for a long, long time," she said sweetly.

For a few moments I regretted not having four hands. There were so many smooth and yielding parts of her to feel, and I was burdened with the need to undress myself. I persevered and soon my clothing was also scattered on the floor where she had carelessly thrown her own.

There was something clean and heavenly about her. Unlike any other woman I have ever been with. She seemed to demand all I had to offer, and having her all to myself, I had much to offer. Every ounce of health and vitality, of which I was in no short supply, I turned loose on her.

All too soon it was the end of round one. "What a woman!" I said, partly out of breath.

"Oh, Tony! You'll kill me, but what a wonderful way to go. What a man!"

She wiggled and shook herself like a barnyard hen who had just got a very large rooster off her back. Then she grabbed me around the neck and stuck her tongue deep into my mouth again.

It took a few minutes for me to settle her down to where she took a drink of scotch with me.

"You know something, Tony. I am not going to let you get away from me, ever."

She put her drink down and faced me. I could tell that she wanted to drop the frivolous attitude that she had until then displayed to me.

"You and I, we are still young and healthy, and I just know that we complement each other.

"I know you real well, Tony. I made it my business to find out all about you. For one thing, I thought you were going to need the best lawyer money could buy to get the Army off your back.

"You really messed up, Sergeant, when you went into Laos. I can't tell you why it was such a big thing, it's classified, but believe me, you nearly kicked the rug out from under a very large operation."

I wanted to say something, but she put a finger on my lips. "Just let me talk, Tony. I have something big to speak to you about."

She poured me another drink.

"I am 35 years old and you are 48. Both of us are free to map out any future we want. The Army is not going to let you remain on active duty. General Collins, the man I work for, let it drop that you are to retire as soon as they can smooth over the mess you made of things.

"No one is going to prefer court-martial charges against you, even though there are a few officers who would love to send you to prison in Leavenworth.

"We are healthy, strong and love life. I have more money than we two could spend in a lifetime. Let us team up. Please, Tony. I want you and I need you. I'll not be bossy nor place handcuffs on you."

Just the smallest glint of moisture started to show in her eyes. I was overwhelmed and did not want to comment, so I just took her in my arms, and when I saw the first sign of a smile on her lips I kissed them.

"We'll talk about it, Penny. Like I said, you are the best thing that has happened to me ever, and I see no reason why I should willingly let you. I can at least go to you.

"Now, young lady, since it seems that I have won your heart and mind, let me have your body as well."

She giggled happily and pulled me on top of her. It seemed as if her hands were as busy feeling me as mine were feeling her. Afterward she lay in my arms with a glow of happiness shining in her eyes, looking up at me.

"Tony," she whispered, "for the first time in my life I find myself in the arms of a real American hero."

"Nuts. No such thing as a hero," I answered back.

"You would say that."

Then she sat up and looked at me. My eyes fastened on her firm breasts and I could just barely cover those lovely things with my two large hands.

"Do you know what the brass said when all those crazy messages of yours started to clutter up the air? They were thrilled and fell all over each other to get the order out to support you. One general said, and I quote him, 'We need more fighting men like that sergeant.' Yes, we were all on your side, Tony."

"Now let me please you while you lie still like that little fluffy you grabbed in Laos probably did when you screwed her."

She exposed me to a few neat tricks of her own invention. There was no way that I was going to ask her where she learned the maneuver she so perfectly executed to my satisfaction.

When she was finished with me, all I could say was, "You win, Penny. I'm not going to let you get away."

When the bottle of scotch was empty, so was I. Penny was just a little more than I could handle, but there were no complaints.

She left me at sunset. "You have not seen the last of me, Tony. What I want, I get. And I want you."

Because of Penny, I no longer saw those small, sad black eyes before me. Just as well, for I needed the rest for what I knew was going to follow.

I had stopped considering the consequences to myself. I was sure that I was at the end of my life, for I knew that Van Trang was not going to give me the two Yards to go after the cache alone. He would send Rangers, and I would have to shoot it out with them.

I also thought that they might keep the scouts in the Huey, and just cruise over the area, not letting the scouts down.

Another consideration that I had to take care of kept plaguing me. I had promised Tom to get the money to his wife.

"How will I know which grave?" I asked myself.

There was yet another problem, one I hated to think about. The Army was not going to let me get away with the undertaking. If I did manage to live through the mess, I would get the book thrown at me. How would that help Tom's family?

The night slipped away like the day, while everything else seemed to hang in limbo. When the first rays of the new sun spread their warmth across the land, and the traffic noises of Saigon took over all sound, someone knocked on my door.

"Come in, it's open!" I hollered and regretted it immediately, for I awoke with a splitting headache.

"Sergeant, I've got a message for you from the Duty Officer. He wants you to get ready to report to some unit. He has the orders," said a young, smartly dressed, Green Beret Charge of Quarters runner.

"Okay. I'll be right over. Do you guys have some coffee?"

"Sure, Sergeant. Freshly brewed."

"What kind of message do you guys have for me? Good or bad?"

"I don't know, Sarge. They just called and told us to have you report to MACV Headquarters ASAP."

I took the time to shower and shave, then changed into the clean fatigues that a considerate sergeant of San-Loo's supply room had provided.

In the orderly room I drank a coffee and was informed by the Duty Officer that I was to report to the MACV duty officer.

"I need four full M-16 clips, Sir, and 20 rounds for my .45," I told the duty officer.

He nodded to the runner who sprinted to the ammo bunker. Within a few minutes I received what I asked for.

"Anything else, Sergeant?" asked the officer.

"No, Sir." I thanked him for their hospitality and jumped into the waiting duty driver's jeep. I was taken through the winding crowded Saigon streets where the smell of human and animal excrement mixed with exhaust fumes to such an offensive extent that I did not want to take a deep breath.

The constant hum and drone of vehicle engines set a pattern unlike anything else on earth. The humid putrid air muffled all sharp sounds, but amplified the rumbled noises. What a place to live, I thought. Better fight it out with the NVA and VC in the dark mountainous jungle than to struggle for space to breathe in the pungent but pacified city of Saigon.

It was 0700 on the dot when I reported with a smart salute to the MACV duty officer.

"Sir, Master Sergeant Blondell reporting to the duty officer as directed, Sir."

Usually I gave that last Sir an extra military ring in reporting to an officer to let him know that I had a pair. It kept the relationship between me and an officer I did not know in proper perspective — at least long enough to find out what type of officer I had to deal with.

The Leadership Committee at Fort Benning's Infantry Training Center would have been proud of the way I reported to that Duty Officer. It shook him just a little, for he was a staff officer with little or no official direct contact with infantry, Airborne, Ranger, and Green Berets. I was all those wrapped up in one.

He returned my salute the best he remembered from his training in some Reserve Officers Training Course, then extended his hand in a friendly greeting.

"Nice to see you, Sergeant. Coffee?" He came from behind his large shiny mahogany desk and handed me a cup of coffee. "Sugar?" he asked.

His demeanor made me wonder why he was uncomfortable, when it was I that should be uncomfortable in his high headquarters.

"No, thank you, Sir."

"Your orders have just been cut. TDY to Headquarters, 7th ARVN Ranger Battalion. They're here in Saigon. That shiny jeep outside is theirs and is waiting to take you to the Ranger Battalion. No hurry, though. Finish your coffee, Sergeant.

"It says here that you are to report in person to a Colonel Van Trang, Commanding Officer, 7th Ranger." Then he smiled. "Of course, you can read it for yourself."

After a few minutes I walked out to where the Ranger jeep was waiting for me. How they managed to get all the necessary approvals for the TDY so fast was beyond me. Usually it took more than a week to worm something like that through all the brass.

The duty officer, in his smartly fitted uniform, an Army G-4 Captain, followed me outside.

"Sergeant..." He seemed hesitant in saying what was on his mind.

"The order came through some strange channels — not from your Special Forces Group Headquarters in Nha Trang, or from Eighth Army. I merely received the directive to have it cut and sign it for your commander." He sounded apologetic. "Sorry to hand you that order, knowing the

260 Honor and Sacrifice: The Montagnards of Ba Cat

circumstances surrounding the deaths at Ba Cat and the subsequent trouble your people had. It does seem strange indeed, that you should be receiving them."

"Thank you for your concern, Sir. It is going to be okay." I added, "I guess."

"Your people at Group did not seem to think so, and I think they are going to have you return to them shortly. The group commander was quite unhappy about it, but it seems nothing he can do about it at this time."

"Yes, Sir. I can well imagine our people being unhappy about it, for the ARVN are a strange lot at the best of times. How they feel about Montagnards doing in their SF A-Team, I don't know, but I'm sure that they'll blame anyone and everyone for it except themselves."

The usual hustle and bustle of Saigon's streets had reached its ultimate crescendo in unpleasantness. Fast-revving engine sounds, sharp motor horns and screaming street vendors competed with each other.

Saigon drivers, like those of Paris after WW II, obeyed the one and only existing traffic law — the first driver to blow his horn has the right-of-way.

With that law in effect, all smart Saigon drivers held more faith in horns than they did in common sense.

When we pulled up to one of the massive steel palace gates, the elite, machine gun-armed guards at that gate appeared to be expecting me.

They opened the gate, and waved us through without the usual thorough search and disarming. I retained my rifle and pistol. We went directly to the guardhouse where a number of ARVN soldiers were grouped. Their eyes followed our jeep as we pulled up.

Colonel Van Trang approached me.

"Sergeant, you kept us waiting."

It was the only sign of recognition I received. He stood surrounded by five heavily-armed ARVN Rangers, an infantry fire team. Behind them I saw a pathetic sight.

My two scouts were huddled close together, their arms tied unmercifully tightly behind their backs. Both of them had signs of having been cruelly beaten. Open cuts and swollen black-and-blue bruises covered their little faces.

The face of little Mo was especially disfigured. Where he had smashed his own front teeth out, the ARVNs had completed the carnage. The lower portion of poor Mo's face was caked with dried blood, and so badly swollen that he could not move a single muscle on his face.

Ding did not look better. But his physical appearance was not what caught my sympathy. It was the air of total dejection and futility that he showed. In all the years that Ding and I had been together, not once had I seen him without that sparkle in his eyes.

In defense of my own conscience, I was hard put to find any indication that their lot could have been worse. At least the weather was warm. Any drop in temperature caused them suffering, so much so, that it often culminated in death before the thermometer dropped to 30 degrees Fahrenheit.

Ding and Mo must have sensed the static between me and the South Vietnamese for they retained their totally dejected and passive countenances. No outward display of relief or perception was given, and yet they must have felt that I had some plan to help them. Ding especially had such faith in me that no matter what happened, he would not give up hope while I was near him.

"Sergeant," Van Trang ordered, "Come inside."

He led the way to a nearby office. A military map was spread before us. Colonel Van Trang, the two helicopter pilots, the Ranger fire-team leader, and I were the only ones looking over the map.

"Colonel, we can expect the Army to cancel my TDY orders any minute now. We should get in the air ASAP," I said in a tone intended to sound as if I wanted to abort the mission.

"Why? Something go wrong?" He sounded worried, and had reason to be. The knowledge of the illegal circumstances under which my TDY orders were cut could at any moment land on the desk of the right person.

"They do not believe that the approval came through the normal chain of command."

"I report that to Ambassador Manley's Headquarters myself. I don't stand for U.S. Army question my orders. I ordered you here and that is all."

The fool. What he said was for the benefit of those around him. Somehow he had managed to get the orders cut in a most unorthodox chain of command.

"Show us where you want to land," ordered the chief pilot.

"Here," I answered, putting my finger on the spot about 1,000 yards below the slate creek and approximately two miles from the Laotian border. "The ground is relatively flat, with enough clearance for the chopper blades. Also it is not an area where the enemy could find cover or concealment close enough for small-arms fire to reach the landing pad.

"One fast circle of the area will show enemy activity should there be any. We can also be extricated 24 hours later."

"Twenty-four hours! I want you back in four hours."

"Okay, we can be back in ten hours or even quicker, but we must then land here."

I put my finger on the Laotian border at a spot 1,000 yards from where we had wiped out the ten NVA APCs and where a red circle had been drawn on Van Trang's map.

The pilot started to say something but the colonel cut in.

"Helicopter cannot go into Laos or near the border."

His tone of speech indicated resignation. I felt relieved, and it must have dawned on the colonel that he had to go along with me.

"Okay, 24 hours, but no longer."

He looked at me, but his eyes did not meet mine. It took little imagination to know that as far as that man was concerned, I was as good as dead. His Rangers had orders to do me in when they got their hands on the money and the jewels.

"I need one bandolier of M-16 ammo and two Thermit grenades," I said as if in a passing thought, but I had an excellent reason to ask for them. I wanted to leave the thought with them that we were going to encounter enemy action.

"And also two concussion grenades." It was a normal request for a soldier heading into enemy controlled terrain.

"Why?" asked the colonel. You got Rangers. You no need no weapon even."

He had no sooner said that when he realized the stupidity and suspicious connotations connected to his statement. "I mean...I mean you be good taken care of by my Rangers. You are afraid, Sergeant?"

He stammered in a blundering effort to correct his mistake.

I looked him in the eyes.

"Colonel, what do you have in mind? I am a combat soldier, and not a dummy who..."

He interrupted me. "Nothing...nothing, Sergeant. I just be thinking something else. No problem, you get what you want."

He had become uncomfortable, and was not very good at controlling his discomfort. He told the Ranger team leader to get me the items I had asked for. After the team leader left, Van Trang voiced some puzzlement by asking, "Thermit grenades?"

"Yes, Sir. I use them often."

Soon we were high above the teeming streets of Saigon. Below us stretched perhaps the world's largest single mass of disorganized human misery. Millions of tiny dots swayed under the sun like magnet-controlled grains of sand.

On narrow one-way streets the magnets would exert an endless pull, while in the opposite direction other magnets exerted their energy to pull yet another mass of humanity along their seemingly useless paths.

We flew toward the mountains, staying a few yards below the white fluffy clouds. As we climbed higher and the temperature dropped, I saw Ding and Mo pull their little bodies into tight balls by crouching forward onto their knees.

It won't be long now, I thought. Just hold on a little longer you two... dumb, useless, damn Yards.

Soon we'll be either safely dead or free, I whispered softly to myself while the helicopter's blades slapped a constant pattern against the cool morning air.

Silently, I gave thanks for the many years of hard military training I had endured. At Fort Benning's Infantry Center, blood and sweat often stained my fatigues as mile after mile I plodded through the seemingly endless array of infantry attacks, withdrawals, retrograde movements, combat and reconnaissance patrols, compass courses, hand-to-hand combat, and physical training that squeezed out every ounce of mental and physical endurance I possessed. Every detail was designed for a soldier to close with and destroy the enemy.

I looked the ARVN Rangers over. I had to assume that they had received good training. I dared not make the mistake of underestimating their capabilities. I remembered that I also had given some of them Ranger training at the outset of the war. And I realized that Van Trang would pick his best men to handle me.

They looked as if they had all graduated from the Ranger school, and were not just influential and privileged soldiers. Something pointed toward their crude nature. They were the type who would bite off the head of a live snake without hesitation, one of the graduation requirements of the ranger school. But, instead of spitting it out, which was permissible, they would chew it and swallow it while soldiers with weaker stomachs would vomit.

We'll soon see how you match up with an American and two Yards, who have nowhere to go but to hell, I said to myself.

First I had to get the two miserable Yards in better shape so that they could help me.

I showed the fire team leader my bayonet and made motions for him to cut the bonds off the Yards. At first he hesitated, but when he saw me move to do it, he pulled out his own razor-sharp bayonet and quickly slashed the ropes holding Ding and Mo's arms.

I motioned to the ropes around their necks that were so fastened as to preclude their pulling too hard on their lashings.

I detected a small crease around Ding's mouth, which I knew would break into a big toothless smile if our eyes met. His unfathomable faith in me had not given way to despair as long as he knew that I was alive.

The helicopter made a fast swoop around the designated landing place, with the two door gunners and two Rangers, one at each open door, straining their eyes downward with fingers on triggers. They were ready for anything that moved below. With a stomach-jolting move downward, we scooted to a hovering position close to the ground.

In seconds, the two scouts and myself were on the ground with the Ranger fire team behind us. We were temporarily engulfed by clouds of dust and flying debris. The chopper swung sideways and headed away from us. In the commotion I stuffed a concussion grenade into Ding's hand.

Immediately, I felt at home. A wonderful silence joined the lovely sweet mountain air to shoot energy and vigor through me. From where we stood, the mountains did not look like mountains. They appeared to be flawless lush green carpets on which one could walk. So dense and commanding was the flora that the mountains seemed to have drawn the sky down to them.

My grip on my rifle tightened. I felt a solid sense of belonging where my boots touched the earth.

"Now, you bastards, you have an American infantry soldier to deal with. Not two dumb Yards," I said out loud, and did not care what the ARVN soldiers thought of my words.

For just a split moment, I considered swinging around with the selector lever at full automatic and cutting the five Rangers down.

It was best that I waited. They were nervous enough to start shooting at any time in any direction if some irregularity occurred. I had earlier decided to toss a Thermit grenade before I started to shoot, so it was imperative that I separate us from them.

"This way," I ordered. "Ding, you and Mo take us to where we catch Shylock." I thought of something else, and held up the Rangers. I turned to the team leader and hoped that he could understand what I wanted to get across to him.

"All be okay here. NVA and VC no know we be here. But if we shoot, they will come quick and we all be killed. You hear me good?" I wanted to add, "You bastard," but reluctantly refrained.

He nodded his head and I knew that he understood and also believed me, even though there were no enemy soldiers for miles in any direction. I wanted him to be afraid. He spoke to his men, and I could tell they believed what he said about the danger of firing their weapons. It was just a little edge for me when the time came. A split second hesitation on their part could mean a clean slate for us.

Ding's eyes had assumed a measure of their former luster. I knew that he had become fully alert for any sign of communication from me. He and I had long shared a private means of contact. It often reminded me of the strange signals I once saw being exchanged between a shepherd and his dog.

Each movement of a hand, head, shoulder, or eye had its own message. I could not explain how our means of passing messages, which verged on mental telepathy, came about, but it was real and effective. Before the ARVN team leader could object, Ding and Mo jumped forward and in a second were 20 or so yards ahead of us. Ding stopped just as the team leader leveled his rifle at them.

I stepped in front of him. "Scouts do not run. They take us to money. Also, VC and NVA shoot them first so they stay ahead of us. Better they be killed first."

That calmed him a little. He was somewhat overwhelmed with the fast pace with which I took control away from him. It was just the way I wanted things to go.

He looked confused as to how he was going to handle me and the scouts out there in the enemy-infested jungle. I settled matters for him, much to his further consternation.

"You fire your weapon and we all die here. VC and NVA all over this area," I lied again.

The nearest enemy unit was at least six miles away toward the west.

He seemed to like the thought that the enemy would kill the scouts first. Even so, he stayed close behind me just in case I tried to pull something. I could imagine the trepidation the Ranger infantry fire-team leader felt.

He must have felt surrounded by the enemy. To make things worse for him, the terrain was such that he could not keep his eyes on all three of us at the same time.

When he had received his orders from Colonel Van Trang, he and the colonel had been standing in the open, flat courtyard of the palace grounds. There it looked so easy to follow two Yards and an American sergeant to a money cache and then shoot the three of them, pick up the money and the jewels, and return to the helicopter. Bingo, the business would be done. It was an easy, simple, safe, and quick job.

I signaled for Ding to move out faster. I intended to find out in what physical condition the ARVN Rangers were. The animal trail that we were following was slanted about 30 degrees upwards with many small loose rocks under foot. It made it difficult to keep eyes searching for signs of the enemy and at the same time keep eyes on the three of us.

An hour after we had started the climb, we were well up the mountain inside the same slate creek that we had negotiated a few times before.

I glanced back and saw that the team leader could no longer keep up with us or keep his eyes on me. He had fallen 15 yards back and his eyes were on the ground in front of him, a true sign of a man finding it difficult to keep up with the pace.

One area that we were in had been exposed to a shelling. Agent Orange had also been used. Overhead jungle growth had been thinned out so that some sun filtered through.

A few times we came to a stretch of the animal trail where visibility was such that I could see all five Rangers. It was in such a stretch that I wanted to act.

From time to time the trail curved, and I lost sight of the scouts and also the trailing Rangers. On one such bend I gave the warning signal to Ding. It was a turtle dove's love call. Seconds later he came into sight. I nodded my head and Ding sprinted around a large rock. At the same time he pulled his grenade pin.

The timing had to be perfect. I had a concussion grenade in my left hand. The pin was out. I held the arming handle under my thumb. My rifle was held at the ready. I also had another 30-round full clip stuck into my belt where I could quickly get it. My pistol was cocked, a round inserted, and the holster flap open.

What was to come bothered me not one iota. I was the professional — well-trained and often put to the test. It was a test where only straight As were honored. Earn a B, or even a B plus, and the report card got mailed to your next of kin.

I knew what Ding would do. He would go around the rock, swing back to either the left or right, wait till the Rangers came abreast of him, let go of the arming-handle of the grenade, hold it for two seconds, and throw it among the five Rangers.

I increased my pace to separate myself further from the following Viets. A second sense told me that Ding was no longer ahead of me. I acted.

In one quick movement I pitched the hand grenade backward among the ARVN soldiers, then went down low on the ground. Even before I hit the ground I had sprayed a full 30-round clip into the Rangers. Luckily I had caught them in a single file.

In the corner of my eye I saw Ding almost jump into the blast of the two exploding grenades. I ejected the empty clip and slammed a full one in, but it was all over. Five ARVN Rangers lay dead. They had had no chance.

The action took but a few split seconds, not even long enough for a hand grenade to use up its four-second delay. Ding and I did not toss our grenades until two seconds length of the primer cords had burned.

A quick look at Ding to make sure that no pieces of shrapnel from the grenades had hit him, and my body and mind relaxed. I was glad that Mo had not gotten involved with us, for that Yard had an uncanny habit of doing the wrong thing at the wrong time, and at the wrong place.

It was over and done. I had acted in a positive manner in something which was going to have grave consequences for me. What it was going to do to my military career I did not care to contemplate. Ding and Mo were free.

For a few seconds my mind dwelled on the luxurious thought of calling Colonel Booby Trap on my none-existent short-wave radio transmitter and telling him what I had done. It gave me a thrill to imagine Booby Trap also coiling himself into a fetal position to remove himself from reality as that American creep had done. I smiled at the pleasant but passing thought.

My mind wanted to rest. I wanted to be at peace for just a moment while the world continued to turn. Let events somewhere else stagger blindly without me being part of them.

If only I could have washed my hands of guilt, as did that gutless Pontius Pilate, then I too could have found absolution in stupidity as did the guilty Romans.

Mo came to me with tears in his eyes. He was only twelve years old, and all life's values had been completely destroyed. He came into my arms and lingered a while, the only human warmth he was likely to know.

"You two damn scouts, you get clothes, weapons, and rations from ARVN Rangers. Dey no be need nothing where they now be."

Ding found patrol rations on the dead soldiers and gave Mo one. They sat on the ground, hungrily eating the rations. The way they ate the sausage-like rations, I knew that they had not been fed by the ARVN soldiers. Their eyes did not wander from me for an instant. I plainly read their complete surrender to me in their little black eyes. It was so upsetting to me that I wanted to scream for them to look somewhere else.

I let my mind focus on the scattered clouds that hung motionless against the small patch of blue sky that barely had room to show itself through the triple-canopied jungle. For a sorrowful moment, I indulged in the luxury of blaming someone else for the sad predicament that I had finally blundered into. So soothing a sentiment, that of a martyr, that somewhere, someone had forgiven all my transgressions and sins, then thrown open a new door through which I could walk away from this harsh wilderness. In sheer desperation I thought of something I once heard about Catholics. They go to a priest, tell him all that they have done wrong, and the priest wipes the slate clean for them.

I could not very well tell a priest everything, but I could tell him enough so that he could lighten my burden. I dropped that thought for I was not a Catholic, and, with all I had to tell, a priest would surely think that I was bragging.

I shook myself back into reality.

"Come, you miserable dumb Yards. Let me see what I can do for your cuts and bruises."

Their faces were too caked with dried blood and dirt for me to apply salve. Laboriously, I cleaned them little by little. Plenty of water was available from the many full canteens the dead rangers had clipped to their load-bearing harnesses. Not all the canteens were bullet-ridden.

After what seemed hours, they were cleaner than they had ever been in their lives. That is, their faces were. The rest of them still smelled like...like...well, like Montagnards.

I sprinkled zinc and starch powder on the wounds. That was as much first aid as I could give them. It was just a matter of time before they would be healed. We had water, patrol rations, and could find shelter.

It was necessary to remain well hidden from air observers lest we find ourselves on the receiving end of artillery fire or air strikes. We had the NVA, VC, ARVN and our own U.S. forces to worry about.

Damn, I thought. Is anyone on our side?

We left the animal trail, and moved deeper into the underbrush. I wanted to get away from the dead ARVN soldiers. I knew that it would be but a short time before they started to emit smells which would draw predators. We went toward the area where the B-52 strike shook the American creep into a basket.

The three of us carried away with us what ammunition and weapons the Rangers had. They also had one machete with them for which I was especially thankful. Without one, we would have had a hell of a time working ourselves through the saplings and vines. The uniforms that the Rangers had on were so badly shot full of holes that Ding and Mo barely found wearable trousers and jackets for themselves. I hated to leave things behind for the enemy to find, but we did not have the time nor the means to destroy the few useable items that remained.

I led the way for the three of us. I worked off much of my pent-up emotion on the profuse vegetation through which I had to cut a tunnel. Left and right, and up and down, I swung the machete until it felt as if my right arm could take no further abuse. It took us three hours to get close to where I wanted to be.

As we approached our former bivouac area, I signaled for Ding and Mo to hold back and lie still while I moved ahead to reconnoiter. Ding showed disagreement with my order. He wanted to take his place as the scout, which he considered his rightful duty. He was still in sad physical condition, but his strength seemed to have picked up. I insisted that he obey as I slowly crept ahead.

Being alone, I became aware of how easily and with what natural coordination of all my senses I slipped through the undergrowth. I was at one with the terrain and wildlife, and my instincts seemed to spread like a protective shield around me.

I was attentive to what went on around me and fully cognizant of what there should be. The absence of some jungle sounds was as much of a warning as was the presence of some. From a vantage point slightly above the old bivouac area, I observed the surroundings. A dark spot on a nearby tree caught my attention.

Slowly I lined my rifle sights on the area and waited.

I let my eyes wonder around the primitive hootch that was still standing, although its former green coverings had turned brown. It would need some attention before it could serve our purpose. All remained quiet and normal except for the dark spot in the tree that was overhanging the hootch.

A deer came into sight. It caused me to relax. The small deer grazed unconcernedly on the green saplings while it stepped daintily over loose slate slabs. It acted unafraid and relaxed.

There were no humans within the immediate vicinity, but the dark spot in the tree still kept my attention. It was always possible that someone might remain unnoticed by animals if that someone lay still and was downwind.

A slight movement and the outline of a black panther showed. Its blackness stood out clearly against the green flora. Closer and closer crawled the panther until he was over the grazing deer. There before my eyes unfolded yet another of life's dramas in nature's own operational plan — survival of the fittest.

My own predicament was not unlike that of the hunted and the hunter. I needed meat and a skin. I lay still until the panther pounced through the leaves onto his quarry.

I acted. The panther jerked upward and away from me as my bullet ripped through his brain. With one single shot I perpetuated man's masterdom on earth. At the same time I was aware that the sound of my rifle shot could reveal our presence.

We had deer meat that night and enough left to feast on the following day. The panther and deerskins served as blankets. They were the first of many we would get as the days dragged into weeks.

The visible wounds of Ding and Mo healed. What damage had been done to their minds at the hands of the ARVN I could not gauge, but felt that neither of them would ever forget or forgive what the ARVN had done to them.

The mountain tribe from which Ding came, the Rhe, was known to carry a grudge sometimes from generation to generation if it took that long for revenge. When the time and opportunity came for Rhes to settle a wrong, they were ruthless.

I had no knowledge of how to treat mental ailments. Visible wounds were something I could cope with, even if it was only to slap on a bandage. How does one slap a bandage on minds?

With the thought that perhaps it would help if I got them to tell me what happened, I asked Ding, "Ding, you be wit Viets, they be talk you?"

"No be, Sargy. Viet, same same Ranger be charge fire team we be do in, he be kick me an Mo in face him boot. Same, same Ranger come we helicopeter, dey be de Viets beat Me an Mo," Ding said bitterly.

"And that colonel, you be see me talk him?" I asked.

"Colonel same same Van Trang he be laugh an spit us many time. Me be sorry him colonel no be come wit on helicopeter."

"Yeah," I answered. "He be come you, me, Mo, we be cut him balls and stuff not in mouth, we be stuff into him ass, den sew ass close wit barb wire."

I could tell Ding liked that. He could not smile because of his busted up face, but I could tell.

As to what could take place in Ding's future, well, some Vietnamese persons may one day find out. He had a singular capability to kill, and his hatred for the Vietnamese had reached a dangerous stage. I knew that I could control him, but only as long as I was close to him.

A pleasant restful lull in our lives ensued as we lay hidden from reality out there in a world of our own. I wanted to stay with the two Yards long enough for them to become physically able to care for themselves.

Having added a few fresh sticks and boughs to the makeshift hootch, it was comfortable enough. We stacked our weapons in a corner and the nights were made friendly by the warm glow of our fire over which we roasted fresh meat procured during the day. There was enough of that famous Montagnard concoction which substituted for salt. The sweet memory of Cathy was stashed in that dark corner across from where I sat.

Usually, shortly after Ding and Mo ate, they fell asleep, and I took over the duty of manning our perimeter security. Early afternoons, I slowly worked around the hootch for a radius of about a quarter mile. At no time did I notice enemy activity or signs that the enemy had negotiated the area for at least two weeks prior to our return to that area.

It was safe to remain for about two weeks before moving further north and east. We would move after I had taken care of another matter, and my wards had regained their health and strength.

A few times, I sat at an advantage point overlooking the area where the nine graves were. I could not see the graves, but I had reason to believe that they had not been molested by the enemy or wild animals.

It had only been eight days since we had buried them. Decomposition could not have reached the stage where much odor could have penetrated upward to attract predators. Scavengers would not dig holes through to the bodies until well after the tenth day.

I did not know in which one of the nine graves Tom had buried the money and the jewels. Because the odors could not help me, it was going to be awkward for me. I needed to wait longer to let the smells guide me to a grave that did not emit an odor.

I did not want to involve either Ding or Mo. They could again fall into the wrong hands and blabber out the information, that would get them into extra trouble. I was going to go it alone, carry what I could, and if necessary leave the rest.

The pleasant days that constituted the convalescence of the Yards spread into a week, then another week. What was I ultimately going to do with Ding and Mo?

That I was in trouble with the command, I did not hide from myself, but I knew that, as long as I kept my mouth shut as much as possible, things might not go too badly for me. Let the command make the decision as to just what I had done wrong. After all, who got me mixed up with that damn Colonel Van Trang?

And also, who was there to testify against me? No one saw me kill the five Rangers. We were in enemy territory and the VC did not like us.

In the final analysis of my position, I saw a small ray of sunshine in my troubled mind. I believed that if I was careful about what I said, I might still salvage some pieces of my career. I had decided to ask the Army for a clean discharge and retire. I hoped the Army would forgive and forget.

Because of my careful attendance to Ding and Mo's body and facial injuries, they healed well. Ten days after our dispatch of the five Rangers, they were in a fair physical and mental state.

Many reconnaissance aircraft came overhead, but we were so well hidden that we remained undetected. We were also lucky that the five bodies of the Rangers were not observed from the air. The area where we did them in had showed patches of blue sky. We had not taken the time to hide the bodies. It was an error that I hoped not to pay for.

"Perhaps," I said out loud to the consternation of my Yards, "a person does not always have to pay the piper."

Ding looked at me as if he wanted me to tell him what I found so amusing, and I was just about to do so, when we heard an unfamiliar sound. It was that of a branch snapping. A definite snap, not as would happen when an animal stepped on a dry branch.

The three of us grabbed our rifles and a bandoleer of ammunition and down on the ground we went. Silently, we crawled away from each other, but stayed in eye contact. Ding and Mo's heads jerked from side to side as birds' heads do. Between each jerk their heads would remain dead still, listening, looking, and smelling for whatever had made that snapping noise.

After a few minutes, Ding motioned to me and pointed to our front. He showed me two fingers, lifted his rifle and shook it as a signal that there was no enemy in sight. I understood that whatever there was, was not hostile. I also understood that it was human.

Ding stood up and walked through the underbrush as if he owned the place. I heard him say something out loud in Montagnard chatter. More noise came from the brush, and first one old woman and then another showed herself.

A lot of talk took place between Ding and the two women and also some pointing in the direction from which they had come. I waited as long as I could and stopped them.

"What the hell are you three talking about, Ding?"

"Sargy, mama be tell me dey be dis many," He showed me eight fingers. "be run from Viets, maybe small time afta plywood. Viets be kill all oder fambly. Dey be oder damn Yards little way us. I be go gets."

When I nodded my approval Ding disappeared in the direction they had been pointing. The two old women stood looking me over and it made me think that it was the first time they had ever seen a European. I must have looked like a giant to them. Neither of the women stood more than five feet tall.

Mo also babbled to them and it seemed as if they felt comfortable with him, and he with them. They moved close and reached out for his rifle. Mo let them run their hands over the rifle and they looked puzzled and seemed to ask so many questions that Mo stood there without being able to get a word in.

They felt his fatigues, his boots, and the web equipment. It was obvious that each item they centered their attention on was something new to them. One of the women stuck her fingers into the bullet holes in the jacket Mo had taken off a dead Ranger. She put her nose close and smelled the dead blood. It took a lot of explaining from Mo to settle them down after that. I believe they thought that the jacket protected Mo from spears.

Both the women were scantily dressed. They had nothing on above the waist other than a few brass bangles around their arms. Their floppy breasts were dangling down to their navels. Once, one of them flipped a breast over her shoulder in much the same way I've seen women flick a lock of hair out of the way.

Below the waist, they wore deerskin skirts that came down to their knees. The skins were loosely wrapped around them, and as the women walked the skirts revealed what was left of a woman to see. There was no way for me to gauge their ages; however, to my western eye they each looked to be about 100 years old.

I was the next to be examined. They did not show compunctions about feeling me and my equipment. Mostly they centered their attention on my blond hair and blue eyes. It was a strange experience to have two old, wrinkled women stare me in the eyes only after they had pulled me down by my load-bearing harness to their eye level.

A sound reached us from the direction in which Ding had disappeared. He broke into view and behind him came six Yard girls. Two of them wore brightly colored skirts that had seen better days. The others had on only deerskin skirts. All of them had silver and copper bracelets around their wrists, necks, and ankles. Their adornments indicated former affluence.

All six of them had reached maturity, judging from the appearance of their breasts. The old women were the normal Montagnard females from the highland Rhe tribe, the same tribe as Ding belonged to — small, ever ready to smile and laugh, and not too interested in personal cleanliness.

Once they had had a chance to examine what they saw, they reverted back to their normal life style. They did not show a long attention span. Characteristic of the Montagnards was the quick way they accepted and adjusted to something.

They acted at home in the jungle and quite at ease with their primitive way of life, which was free of burdensome property. What they needed and owned was what they could carry with them, and in most cases that was very little.

"Now what, Ding?" I asked while all the girls circled me with giggles and wide-eyed wonder at what they must have considered to be some apparition.

Two of the girls had crossbows slung over their backs, and arrow quivers made of bamboo were fastened around their waists. One of the girls carried a wicked-looking mountain ax in her right hand. That one I kept a sharp eye on. Another girl had a spear that was only about five feet long. It was much shorter than those normally carried by the highland Rhe tribe.

Before I could get an answer from Ding I had to ask him again, "Now what, Ding?"

"No be problem, Sargy. Dey be all leff small hamlet. All oder be kill long time afta plywood. Two, be mama san, dey be run all girl for Viets no be gets rape she. Dey be say dey be stay we. We be take care all she."

Ding seemed to take it all in stride. He acted as if it was a normal situation. After all, he was in his own backyard, whereas I was in Vietnam fighting a war. To me, it was one hell of a mess to get involved with.

"Okay, you," I said sternly. "You want to be a damn fool, you go for it, but you better tell them that we are in an enemy-controlled area. They draw enemy down on us, I be shoot them all. And Ding, take that ax away from that girl." I had to repeat what I said because I spoke too fast for Ding to follow.

Ding gave me a shit-eating grin. He did not know what to say and I thought that he, like me, was just a little confused as to what to do about the women. He took the ax away from the girl and was awarded with a smile by her. He herded the eight women back towards our hootch.

In the hootch we gave the women meat and they added roots and berries that the youngest girl carried in a skin bag. It was not long before our gathering settled down to look as if we had been a congenial family for years.

Darkness had enveloped our hootch, and the temperature started to drop. Inside we enjoyed the warmth and light of a lovely fire. We had all eaten enough, and I was just about to roll myself into a deerskin and go to sleep when the silence was shattered by the loud explosions of an M-16 rifle at full automatic. Thirty bullets tore through the hootch's walls and tracers streamed into the night air.

Both Ding and I landed on top of one of the girls and wrenched the rifle away from her. She had been playing with the rifle and pulled the trigger. When the thing went off she became so shocked she just held on for dear life. We were lucky that the rifle was not pointed at us.

Ding let out many Montagnard cuss words, pushed all the girls and the old women into one corner of the hootch, slapped a few of them, and he, Mo, and I scrambled out into the darkness.

That night we did not sleep. We had to search the surrounding area for the enemy. The rifle fire could have drawn the enemy to us and we dared not let them find us first. Only when daylight started to penetrate down to the damp moss-covered earth did we return to the hootch where we found eight snoring females under our deerskin blankets.

I shook my head and muttered, even here in the dark, unfriendly jungle, the role of the male is understood by people who are a thousand years behind in civilization.

The days that followed were disorganized. No matter how Ding and I tried to get it though the women's heads that we were in a dangerous situation, they insisted on enjoying the days as if we were on a picnic.

Ding and Mo hunted well away from where we had our hootch so as not to draw attention to our area if and when they used a rifle. We had food in abundance, and the ease with which the women provided us with an assortment of edible vegetation amazed me. They never seemed to be worried about water, not even to drink. The dampness of the berries, leaves, and roots they ate must have supplied what moisture their bodies needed.

With Ding's help, they explained to me where we could find water that came out of a rock on the side of a steep cliff. Two of the girls took our empty canteens to fill. I went with them to clean myself. In my combat pack I had toilet articles.

On the way to the spring I wished I had some sticking tape to shut their mouths. They babbled and giggled incessantly, as young females are apt to do the world over, and I wondered if there was some cure for that affliction other than the enemy bullets they were inviting.

Once I tried to shut one of them up by grabbing her and putting my hand over her mouth. Her reaction to that was a surprise. She pushed herself against me, showing that she was ready for sex. She was, and so was the other one. The two of them acted completely devoid of inhibitions in regard to sex.

The spring spouted well away from the rocks and was high enough to act as a shower. The primitive surroundings and the fact that I could not get the two girls to give me privacy caused me to say, "To hell with it."

I got undressed and stepped under the cold mountain spring water with my bar of soap.

Soon both girls were also under the spring, wearing only their giggles. It was perhaps the first time in their lives that they had ventured into such a novel experience. The soap completed the wonder of it all to them, especially the sweet odor that took the place of their usual rancid smell.

I did the best I could with my fatigues and web equipment without using up all of my precious soap. I shaved, and combed my hair, much to the amazement and amusement of the girls. To them such care of one's body must have seemed a useless exercise.

On the way back to our hootch, I had to push the two of them away from me a number of times. The smell of the soap seemed to act as an aphrodisiac, if indeed they needed it.

They wanted sex and I wanted to stay alive. I needed Ding and Mo's respect and was not about to trade that for a few minutes of pleasure. We SF did not touch the Montagnard women. If we had, they would brag about it, and that would be the end of our control over them.

The days that followed became full of problems with those six girls. Ding merely laughed at their antics to get me to service them. I guess the six were just too much for him. However, not once did he complain. He seemed to be enjoying a full life, while Mo appeared so disgusted with the entire affair that he stayed close to me all the time.

Once Mo showed his bayonet in a threatening manner to one of the girls to get her to leave me alone. It was when the two of us were curled up in a corner of the hootch wanting to sleep, and one of the girls, with nothing on, wanted to crawl under the leopard skin with me.

The women had made candles out of beeswax and betel nut, which they burned all night inside the hootch. I would not have minded, but with it went a constant wagging of female tongues, the chewing of betel nuts and the offensive smell of their pipes. It seemed that they never ran short of tobacco. Tobacco leaves grew among some of the manioc plants.

The manioc is of the cassava family, from which the Yards made bread and tapioca. These foodstuffs, added to the many other edible roots, plants, and an assortment of mushrooms improved our daily diet. Ding and Mo were incapable of providing as good a meal as the women did with little effort.

There were two approaches to our area, and we dug booby traps in the form of concealed holes with sharp punji sticks inside. The women made a concoction of resin scraped off a persimmon tree, some crawling insects, and red peppers. They cooked the mixture inside one of our canteens until they could extract a black, evil-smelling mixture. This mixture they smeared on the points of the punji sticks and allowed it to dry.

"Dis black be stuff be much much bad." Ding said.

He further explained to me that within a few seconds the poison would kill anyone who got stuck with the punji sticks.

"Dey no be walk one, two maybe step, dey be scream den dey be go ancestors for to tell Sargy be boo coo bad Sargy," said Ding.

He was enjoying his new-found status as hamlet chief.

Chapter 9

Absolution

B ack at 5th Special Forces Headquarters, a number of important happenings were taking place, as I learned later. Initial complaints against me had spiraled into a maze of confused and contradictory accusations.

Colonels Wallace and Wakefield shook up the military and civilian commands all the way to Washington and the Pentagon. Their reports condemned the manner in which the investigation had been conducted. One issue with which they were at odds was the immediate command's cover-ups.

Colonel Wakefield became outspokenly hostile toward the authority that exerted pressure to place me on TDY to the Palace Ranger Battalion.

He had gone on record as demanding a congressional inquiry into corruption, coercion, and blackmail activities where State Department personnel were involved. At that time, I was unaware that Group had finalized a comprehensive report on all the activities of my ill-fated patrol. Till this day I have not been privy to the contents of that report. What I know I found out later and second hand.

Group had studied my patrol's actions chronologically, and determined each tactical operation as having been conducted effectively. When they came to administrative matters, it was less flattering. My entering Laos on two occasions was condemned as a blatant disregard for authority, and the matter placed on hold to be dealt with at a later date.

Our method of handling POWs was suspect, but because no witnesses could be found to contradict my report, no derogatory references were made in any unclassified report. That part was swept under the rug for good.

It was determined that the late Captain Mock could have been the only one to give information as to the whereabouts of one World Council of Churches' interpreter.

The final report was placed on the desk of General Collins, with the reply that the Army had received from our military attaché in Saigon. The general leaned back in his chair and looked over Lieutenant Colonel Becket, aka Booby Trap, from head to foot, while making no effort to conceal his disgust.

In the spacious office of the general were three other field grade officers — Colonels Wallace, Wakefield, and the over-worked Brooks.

"Colonel," the general leaned forward and looked Becket in the eyes. "Just so I get things straight, I am going to repeat what you told me. If I should quote you wrong, please feel free to correct me."

The general waited for Booby Trap to acknowledge.

"Yes, General," came meekly from Colonel Becket.

"You asked that ARVN colonel, you say his name is Van Trang, where Master Sergeant Blondell was. First he said that the sergeant was busy. Then that the sergeant was not in Saigon. Then that the sergeant went back to your Group. Then that the sergeant left the Palace Compound without permission. Then that the sergeant never reported to him in the first place. Then he finally topped things off by saying that he was not responsible for no damn U.S. Army enlisted man."

There was a long silence in the general's office, which hung like a poorly tied bomb from the ceiling.

"Is that what you were told?"

The general hit his desktop hard with his fist and kicked his chair backward against the wall. Then, with the knuckles of both his fists pushed hard on the desk, he went on.

"I am disgusted with this affair. Wakefield, you and Wallace remain. You other gentlemen get the hell out of my office."

When the two colonels were alone with the general, the general took out a box of cigars and offered each one.

"Please be seated, gentlemen. I have the ability to regain my composure quickly," he said in a relaxed manner.

"Colonel Wakefield, I want you to compile a completely new and thorough report on what took place leading to the killing of the eleven ARVN SF men, and then continue with the patrol actions, ending with the order that was given to the sergeant to report to the ARVN Ranger battalion."

Colonel Wakefield spoke up. "General, what I have thus far been able to establish is that some of the operations of our Special Forces could very well stand scrutiny. With this in mind, General, I request your permission to look into their operations.

"The fiasco that took place in Ba Cat is but one regrettable incident. There could have been others, and I dare to predict that there will be others in the future. Even though the actual operations they are involved with are, in themselves, not to be considered discrediting, it is the methods they employ which are."

"Please qualify." General Collins had become interested.

"With your permission, General, it is the great care and trouble they go through among themselves to preclude any knowledge of failure becoming known outside their own circle. It seems as if they have set themselves up as an army within an army incapable of admitting that the impossible does exist.

"This method of operation has caused unnecessary killings and numerous intra-theater transfers of personnel. The case of Sergeant Blondell would never have gained your attention, General, if it were not for the killing of the eleven-man ARVN SF A-Team."

"Do you tell me that the obvious discontent and animosity that existed between the Montagnards and the ARVN SF in Ba Cat, would not have prevented our SF from formally turning the camp over to the ARVN?"

"Yes, General. I have a copy of the final orders relinquishing U.S. Army control of Ba Cat, and of the ARVN assuming control of that installation. It is dated three days before the killing of the ARVN soldiers in Ba Cat."

"My God, man. What is the SF trying to pull? Their mission expressly demands, among other prerequisites, that harmonious, amiable circumstances be present prior to the transfer. Without that, the entire time-consuming and costly undertaking would be a failure."

"Exactly, General. That is why such great care is exercised to falsify reports, especially those dealing with ARVN-U.S. relationship."

"I see. Well, perhaps we cannot correct some past errors but we can prevent future ones. You have your orders, Colonel. Only try and keep things on a level where I can take care of them."

282 Honor and Sacrifice: The Montagnards of Ba Cat

General Collins turned his attention to Colonel Wallace.

"For you, Wallace, I have another assignment. I want you to represent Master Sergeant Blondell's interests. His present status is Missing In Action. You take it from there. It seems everyone I have spoken to thus far, except the two of you, has been dead set on blaming the sergeant for everything from dropping pigs and cows out of an aircraft without parachutes to going into a foreign country without a visa.

"That man did more damage to the enemy in one week than did half a million U.S. servicemen during the same period. I would say that he could possess some redeeming qualities. Your mission is to find those qualities for the record. What a pity I could not have known the man."

The general closed his eyes, deep in thought. Then he continued, "Wallace, you may start with a young lady by the name of Catherine Friem. She came to see me. She had a most interesting point of view and also quite an interesting analysis of the sergeant's character. You will find her in the BOQ at the 5th Special Forces Group Headquarters. Any questions on what I want you to do?"

"No, General. I understand and will have a report on your desk within a few days."

The two colonels exchanged salutes with the general and left his office through a door that seemed to have opened automatically at the close of business. The general's aide escorted them out. He handed the two colonels each a piece of paper on which a series of numbers were typed.

"Fund citations in the event they are needed, Sirs."

They looked at each other.

"It seems as if we have a job," said Colonel Wallace.

"No doubt about it," answered Colonel Wakefield.

The two colonels flew to Nha Trang. It was the best place for both of them to start their investigations. The SF Group Commander had gathered what was left of my A-Team, and they were waiting to be questioned.

In Nha Trang, Colonel Wallace's jeep slowly moved between the barbed wire entanglements along the oil-sprinkled dirt road that wound around the many plywood buildings of 5th Special Forces Group.

"Stop at the club, Driver," ordered Colonel Wallace. "And get something to eat before you seek billets. Chow time will be in a half hour."

"Yes, Sir, and will you be needing the jeep again today?"

"No, but be at the club at 0800 hours tomorrow."

"Yes, Sir," answered the driver, somewhat relieved.

It had been a long day for both the colonel and him. Colonel Wallace had interviewed more than two-dozen men who knew me. Each had been required to submit a separate sworn statement attesting to my military qualifications and moral character.

Some of these reports I saw later. It made me blush to read what most of the men wrote. I did not for a moment flatter myself that I was as perfect as they made me out. I was quite aware that every man who made a statement believed that I had been killed and no one was about to make derogatory statements about a dear departed comrade-in-arms. Not every man gets to read two-dozen of his own eulogies.

Colonel Wallace had been warned about Catherine Friem and her connection with the World Council of Churches. That organization had caused much trouble in the past for the United States and other western countries. The Council's power was often supported by the religious title, whereas, in reality, not many churches cared to be associated with it.

The United States Army did not care to have a situation develop where derogatory reports on military operations in Vietnam further muddied its image, and it was correctly assumed that Cathy could very well throw the mud.

The order was out. Treat the lady with kid gloves and make her a VIP as long as she played by the Army's rules.

Colonel Wallace found Cathy sitting alone at a table in the SF dining room.

"Miss Friem?" inquired the colonel.

She nodded her answer.

"I am Colonel Wallace, Daniel Wallace. I have been ordered by General Collins to conduct an investigation on Sergeant Blondell. May I join you?"

"Please do, Colonel. General Collins told me that he would do something to help Tony — Sergeant Blondell. I hope you can."

Colonel Wallace sat down slowly and looked Cathy over cautiously. He saw a very pretty woman, about 23 years old. She had beautiful blue eyes and lovely blond shiny hair that hung down to below her shoulders. She was neatly dressed in a skirt and light sweater that outlined a seductive body.

"Sergeant Blondell is a lucky person," he said.

"Lucky?" Cathy looked intently at the colonel.

"Yes, lucky to have gained your friendship. You see, I have already managed to get a pretty clear picture of your character, personality, and moral courage. As I said, Miss Friem, I am investigating the sergeant, and you are one of the persons knowledgeable of facts of interest to me."

"Then I meet with your approval, Colonel?"

"You most certainly do, Miss."

"Thank you, Sir," she said sweetly. "Can you tell me when I can see him?"

"You don't believe he is dead, do you?"

"No, I don't believe he is dead," she said with conviction and feeling.

"Is it just your faith, or do you have knowledge that I do not have?"

"I just feel that he is alive. After all he has gone through, surely God would not let him die now."

"You believe very strongly in God, do you not?"

"Yes, Sir. I believe."

"Would it not then have turned you against the sergeant, having witnessed him killing?"

The colonel was interrupted.

"Killing?" She again evinced confusion. "I did not see him kill anyone."

"What about the enemy POWs and the other members of your World Council of Churches?"

"Tony did not kill them. Are...are you trying to tell me he did?"

"No, Miss. I am not saying he did. I was merely referring to the killing in action against the enemy."

"I don't think I'm going to like you, Colonel Wallace, unless you dispel the suspicions you just now instilled in me. You tried to trick me into admitting something that wasn't true."

Colonel Wallace knew that he had made a mistake, but he also knew that he could reason with her.

"Please forgive me. It is a difficult job for a man of my age to change undesirable habits. One such undesirable habit just manifested itself and I hate myself at moments like this."

"You are forgiven, Colonel. And furthermore, please understand that I am in love with Tony, and will do anything to help clear him of whatever trouble he may have gotten himself into with the Army."

That she was obviously a biased witness did not disturb the colonel.

"If my report carries any weight, Miss, then the sergeant should not be in too much trouble with the Army. I want to help him where I can."

The waitress placed two menus in front of them.

"Shall we have dinner, Miss Friem?" asked Colonel Wallace. "It has been a long time since I enjoyed such lovely company at a dinner table. Please do me the honor."

She smiled and said simply, "It would be a pleasure."

"Good. Over our coffee, while we wait for dinner, may I tell you what I would like to learn from you? Later you can either send me off or answer my questions. Everything I do is toward helping the sergeant."

"Is he in trouble with the Army?"

She was just a little puzzled about all the attention that she was receiving from high-ranking officers.

Colonel Wallace smiled. "There are some problems. I think my report will carry weight, but I need your help to write it."

"Oh, I see. All right, I'll answer your questions."

"I'll be honest with you," said the colonel.

"I should certainly hope so," she answered with a smile.

"Yes, well, in regard to your membership in the World Council of Churches, I need to know how deeply you are involved with that organization."

It was some time before he continued. Cathy made no attempt to give him an answer. She waited for the colonel to continue.

"Next. I would like to discuss with you just what happened at the helicopter when you were extricated from the jungle."

Cathy smiled.

"Why are you smiling?"

"I smile at the thought of how softhearted you men really are, and at the same time how terrible in the face of danger. Tom, Doc, and Tony. None of them would have admitted, either to himself or to another, that he loved the Montagnards too much to leave them in the jungle to fend for themselves."

"You've answered that very well, although I would rather state that they felt that the United States Army's interest would best be served by their remaining in control of the Montagnard force, and they were not able to convey that fact to their command prior to the arrival of the helicopter. Therefore, like dedicated United States Army combat leaders, they acted commendably in the face of the enemy."

"You know, Colonel, General Collins is a great judge of character by assigning you to conduct this investigation."

He smiled and continued, "And finally, Miss Friem, did you personally observe atrocities being committed while you were with the patrol?"

She turned pale. "I don't think I could eat dinner now."

She stood up. Colonel Wallace took her by the arm to steady her. He guided her out of the dining room.

"I...I can answer that," she said as they walked into the lounge. "I saw a small Montagnard horribly mutilated by the North Vietnamese. There were...Tony said, three more just like the one I saw."

"You don't need to talk about it any more, Miss. And I shall not bring the subject up again." Colonel Wallace was aware that many curious eyes were on them as they walked out.

"Miss Friem, all that remains is your comment in reference to your affiliation with the..."

"I can answer that in short order," she interrupted him. "I have severed my connections with that organization. Prior to meeting Tony and his men, I had only been exposed to one side of the problem here in Vietnam."

She hesitated.

"Colonel, "you seem sympathetic toward other people's probems."

"Try me out, Miss," he said with a fatherly feeling toward her.

For just a moment he wanted to put his arms around her to comfort her. "Colonel, I feel guilty for having been part of the World Council of Churches in their sympathetic dealings with the enemy of my country. Can you understand that?"

"Yes, young lady. I can understand. The significance is that you have the courage to face things as you see them. Many people go through life lying to themselves or refusing to see the other side of a problem."

She squeezed the colonel's hand in gratitude.

"Is there anything I can do for you, Miss Friem?"

"Yes, Colonel, there is. I would like to remain here for a little while longer. At least until Tony returns."

"That will be no problem. Besides, General Collins would like you to remain in the event that we need additional information. I'll give the necessary orders to establish you as the guest of the general. You will be moved to VIP quarters in Saigon, which should be more comfortable for you."

"Thank you. You are a darling."

"Oh, yes. Just one more question and you need not answer it. Did anyone try to influence you on your statements to the military?"

"Yes. Directly and indirectly I was informed by my previous associates that I was in shock when much of this happened, and therefore should not discuss matters with our military. The reason, they said, was that the military had the habit of twisting facts to suit themselves.

"And listen to me carefully. I am not going to repeat it ever. They did not want me to tell about money that they gave the North Vietnamese Army. Money in U.S. dollars. A large amount... perhaps a half-million dollars."

Wallace looked at her intensely for an awkward moment, put his hands tenderly on her shoulders and said, "This is serious, little girl. Let me help you. Let me guide you, tell you what to do with that information. To give money to the enemy..."

Cathy interrupted. "I do not ever want to talk again about that money." Her demeanor left no doubt in his mind that she was serious and he had better drop the subject. He also understood that she was by law protected from self-incrimination.

"Thank you, Miss Friem, and goodbye. I'll keep in touch and keep you posted on developments as far as Sergeant Blondell is concerned. Contact General Collins' office should you need anything."

Later that day, Cathy was transported to the VIP quarters of MAGV Headquarters. She had no sooner walked into the plush quarters when her doorbell rang.

"Come in," she said wondering who it could be.

In walked Penny, dressed in a very fashionable suit that was obviously expensive. A lovely diamond necklace adorned the top of her cleavage and dainty bands of diamonds sparkled from her wrists. She carried herself with obvious confidence as she stood for a few seconds in the doorway so that Cathy could get a good look at who it was she had to compete with.

"Hello. My name is Penny. I am here to welcome you to Saigon for General Collins, and to see that you do not want for a thing," she said in the sweetest voice she could manage.

She looked Cathy over from head to foot as if Cathy were a newly purchased concubine for a harem, and she the sheik's favorite.

"How nice of you and General Collins. Please sit down, and can I offer you something? The liquor cabinet seems to be well stocked. I did not realize that this type of luxury existed here in Vietnam."

Cathy had a feeling that all was not as her visitor wanted her to believe. Perhaps a woman instinctively recognizes threats. She started to look on Penny as such.

"A scotch, please, with a dash of ice water. The way Tony drinks his."

Penny pretended that she did not see Cathy jerk up and almost tip the liquor cabinet over.

"Tony, do you know him? Do you know where he is?" Blood had drained from Cathy's face. She felt faint, and sat down.

Penny sat down next to her. She took Cathy's hands in hers, and pulled her close.

"You love him, too. I know. I came here to challenge you for his love, but looking at you...I see a person that I do not want to hurt."

To Penny, Cathy presented no threat or challenge. The two of them were miles apart in character. Penny sailed through life, fully aware of what she wanted, and she usually got what she went after. Cathy lived in a dream world, and received only what life might send her way.

"You relax, little girl. I'll take care of you," Penny whispered softly to the distraught Cathy. "Don't think about him now. Later, perhaps, we'll talk about him."

It did not take Penny long to make Cathy relax. She followed with such a smooth incitement to talk, that Cathy readily confided her innermost thoughts.

You poor, dumb, naive girl, Penny thought. Where have you been all your life? I am going to teach you a few things about survival, and inject some sparkle into your dull life.

Hours later Penny returned to her own quarters. She skipped two stairs at a time as she bounced up to her rooms on the second floor.

"To hell with the elevator," she said aloud and did not care if someone wondered to whom she was talking. She was in high spirits, and loved the world around her. She had made up her mind about me, and she found Cathy perhaps the easiest opponent she had ever had to cope with. Later, I was to find out all there was to know about that fun-loving Penny and her singular ways of getting all she set her sights on.

Chapter 10

Values

O n the 15th day since killing the five Rangers, and the sixth day
since becoming involved with the women, Ding, Mo, and I were
sitting outside the hootch, enjoying a lovely morning. We had
found a spot where some sunrays could filter down to us. Having eaten
leftover meat we had fried the night before, we were lazy enough to delay
making the necessary daily security sweeps.

The women were happily chattering away among themselves inside
the hootch. They had reason to be happy, for they had found three men to
take care of them. For one of their wants they must have maintained high
hopes, for I often read that message plainly in their eyes each time that
they looked at Mo and me.

I don't know how successful Ding was with satisfying them. Mo had
been of no help to Ding. Come to think of it, I wondered just what Mo
really was good for other than giving me problems.

Each day we had to look carefully for signs of enemy activity. The distance that we were separated from friendly forces and the type of terrain
presented challenges that had to be met.

Once I saw, or rather, heard a small enemy patrol working their way
through the underbrush. I could not determine with accuracy the number
of soldiers in that patrol, so I discarded the desire to ambush them.

Ding was all for trailing them and wiping them out when they stopped to rest. It was that incident which made me think that it was time to call an end to our vacation.

"This morning Mo, you be go look VC and NVA. You be gets boo coo fat. You be too lazy."

I waited for Ding to translate what I said. Mo was not capable of learning a single word of English. I had long since agreed with Ding that Mo was indeed the dumbest Yard ever.

"Mo him be say he want know why we be kill some and no be kill some."

I noted that the question of Mo doing the security sweep was left hanging. Perhaps Mo wasn't so dumb after all. I knew that he was very lazy in addition to being dumb.

"How in hell I be tell him that? comnist...damn, you are getting me to say it like you do. Tell him he see VC, he see NVA, he be kill them. That's all he need be know. You tell him he no sweep perimeter, he no be stay alive long enough to worry about what the hell a communist look like."

All that my threat brought was a toothless smile from Mo. He firmly believed that he had me wrapped around his finger.

"Mo him be say Sargy be tell he differ VC, NVA, ARVN. Mo he say he not all time know who he be shoot. Mo say Sargy be piss off he be shoot wrong one."

"Oh, my God," I muttered under my breath. "How many more were there among these tribes that we had corrupted blindly into such a sad state?"

I stood up wanting to take a walk alone. Away from having to look the two of them in the eyes while I continued the lie that I had learned to live with. The lie that we were saving them from communism and therefore giving them freedom.

"You tell god damn Mo he be ask too many question. He be go sweep before I be kick him ass all way to VC camp."

Ding did not translate my words, instead he looked me in the eyes and imploringly said.

"Me too, Sargy. Me too want know difrent VC, NVA, ARVN. Now, we be kill Sargy say. One time Sargy no wit we, we no be want kill wrong one, Sargy be gets boo coo piss off we." Mo and Ding's values were somewhat different from those of the women of Ba Cat, where I had effectively used mystic water buffalos and sad hamlet chiefs by way of explaining communism.

"Ding, you and Mo. You be soldier all same me. Okay? You be take order. I say kill, you kill. Me boss say me kill, I kill.

"All soldier he like take him order. Mo him be ask boo coo question. Now you be tell that dummy he no go out sweep, him ass gonna be one sad mess to be sit on."

A faint smile from Ding told me that he understood that I could not give a good reason why we were out there in the jungle slugging it out with an enemy.

All during the day I insisted that both of them comb the area for enemy signs. I had decided to go after the money and jewels that night. I wanted them tired when evening came.

The distance I had to travel to the graves and back was approximately six miles. The ground over which I had to go was relatively easy, so I did not expect problems making it there and back while they were asleep.

When the sun disappeared behind the western hills, I told them that I would take the first portion of the night's security. They were glad to have me do it, and did not suspect that I had ulterior motives. Neither of them noticed when I took one of the bullet-ridden combat packs that we had taken from the Rangers, swung it over my shoulder, and casually stepped out of the hootch.

One of the girls wanted to go with me, but Mo scared her off with a threatening gesture. She looked at him with daggers in her eyes but dared not defy him. Reluctantly, she backed off and reentered the hootch.

I worked myself through the thick brush to the creek-bottom where I could move faster. The first two miles I covered quickly, for I knew we had swept that area, and no enemy activity had been noted. When I came within 200 yards from where I thought the graves were, I slowed down, and carefully felt my way closer. I did not expect the enemy to be around, but my training did not allow for blunders.

Twenty yards from the graves, I flattened on the moist ground and remained still. Every sound that reached my ears I listened to carefully, and identified as being natural in pitch and frequency. When I was satisfied that no sound could possibly be caused by human intrusion, I ventured closer to the spot where I knew the graves to be. The area was dimly outlined in the darkness. However, I could make out the slight depressions. The grass that was used to camouflage the graves had turned a dirty yellow and now gave away the location. Not enough wet dirt had been removed with the grass to keep the grass alive until it was replaced over the filled graves. Just one more oversight in a seemingly never-ending chain of things in jungle warfare that needs correcting in the future.

I crawled to the graves. At each grave I lowered my nose close to the ground to smell for human decay. To my consternation no offensive odors were present. Why?

Oh yes, I thought. The bodies were firmly wrapped in ponchos. It was going to be a long, hard night for me, so I went to work immediately.

I cleared the dead grass off a grave. With my entrenching tool, I went to work. After 30 minutes I hit the poncho and broke through it to release a terrible nauseating smell. Quickly I re-covered some of the body and moved to the next grave. While I was busy, the moon had moved lower and it no longer filtered light down to the small clearing where the graves were. My night vision was great at the time, so I could see far enough to satisfy myself that I was alone.

Once more I hit a poncho about five feet down and again a nauseating odor seemed to jump up into my face. I felt like vomiting, but kept myself engrossed in what I was after.

"Tom, damn you, Babe, wherever you may be, look down on what I'm doing for your wife and boys," I whispered, and went to the third grave with sweat pouring down my face.

I was engrossed with what I was doing, but a second sense warned me of something, so I roamed my eyes over the dark surroundings. Something was there. What it was I could not immediately determine, for I had heard no sound other than that which I caused with my digging.

Then I saw a movement. It was as black as the night but I saw it move. It had moved ever so slightly but I had seen it. Something was there.

Only my right arm moved. I folded my fist around the grip of my pistol and slowly pulled it out of my holster. I slid the hammer back and waited. The back of my neck tingled. Every muscle in my body was coiled for instant action.

It was the silence that disturbed me most. It seemed to me that a heavy, ominous, dark blanket had descended over me and wrapped me up with the surrounding jungle. Not a breath of wind stirred through the dark undergrowth. Everything was still.

I had been exposed to too many unknowns in my life to let a little thing like opening graves in the middle of a black night, even deep in a hostile jungle, make me see things that did not make a noise.

With my left hand I felt the ground around me for my M-16 rifle, without taking my eyes off the dark spot that I had seen move. When my fingers touched the rifle I brought it to bear and eased my pistol back into the holster.

With my rifle I felt safer. The 30 rounds that I always kept in the clip could settle all my troubles when it became necessary for a shootout. It started to dawn on me that perhaps it was something out of our world and somehow connected to opening of graves. I wanted to laugh, but I saw it move again.

It was closer to me, and it was low on the ground, about ten yards away. I did not hear a footstep or any other sound. I thought that no living being could approach me that close without me hearing it. By then, I was ready to kill at the slightest sound.

A sound came. It was the sound of breathing. Fear froze me for a split second before I fired and rolled quickly three times to the side. A full clip split the night's silence, and tracers temporarily blinded me as the bullets ripped the area where I had seen the movement.

Silence settled once more while I slammed another clip into the magazine and continued to roll yet further to the right. No one returned my fire.

I lay still for approximately 20 minutes. Nothing stirred. Reality and my military mind told me that whatever was there, was there no more, for I could not miss at such a short distance and leave a living soul to bother me. I told myself that it was the strain and my fatigue that had made me see things that were not there. I did not altogether believe that, but I had work to do.

On the sixth grave I hit a canvas bag and no offensive smell came up to me. It was the money and the jewelry, a large bag full. It was a pleasant relief to have another unknown settled. It was the ninth grave that Tom had dug, and a warm feeling of what it would mean to Tom's wife, Maggie, and his four boys stirred a sense of well being within me.

The money I stuffed into my combat pack, and a few packs of bills went into my fatigue pockets. I was surprised at the large amount of money. There was less jewelry than I had expected, and I managed to hide it in my first-aid and ammunition pouches. I recovered my weapon and with my eyes I searched the surrounding area before I stood up.

There it was again, that dark spot that moved slightly. I had no doubt in my mind that I saw it. It was located at the very same spot where I had seen it earlier. I backed off, ready to shoot if it approached me. I knew then that I was dealing with a strange phenomenon.

I had to back around in a circle to head in the direction from which I came. I wasn't sure if I was afraid of the enemy at that time or something out of our Montagnards' dim past. I had been listening to too many Yard stories, I told myself. But this did little to dispel the knowledge that with the one burst I had definitely killed whatever was there — that is, if whatever was there was not already dead.

I came close to panicking when once again I saw the movement after I had progressed about a half-mile and had just begun to dismiss the entire incident. I spotted it to my rear. I lined my sights on it, and waited.

When nothing happened, I first moved slowly to the right, then toward it to offset whatever was there. Suddenly I saw it, ten yards from me, and it seemed to rise from out of the ground. I held my fire and stood still. My breath stuck in my lungs, refusing to come out, I was so tense. Again I heard the distinct sound of heavy breathing, or perhaps it was my own breath that I heard. I crouched lower and waited.

Whatever it was also stood still and I had a definite feeling that I was being observed. Again I backed off and saw whatever it was remain standing still. It did not follow me. When it was out of sight, I turned and ran. It was the first time ever in my combat career that I ran from something that I could not identify.

Approaching the hootch, I behaved like a soldier. I shook off the strange feeling of having lost my mind and searched the area to insure that all was still as I had left it. There were no sign of enemy activity and no indication that Mo, Ding, or the women had missed me.

The eight women were fast asleep inside the hootch. Ding was inside with them and Mo was wrapped in a deerskin and curled up in a ball some distance from the hootch. I felt sorry for him being pestered by the girls.

The dawn was just starting its daily battle to penetrate down through the canopies. I hoped for an uneventful day unlike the many we had had to endure since the women came. I wanted to lie down in blissful slumber, knowing that the difficult part of my promise to Tom had been accomplished.

"Wake up, you miserable scouts. I be want some meat for breakfast. Scat you two."

Mo rubbed his eyes and hung back, but when I approached him and aimed a kick at him, he gave me a toothless smile and made off after Ding.

The women must have stayed awake chattering all night for they lay curled up in the skin blankets. I took advantage of them being asleep, and looked at what I had stuffed into the combat pack. I also emptied my pockets of money and jewelry. I stared at a very large amount. The bills were 100s and 20s. I did not count them, but was sure that Maggie and Tom's boys would never have to worry whether they would have food enough.

I had to hide the many rings, necklaces, and bangles of gold as best I could. Quite a few diamond rings that I estimated of real value, were among the lot. I was ready for the real world. I had done what I had set out to do. Ding and Mo were safe, and it was high time I gave some thought as to what I could do for myself.

For the first time, the women became an asset. Their being with us gave Ding a reason to want to live. It also had some effect on Mo, even though he took a dim view of their dumb efforts to get him and his Sargy to bed them.

We had extra rifles and many full 30-round clips. I spent some trying times teaching the girls how to use the rifles. At no time did I want them to get near a grenade. I had nightmares about one of them playfully pulling the safety pin and handing it to me to put back in again after she had released the arming handle.

It took only a few hints and outright conversation between me and the two Yards to pave the way for a sensible agreement between us. It was not easy to make them understand that it was imperative that I return to my people. They did, for a short time, believe that I was going to spend the rest of my life in the jungle with them.

"Sargy, you be order me, I be gets boo coo damn Yard. You be tell how be fight all Viets. Sout Viet, Nort Viet, all VC. Sargy be big, big, much good be hamlet chief." Ding had warmed up to the thought of being an Assistant Hamlet Chief.

I did not have a problem with them wanting to return with me to Saigon. The memory of their treatment at the hands of the ARVN Rangers was going to remain with them forever.

When they returned with a young deer, I had taken off my clothes to dry out from the sweat of the night's work. Later I would again visit the spring and endure another session with one or two girls. I had become as much a master at fending them off as they were in perseverance.

"Ding, what do ancestors do when you dig him up grave?" I asked even though I did not want to hear his answer.

He looked me over with fear showing in his face. "Ancestor him no be like Sargy be dig em up grave. Dey be look over Sargy good. Dey be no forget."

"What will they no forget?"

"Dey be no forget Sargy look."

"That all?"

"Yes be, Sargy. Dat be all. Dey no be forget."

"I asked you, damn you, what they no be forget?"

"Dey no be forget Sargy look. Sargy be dead dey be lemember Sargy look, den dey be kill Sargy."

"What are you talking about? I'll be dead by that time."

He thought that over for a while then said. "Sargy, no be unstand. You be die, killed, you no be dead. You be go ancestor. Ancestor no be real dead, dead. Dey be wait we come, den dey be happy greet we. We be dig out grave dey be boo coo pissed off. Dat way dey be look you, you dig up grave."

"Okay, okay. Forget it."

It would explain something to me if I were a Montagnard, the fact that I was looked on that night with nothing else taking place. But I was not a Yard and remained as confused as I had been when I saw that black form.

By that time the women had joined us. The deer meat was fried over a lively fire and they sprinkled the meat with their concoction of spices. All in all the taste was as good as any one would get at a well-organized picnic back in the States.

When we finished eating, I said, "Ding, now we move. Take one rifle each. Other rifles women be carry, also extra ammo. No be have ammo clip in rifle women be carry. Dey be shoot us for be sure. Boo coo dumb be women."

He smiled his agreement with what I said, for he remembered just too well that dumb stunt one of them had pulled which had almost got us all killed.

It was noon when we left our dilapidated hootch with the eight women in a single file behind us. We set off toward the east where flatter land and less jungle would make movement easier. We cut our way through the dense growth down the mountainside all afternoon, then well into the night, before we took our first rest.

I was fearful of discovery by electronic detectors, which would invite our being fired on. After all, we were inside an A-Camp's AO, and I knew our method of operation well. By daylight we were in kindlier terrain, where we were able to move faster.

All through the early morning, long stringy clouds like mare's tails had shown themselves high in the sky wherever a clearing presented itself overhead. A heavy, stifling atmosphere seemed to have blanketed the countryside in ominous foreboding of a storm that was about to break.

It was late in the afternoon when it came. Thunderclaps tore through the sky as strong winds ripped over the jungle and black clouds darkened the day. With extreme violence, a cloudburst shattered the former tranquility to send torrents of big horizontal raindrops slashing from the mountains to the South China Sea.

Quickly, I undressed to let the rain wash some of the smell from my body. It felt good to feel the cold water pelt my naked body and watch the large raindrops wash away the mud and dirt I had accumulated on my fatigues and web equipment while digging out the graves.

Ding, Mo, and then the women did the same as I did, but with happy laughter that rang in ripples through the dense underbrush. To all of them it was a new experience to stand in the rain when a more sensible action would have been to seek dry shelter.

For the rest of my life I'll carry the hilarious mental picture of eight naked women and two naked Yards laughing and dancing in the rain. The two old women provided the most fun with their long, floppy tits flying around their necks and over their shoulders as they danced in circles around me.

In ten minutes it was all over. The sun came out and sent friendly rays to flicker playfully through the overhead canopy onto the wet, glittering grass below. The air smelled sweet as we doggedly walked along a winding footpath. We set as fast a pace as the women could manage. They seemed fairly tough. Even the two old women surprised me with their stamina. Perhaps they were not as old as they looked to me.

It had taken a long time to explain my plans fully to Ding and Mo. But when Ding asked me, "We be kill Sout Viets too, when you be come back?" I answered in the affirmative, and it brought smiles to both of them. I knew then that they had hope.

Hope is a very powerful and often a necessary incentive to make people want to stay alive. Especially where we were.

Our entourage traveled together for two days. When the mountainous terrain gave way to gentler hills, we separated. I had to remind them that it would not be long before all U.S. forces would leave to return to our own country, and it would be best if they started to live again freely in the mountains. It was a poignant parting.

The terrible experience they had gone through at the hands of the South Vietnamese Army was too vividly imprinted on their minds for them ever to forget. Because of that, they readily accepted my statement that I intended to return.

Two of the girls wanted to go with me, but with Ding's help I pried them off me and went on my way eastward toward a world that I knew better. It felt good to get away from the Yard girls who were bound to get me killed.

The Viet Cong had various strongholds in the numerous hamlets along the route I had to travel. While still close to the mountains I did not travel during daylight.

All through the night I settled down to a mile-consuming airborne shuffle. It carried me a great distance eastward toward the flat areas where U.S. Forces controlled the land. During the day I hid myself in thick brush. The days went fast, for I slept my famous twilight sleep, gaining all the rest I needed.

When I had traveled about 50 miles from the mountains, I could travel by day. With my airborne shuffle, I knew that I was covering approximately five miles per hour and could keep it up for six hours each day.

My stomach had contracted to a painful emptiness, but I refused to stop long enough to find something to eat other than the raw wild rice I managed to snap off as I ran. I was traveling through Viet Cong-held territory, but I knew that they lacked the communication equipment and ability to act on a target of opportunity. By the time they grabbed weapons and organized themselves, I was out of rifle range or out of sight.

I was at no time sure as to where I was, other than that I was west of most of the U.S. Army installations and had to travel fast before an ambush could be set up.

On the sixth day after parting from Ding and Mo, I sighted what appeared to be a large city silhouetted against the early dawn. I also thought I was smelling salt air, but dismissed it as a trick my tired mind was playing on me.

I reasoned that if I was near the South China Sea, then I was near where I wanted to be. I waited for the eastern sky to turn red, then cast a gray glow which quickly chased the darkness westward, before I recognized where I was.

Somehow I had wandered too far north, and had come to the provincial capital of Quang Ngai. This city, of approximately 20,000, lay straddled across the north-south coastal highway and within the AO of our powerful U.S. 23rd Infantry Division, the famous Americal Division. Its headquarters was 20 miles to the north at Chu Lai.

At a nearby stream, I joined a number of washerwomen. Among their excited giggles I cleaned myself as best I could. One extremely fat woman gave me a piece of soap, which came in handy, since those sex-oriented six Yard girls had used up the single bar I carried in my combat pack.

After I had cleaned myself, I felt refreshed and certainly smelled better as I sauntered as nonchalantly as I could manage through the narrow, dirty streets toward where I knew a U.S. Military Compound was located.

Once inside the compound, I straightened the green beret on my damp head and let it be known that I had 20 Montagnards in the city, resting after a long patrol. I said that I, too, wanted to rest and needed logistical support, especially food, clean clothes, and rest, all of which were pleasantly provided.

The commanding officer, a young captain, said, "Sergeant, anything you need, just order it. I assure you that my men will see that you get it. If they do not, you let me know."

Shortly after I had received what I needed, I was between two white sheets. The humming noise of the city was immediately wiped away by a blissful sleep which engulfed me seconds after I laid my tired head on the pillow.

Once, during the night I woke up in a sweat after a nightmare in which I had four Montagnards girls in bed with me. One of them had held a rifle barrel to my throat, while two other girls played catch with a hand grenade minus its arming handle.

I awoke up to hear many machine guns and grenades shatter the silence around the compound. Some problems with the Viet Cong. I turned over and went back to sleep, much relieved that it was not one of the girls shooting at me. Our American soldiers were in charge. I was safe and not needed.

Early the next morning I stole a jeep. Within minutes I had joined a military convoy guarded by Military Police. They were on half-tracks, jeeps, and sand-dune-tired patrol vehicles. The MP vehicles were mounted with M-60 and 50-caliber machine guns.

The route was beset with danger to U.S. servicemen. The VC would hide in the populous villages and towns along the way. Only a few unreliable indicators would warn of VC presence. The best one was the absence of children. If there were no children, then be alerted.

Another indicator was an unusual blockage of a street. The VC wanted easy targets and confusion before they took a chance with us. Most of the time it was very difficult to know just when or how they would attack a U.S. vehicle.

In one village we were blocked by a number of water buffalos, which I thought strange. Usually these buffalos were not found in large numbers, and seldom in the center of a village.

I was behind a two-and-one-half-ton truck. Behind me was one of the MP vehicles, armed with a M-60 machine gun.

When the convoy came to a stop, I was alerted. No children, except one little girl could be seen, and there were too many buffalos. The usual street noises were absent.

"Enemy!" I screamed and fired a burst of my M-16 rifle into the air. Every man in the convoy grabbed weapons.

"VC in control!" I hollered at the MPs behind me.

At the same time I saw that small girl at the side of the road swing her arm and toss a snake into the cab of the army truck ahead of us. The snake swished through the air and landed on top of the soldier driving the truck.

Behind me, one MP had also seen it, and with instant reflexes the MP pulled the trigger on his M-60, sending a stream of bullets into the girl and dropping many bystanders to the ground. The area cleared as if by magic. Other machine guns fired but most of the MPs were not sure whom or what to shoot at.

The road ahead was clear. The two GIs ahead of me vacated their truck and ran toward my jeep. One held his upper arm where the snake had struck him.

"Cut the place where the snake bit him and do what you were trained to do, damn you," I ordered another GI close by.

The truck ahead had blocked the road for us, and I saw the dangerous situation. We were stuck in the middle of a village with hostile people all around us.

I grabbed a soldier and pulled him with me into the truck.

"Where is the snake?" he asked in a panic.

"You look for it while I drive." I slammed the truck into gear and moved out of the village as fast as the thing would go. I felt good and wanted to have some fun with the MP who was standing beside me on the seat of the truck, frantically searching for the snake while waving his pistol all around.

"You're not going to give me a ticket for speeding?"

He looked at me sideways. "Jeez, man. You're some kind of a ..." Then he caught himself, seeing my master sergeant stripes.

"I can't see the snake." He was nervously jumping around on the seat of the truck, pistol pointing wherever his eyes went.

Through the rear view mirror I saw my stolen jeep with an MP half-track close behind it.

Chasing a stolen jeep, I thought with humor. The positive action had lifted my morale.

"The snake must have gone into the back," said the MP.

"Why don't you go look?" I teased.

"Hell, no, Sergeant. Sorry, I mean let's wait till we stop."

"No sweat, MP. The snake is not bothering us here, so let's not bother him back there."

"Sure," he said, much relieved that I did not insist on his climbing into the back among the many crates.

"Sarge, that little girl. I think we killed her."

"Yes, I know, and also a few of the bystanders. But did you see the VC running in the background?"

"No, I didn't, were there VC?" He sounded puzzled.

When we pulled to a stop and the vehicles behind us had closed up on us, the sergeant in charge of the convoy came to me with a question clearly written on his face. He wanted directions from me, a Green Beret master sergeant, and I gave them.

"Good work, Sergeant. You handled the situation just fine. Scratch at least ten VC. Sorry about the little girl, but you could not help it. They kept her at knifepoint and made her throw the snake. Your men sure reacted fast and commendably."

He did not know how to switch from feeling guilty.

"You think we did okay?" he asked meekly.

"Yes, darn it. You did just fine. Those VC you killed held the people at gunpoint until the girl threw the snake. Then they ran and would have gotten away but for your men cutting them down. It is their way of getting the people to blame us for killing innocent people, their way of fighting this war."

From behind me I heard a cocky 19-year-old soldier say, "The bastards, I wish they would try us again."

"My sentiments too, MP, and if it is any consolation to you, know that many of us feel the same way."

Again I saw that black and white sign of Ba Cat. "Try us again, you commie bastards."

"MP," I looked at the sergeant in charge of the convoy. "You'd better get on your radio and call for a medevac for that trooper of yours that the snake got. Those bites can be fatal."

That shook the young sergeant. Quickly he grabbed his radio and nervously called his unit. I heard his station ask for his location. The MP sergeant was too shook up to get the necessary information out so I took the microphone from him.

"Request priority Medevac for one...I say again...one U.S. casualty on MSR (Main Supply Route) one mile south of Binh Thanh, over."

Over the air came a repeat of my transmission. "Affirmative. Out."

"Now we wait for the chopper, and sergeant, set perimeter security and do your thing with the traffic. Let's not block traffic on this main supply route."

As I expected, the Medevac chopper was overhead within minutes. Again they impressed me with the expertise with which they got the wounded in the air and on the way to a hospital.

Not a second was wasted. They acted as if they did not give a damn for possible enemy interference with their mission. Down they came, all the way to the ground. Out jumped the stretcher-bearers. Next to the wounded they went on their knees, covered him with a blanket, and rolled him onto the stretcher. They ran with him to the chopper struts where the stretcher was securely clamped, and up they went in a whirlwind of flying grass, rocks, and dust on the way to the surgical field hospital.

If one were to get hurt in an accident in the middle of any city in the U.S., one would not get onto a modern hospital's operating table as fast as a wounded American soldier in combat could.

When we pulled into Nha Trang, the MP sergeant in charge of the convoy approached me with his squad.

"We want to thank you, Sergeant, for the timely warning and also for helping us to get the convoy out of the village."

"Don't mention it. And by the way, you should take my name and unit for your report on that grenade-throwing woman I saw."

"What woman?"

He looked puzzled.

"I saw a VC woman, a small piece of her checkered scarf showing, waiting to throw a hand grenade, but one of your men cut her down before she could. Also those armed VC in the background were shot down by your men before they could do damage to your convoy or kill any of your men.

"The girl who threw the snake was a diversion the VC tried, but you sure fooled them. Commendable action by you and your men, Sergeant." I pulled a pencil from the pocket of the nearest MP and wrote down my name and unit designation. I handed the paper to the MP sergeant.

"The body count of the VC is nine. That was what I counted lying on the ground. There might have been more, but I can swear to a body count of only nine."

"Ah...oh, well. I got the convoy through, men."

He managed slowly to grasp what I had started. His men, too, started to see things differently. They saw what they wanted to see. Certainly not the killing of innocent civilians, which was something no Americans would want to do. It was better to stretch the truth a little. The damage had been done and definitely not because of our initiation.

Silently I gave thanks that there were no civilian news reporters in the convoy. If there had been, they might have further tainted our Army's image, as they too often wrote for the anti-American segment of our world.

The little girl with the snake reminded me of another little girl. It was a little girl who, unfortunately, stood too close to a kerosene stove her mother was trying to light with Army black market gasoline. The stove exploded, and burned the little girl.

The picture one news reporter took of that little girl running naked down a street became a front line story, and proof that the U.S. Army was dropping napalm onto innocent civilians. After all, pictures did not lie.

On parting, the MP sergeant pulled me over to the side.

"Thanks again, Sergeant. I understand now what is best to report." Then he smiled and asked aloud for all his men to hear.

"Any of you seen a stolen MACV jeep?"

No one answered him, but there were many friendly smiles when I drove off in the stolen jeep.

Chapter 11

The Last Laugh

atherine Friem, considered a member or ex-member of the powerful World Council of Churches, was handled with kid gloves by all
officials who came in contact with her. It was believed that she
might open a Pandora's box for the Army, because she was the only person who could have given adverse testimony in reference to the one raid
into Laos. It could have led to adverse publicity for the Army. And of that,
we'd had enough.

"The general will see you now, Miss," said the aide as he held the door
open for Cathy.

"Please take a seat, Miss Friem. It is with a heavy heart that I meet
with you this time." General Collins felt genuinely sorry for her. He had a
good idea what had transpired between her and me.

"General, it is hard for me to believe that Tony is not with us any more."

Tears were in her eyes. She took the handkerchief the general offered her.

"I know how you feel. He was a soldier. Perhaps a lonely soldier, but
he had loved and was loved in return. He died on the field of battle."

There was a long silence before he spoke again.

"I specifically want to tell you myself how and where he went. It was
near where you came to know him and you started to love him. A reconnaissance patrol discovered the remains of the ARVN Ranger Fire Team

who were last with him. They were all killed in close combat with the enemy."

Cathy was unaware that I had returned since she last saw me or that I had gone again into the mountains. Penny had changed her mind about telling Cathy about that. It was not the only thing that Penny had changed. She later proved to be one unique and changeable woman. That Penny was like no other woman I've ever known.

"They were all killed? All those little, dark, incredibly brave friends of his — Captain Mock, Ding and the funny little Mo, who was always cold?" She sobbed softly.

"You will want to return home to your family, Miss."

"Yes, General, there is nothing left here for me."

"I'll have a seat for you on the Pan American flight that leaves Tan Son Nhut at 0900."

"Thank you. That will be fine. Thank you for all your kindness. I'll stay at the embassy tonight."

After Cathy left, General Collins ordered his aide to have Colonel Wallace and Colonel Wakefield report to him. They were waiting in the reception room.

"Please be seated, gentlemen," he said after they had exchanged formal greetings.

"I personally want to convey my gratitude for the splendid and timely investigations which you two conducted. Because of you, I could jump into the middle of the mess and clip some wings before those involved could get their stories twisted.

"And Wallace, I concurred with your recommendation not to prefer court-martial charges against Sergeant Blondell. I do, however, believe that it is time for the sergeant to retire. He has served honorably for many years. It is time that he enter into civilian life, and I hope the civilians can cope with him. There are many Green Beret sergeants like him who may just find the real world a very difficult place to adjust to.

"I would like to state that we have learned a lesson. However, such a statement would be asinine, since we know that this type of thing is normal procedure out here. The only difference is that we beat them at their own game this time."

The general smiled. "A pity you two could not have been present when I had Colonel Van Trang, General Duc Lap Mihn, the black market king, and Mister Sanders, our AID coordinator, all in my office at the same time."

General Collins offered his cigar box to the colonels.

"As soon as I said that not another dime's worth of class-six supplies would go into ARVN clubs, the black market king saw his entire kingdom evaporate around him. Only then did I ask questions and receive truthful answers."

The general paused for a few minutes, then slapped his knees and burst out laughing, much to the delight of the two colonels.

"Do you gentlemen know how that sergeant rubbed two ARVN colonels' and one ARVN general's faces in the mud? Talk about face-saving. I don't believe those three will ever be able to look an American in the face. I made it my business to see that the entire story came out so that most ARVN, American officers and civilians could hear it."

With much laughter, the general related my dealings with the two ARVN colonels to save Ding and Mo. When he was through, none of them could remain seated, and a light-hearted atmosphere ensued in the general's office.

None of them, for a moment, believed that there really were money and jewels hidden. They took it as a clever scam of mine.

The ARVN colonels had said nothing about having received American money since it was illegal to possess greenbacks.

To the three of them, the dealings I had with Colonel Van Trang were viewed with humor, for they alone were in possession of all the pertinent facts. They knew that I had not died with the ARVN Rangers. They further believed that I was not dead, but might very well show up eventually.

They had to pretend that I was killed in action to pacify ARVN officials. The official report read that we ran into an enemy patrol and were killed.

The general relit his cigar. "I wrote the final chapter to the report. What a pity none of us could have gotten to know the sergeant. We learned quite a lot about him, though. If he should turn up we will have to get him home and out of the Army. Retire him. He is just a little out of hand, I would say."

"Yes Sir," said Colonel Wallace. "I would not like to have had him in my command."

"I second that," said Colonel Wakefield. "I would like to have asked him just one question, though."

"And what is that?" asked the general.

Colonel Wakefield thought for a moment.

"I would ask him if he had those pigs and cows dropped on purpose to upset Captain Van Trang, thus instigating that shoot-out with the ARVN SF team. He and his communications sergeant acted so fast that I believe they expected things to happen the way they did."

"Maybe," mused the general, "but I don't think so. I think that A-Team was just swept along by an overwhelming series of circumstances. The two things which caused me to exonerate the sergeant from wrongdoing were the command's reluctance to take action against Captain Van Trang, and that the ARVN command actually connived with the enemy to have Ba Cat fall to them."

It was because of that, I found out later, that I was not court-martialed and sent to Leavenworth. An American soldier does not disobey orders, least of all not in the face of the enemy. That I did nothing indicative of self-gain was a plus for me.

It was two days after a U.S. Army reconnaissance patrol discovered the five dead ARVN Rangers, and caused the command to report me Killed in Action, that I drove my jeep into the smelly city of Nha Trang.

I swung the stolen MAGV jeep to a stop in front of the club inside the SF Headquarters compound. The club was empty except for one over-perfumed Vietnamese barmaid. This was strange, for the large number of men assigned to that unit and their scattered duty hours usually meant some would be enjoying their off duty time in the club.

"Where is everybody?" I asked her. "It's way after 1800. These guys all joined the Baptist or Mormon religions?"

"No, GI no can come crub till afta service," she answered.

"Two double scotches with water on the side. What service? And two more of the same," I rattled off to her.

"You be boo coo tursty, eh Sargy?"

"Yeah, I be boo coo tursty. Me long time no...what the hell am I talking like you for?"

She laughed.

"Service blong Sargy kill maybe two day go."

Another glossy eight-by-ten picture to be mounted on the wall of that shiny hallway at Group, I thought sadly, and settled down with a strong desire to get drunk. I called the BOQ about Miss Friem.

"Sorry, Sir." the Vietnamese manager said. "Miss Friem left for Saigon two weeks ago, and she is now back in the States."

Other than the drinks, everything became less friendly to me. The drinks warmed my insides and chased away some of my apprehensions and all of my fatigue. After a half-hour alone in the club, I became worried and walked to the orderly room to sign in.

My name, rank, serial number, and unit were then officially recorded for the next day's morning report. Where it asked for last station and travel order number, I wrote, "MIA to Active Duty." I returned to the club to let the first man that read that entry flip. On the way back to the club I could hear sad church music and unharmonious singers paying their last respects.

Something seemed to draw me toward the small chapel. I slowly climbed the few steps to the first level. I heard Chaplain Brown, a long-time friend of mine, speaking in a reverent voice.

"And all of us who are gathered here together in the presence of God, ask forgiveness for our dear departed comrade Anthony Blondell, for his transgressions, and ask the Almighty to open His golden gate to him. Yes, Lord, help...Tony! You son-of-a-bitch!"

He shook the entire congregation to their feet. First in confusion, then with all eyes turned on me. It was but a second before the congregation resembled a victorious football team.

We spilled out into the quadrille, then toward the club where the club steward was told that no one paid for drinks and just to pour it as fast as his barmaid could.

I had to answer a dozen questions at the same time until a loud commanding voice ordered.

"At ease!" All became quiet. A full colonel whom I did not know, confronted me.

I reported to him. He returned my salute and extended his hand in greeting.

"I am Colonel Rundell, Group Commander. Take a seat, Sergeant."

He sat down with me. All the men backed away to a respectful distance and remained silent.

"I am especially glad you followed my orders, which said that everyone was required to attend the farewell service."

He smiled in a genuinely friendly manner. I saw a good man in front of me. He turned and addressed all the men in the club. "All of you know to some extent the problems we have had these last few weeks."

Then he stopped.

"Sergeant Major," he ordered, "empty the club of all indigenous persons and shut the doors. No one leaves or enters until I say so." While the sergeant major, with help of other sergeants, carried out the colonel's orders, the colonel whispered to me, "I'm asking and am expecting your full cooperation." He looked around the club. The doors were closed and indigenous persons were out.

"I'm ordering all of you to keep quiet about Sergeant Blondell's return. We have had enough trouble with the ARVNs. They believe the sergeant has been killed, and that is what we want them to believe. So, keep this information classified. If word gets out that the sergeant is here, we might have trouble.

"Sergeant, I'll get you on an aircraft for the States within hours. Are you ready to leave?"

"Yes, Sir," I answered. "I can have our S-4 Sergeant Bellimy take care of whatever property of mine was salvaged out of Ba Cat, and also get the necessary uniforms ready."

"Excellent. Sergeant Major, see that all is done as soon as possible. I shall take care of the rest. And Sergeant, stay here for the next few hours. I'll get your orders from MAGV. You were transferred to them two weeks ago."

He left the club and the former hum broke out again. What an evening it was going to be, I thought.

"Don!" I called Master Sergeant Don Medford, A-Team sergeant of A-107. "Last time I was at your camp I noted your jeep being kind of dilapidated. A brand new one is parked just outside. Got a MAGV bumper marking. It's yours."

"Great." He turned to one of his men. "Get a bottle of whisky and take the jeep to that helicopter company. See Lieutenant Beck. Tell him I want the jeep at Tra-Bong ASAP."

"Okay, Sarg," he answered and left the club.

Sergeant Bellimy from supply came to me.

"The tailor will be here soon. I have all your property taken care of. I mailed everything to your next of kin. Finance will get you a few hundred dollars here in a few minutes. Give us two hours and we'll have uniform, ribbons, and everything ready for you."

"Thank you, partner." I gave him a slap on the shoulder. The men I was with at the time were well-trained professionals and knew what I needed for my return to the United States.

"What are you doing here, Don? I thought you were still slugging it out with the 5th NVA Division."

"Thanks to you. Man, you sure started something there. How much do you know...I mean about what happened after that attack of yours on the guns?"

While Medford was speaking, a circle had formed around us at the bar.

"Not much, other than that I had to fight for my life."

The club had gone silent. About 20 Green Beret NCOs were gathered around Don and me. They were very attentive, as many of them were assigned to Headquarters.

"They, the 5th NVA, kept pouring out of Laos like hornets that had had their nest disturbed. Which you did. The Air Force, and Navy Air, and then our own heavy artilleery, went to work on them, but they just would not go back to their safe haven in Laos.

"Believe it or not, first they believed that the force that destroyed their guns came from my camp, and they believed that they had us trapped, so they came toward us."

"Later why did they go to Ba Cat?" I asked. Something was not right and I smelled a rat.

"NVA POW we took, a lieutenant, told us the loss of A-106 was prearranged between them and the ARVNs," Medford said bitterly.

"The bastards!" I hit the bar counter hard with my fist and did not feel pain. "The bastards," I said again. I had to have a big drink, so I just took the nearest sergeant's and downed it.

What I was told was about the last thing I had expected. It suddenly made many things clear. Above all it explained why the command did not put me in front of a firing squad for what I did. By the time I had disobeyed orders and caused the problems our command had known about the ARVN's treasonous actions.

"Did the authorities pin down just who was involved?" I asked, knowing that none of us would be on the receiving end of such information.

"No, Tony. Like so many other things here in Vietnam, it will never come out in the open," said the sergeant major.

I thought of something that I had to do quickly. I called the sergeant major and Medford away from the other sergeants and whispered to them my problem with Tom's money and jewelry. I had to get the things into the U.S., past customs without the Army finding out.

The sergeant major smiled and said, "Tony, no sweat. In a few minutes I'll have phony courier letter orders for you, and an empty mailbag with seal ready to snap on. It will do the job."

"The stuff is in this combat pack and in my pockets. You guys take it and get it into a mailbag."

I went with the two sergeants into the washroom and gave them the money and the jewelry. They were both surprised at the large amount of money. The sergeant major walked out with the items, and I knew I had solved another problem. Maggie would get Tom's things.

Back with the rest of the sergeants, I saw the tailor. It did not take him long to get the necessary measurements for two summer Class A uniforms and two winter ones. A copy of my Form 20 had materialized, and a young sergeant was detailed to see that I got all my decorations correctly put on my uniforms.

"Tony," Don said, "be assured we mauled that 5th in a real professional way. We helped them with that motto of theirs, 'Born in the North, die in the South.'"

"Say Don, how come Group found out so much about what happened on Black Face?" I asked.

"I ran a recon patrol on it the night after you repelled their attack. I could not raise you on our radios, but we did spot some of your scouts. They mistook us for NVA." He smiled when he saw me wanting to apologize for my scouts' stupidity.

"We had to vacate the area without looking for you further because of the scheduled B-52 strike.

"Tony, you really pulled one. No one, not I, not Group and apparently not the NVA expected you to go back into Laos. And then to top it all off, man, to attack a military compound, the one near Attapue, of all places. The place was a hornet's nest of enemy strength. Close to that NVA Camp-102 and right in the way of all war materiel they move down to Cambodia. Hearing that, I knew you had bitten off more than you could handle, Babe."

I gave them a shit-eating grin.

"You guys know how we all like our women. Well, I just got lonely and went courting after a few of those black-and-white-checkered scarf-wearers, but ran into more of them than I could handle, and they were not very lovable. Every one is entitled to make mistakes."

They laughed.

"The only one that made a mistake was the NVA for underestimating our fire power, Sergeant," it was the voice of Colonel Rundell. He had entered the club without being noticed.

"At ease!" Someone ordered.

"Carry on," said the colonel.

He motioned me to the side.

"Sergeant, I was on the phone with General Collins, the MAGV G-1. He orders you to board a Pan Am Flight at 0900 hours tomorrow. I am to place an armed guard around you until then. We expect trouble from the ARVN if they find out that you are here." He pointed to two sergeants with load-bearing harnesses on and armed as if ready for a patrol.

"They will stay with you temporarily. We have to give the detail to the Military Police. They should be here soon to take over. A MAGV helicopter will pick you up at 0600 tomorrow."

"Sir, the MPs are not going to lock me up, are they?"

"No. I'll order them to let you do as you wish, only you don't leave the compound. You can stay here in the club if you want. They'll be ordered to insure your physical safety, see that you get on that helicopter at 0600, and then stay with you until you board the aircraft at 0900."

"Thank you, Sir." He shook my hand, then turned to leave, but came back to me. Softly he said to me, "Sergeant, you need not answer me, but I'd be grateful if you did, and it would be only between you and me."

He looked around to make sure no one could hear us.

"Yes Sir?" I waited for him to continue.

"About those two Frenchmen and the one North Vietnamese, the WCC members. I have to order patrols into the area until it can establish what happened to them."

"Sir, I'll pinpoint the place within an eight digit coordinates where their bodies can be found for Sergeant Medford." He said nothing further, but looked me over as if he wanted to believe what he had heard but found it difficult. He was an officer and a gentleman and must have found it difficult having to deal with me. He had one thing going for him, though, and that was that I no longer was in his command, and he was not responsible for any of my future actions.

The poor man had asked a question that he should have known not to ask. He became saddled with knowledge he did not want, and something that might haunt him for the rest of his life. But I did not start that damn war either. Booby Trap was not the only one that could say that and get some measure of satisfaction.

"Don, get a 1:50,000 map that covers Black Face. I have something to show you," I said, lifting my glass to him.

He nodded to one of his men, and within a few minutes we had a map spread out in front of us. I marked a spot of the map.

"Here, Don. Go here and look for what the colonel will tell you to look for."

"Okay, Babe. Kind of close to a dangerous area," he remarked absent-mindedly.

It seemed that he knew what he was going to be ordered to go after.

"Hi, you guys," said a young sergeant who had just come in.

"Remember that big snake? This is the sergeant who put that snake in the chopper."

He burst out with loud laughter that was picked up by many in the club.

"What about that snake?" I asked when the laughter subsided.

Sergeant Medford said loudly enough for all to hear, "Quiet, you guys. I'm gonna tell about that snake."

Then he turned to me.

"Tony, you would have laughed yourself sick if you had seen those two helicopter pilots land, shut off their motors and everyone bail out and run away from their machine.

"The snake had wiggled itself free of most of the lashings, and got itself tangled up in a belt of machine gun ammo. Both machine gunners were hanging off the struts when the helicopter came over Group Headquarters. They did not even wait for the chopper to land before they jumped out and ran for their lives."

The Sergeant Major took over the telling.

"You should have seen the mad scramble of the MIKE Force to get out of sight when I screamed for them to catch that snake. We finally had to throw a cargo net over the thing before anyone would come near that much pissed-off snake."

"And the pilot," said another sergeant "he damn near flipped. Last thing I heard him say before he restarted his chopper was, 'You are a bunch of crazy nuts, not only that weird one that put that snake into my chopper but all the rest of you Green Berets.' Then he almost wrecked his chopper on our standoff fence. He was that shook-up."

What time the party broke up I did not know. It was a pleasant evening among friends, one that would last a long time in my memory. It seemed a culmination of all that had been pleasant in my life. Even the four MPs who stayed respectfully in the background did not dampen our morale.

"Sergeant, it is time to get up," said an MP who had stirred me from my sleep. I opened my eyes to see the uniformed military policeman leaning over me. For a horrible moment I thought that I was in the federal prison in Leavenworth, where Booby Trap and a few others wanted to send me.

"Okay, okay," I said meekly and staggered into a cold shower which immediately brought me back to life. I breathed a sigh of relief to discover that I had not been locked up, and that the MP was not a prison guard.

"Damn you, Colonel Booby Trap, what are you doing to me?" I hissed under my breath.

My room was crowded when I stepped from the shower back into the bedroom. Friends of mine, the MPs, and the tailor with hangers of uniforms were there. Even the Sergeant Major was sitting on my bed. He had a half-filled mailbag, officially sealed, and ready to be taken to the U.S.

"How you feel, Babe?" he asked. "I have everything ready for you. These orders will help you get a priority flight home when you get to the states. Hope you don't mind taking some classified material back to the U.S. for us."

All okay, I thought. Maggie will get her money.

"Here are Tom's and Doc's home addresses. I know you would want to see their folks. The courier letter orders will get you a flight to their homes."

The sergeant major talked too much, telling me the obvious. Maybe he just wanted to let the others know that he too was with me.

When I looked at myself in the full-length mirror, I was pleased with the tailor's work, and the way the S-4 sergeant had taken care of my decorations. Indeed, I looked smart enough in my shining apparel to have qualified for the soldier of the month.

After all the well-wishes one man could endure, the MAGV helicopter lifted me and four MPs high above the corrugated structures of Special Forces Headquarters and the many buildings that housed the MIKE Force and two SF B-Teams.

Hundreds of Montagnards, most of whom were from the MIKE Force, were lounging in boredom around their quonset huts. They were gathered in groups distinguished by the brightly colored neck scarfs they wore. Blue, red, green, and black — each color a grade significant to the individual and to his company.

I gazed down for the last time on the barbed wire entanglement, control and fire towers, stand-off fences, fire positions, and the mine field of SF Group Headquarters.

What I saw from the air had become such a vivid part of my life that even with moisture in my eyes I could see two sets of small, sad, black eyes drift though my mind.

"I'll be back, Ding." I whispered to myself.

My mind jumped to the many Stay Behind Coffins that I had supervised the burial of. All the money and weapons. What could Ding and I do with them? I knew that one day I'd find Ding again.

Then SF Group Headquarters disappeared, and the green fields with the many hamlets and villages became blurs below us.

Soon, I saw the teeming mass of disorganized humanity appear like so many ants, as the helicopter scooted over Saigon toward Tan Son Nhut airport.

Putrid air and the dull hum of the streets mixed with jet blasts and helicopter blades slapping air combined to convince me that finally I had been torn away from one world, the world of Ding, Mo, and the many Yards that were happily with their ancestors, and thrown into another world.

The helicopter settled down on the hot tarmac with its blades losing their fast pitch. I stepped out with my mailbag slung over my shoulder and the MPs carrying my travel bags. Then I saw them and my heart skipped a beat.

"More trouble," I said out loud.

A one-star general and two colonels stood at the bottom of the gangplank of a 727 Pan Am flight. They were watching me get out of the helicopter, and as I walked toward them, I recognized the two colonels. They were Wallace and Wakefield. The general I did not know. I came smartly to a halt in front of the general, dropped the mailbag on the tarmac and reported, "Sir, Master Sergeant Blondell reporting to the General, Sir."

He returned my salute and reached for my hand. I received a warm handshake and an equally warm smile. Possibly the smile was to set me at ease, for I must have showed my nervousness. Colonels Wakefield and Wallace also shook hands with me while the four MPs stood rigidly at attention close by.

The scene, as observed from the aircraft's doorway where three airline stewardesses took it all in, must have looked like a cross between the transfer of a condemned prisoner to the gallows and a military change of command ceremony.

"Sergeant, it is a pleasure to meet you. And I speak for these two gentlemen as well. We have compiled a report that exonerates you of all wrongdoing. So we came to say goodbye to you, and I want you to remember, Sergeant, if ever you need something and believe that I could be of service to you, please feel free to contact me."

The two colonels also said goodbye, and I walked up the boarding ramp as if in a daze. Too much had happened to me faster than I could mentally cope with. The honorable farewell that I so unexpectedly received from such high-ranking officers had yet to be fully appreciated.

That appreciation would come later, and would be for all time remembered as proof of how comrades-in-arms often disregard rank to show how much we care for each other.

Those officers did not know about the gray mental curtain behind which I hid my bitter feelings for having lost so many men. Neither could they know how well I had buried the memories of my many fallen friends, among whom were Doc, Tom, and Mock. I took care not to let the thought of Ding and the little, cold, scared Mo break through that cowardly gray veil of mine.

When I had been fighting in Korea, I had seen two American soldiers being led off as prisoners of war by North Korean soldiers. Like the plight of Ding and Mo, it had a devastating and permanent effect on my mind. Dead soldiers I could accept, but not those condemned to a living death. That the three officers came to see me off was an open display of leadership, a commendable quality well developed in the characters of our United States' Regular Army officers.

I walked up the boarding ramp where the three stewardesses met me with extra smiles. They must have decided that I was not a condemned prisoner, even though two MPs had followed me up the boarding ramp and handed my travel bags to them. The mailbag I hung onto tightly, and stowed in a baggage compartment above my head.

Almost immediately the doors slammed shut, the No Smoking signs were on, and I knew that the flight had been delayed especially for me. All the passengers were buckled up when I boarded.

The homeward-bound jet ran noisily down the runway, lifted into the friendly blue sky, and slowly turned its nose eastward toward that great country of ours.

Before it cleared the land, I again saw the many whitewashed sepulchers which were scattered among the thousands of bomb and shell craters...scars we would leave deep into posterity. I did not really see them clearly, for an endless parade of dead Yards and dead Green Beret friends of mine passed before my moist eyes.

"God," I whispered. "Please don't let those anti-war hippies throw rotten eggs and tomatoes at me when I walk out of the terminal at San Francisco."

I heard later that as the general looked up at the departing jet, his aide said, "General, I managed to get through to Miss Friem on the telephone. She was elated. She said she would meet his plane when it lands. She sure sounded a happy girl. Let's hope he does not have a few other girls waiting for him."

They laughed.

The general said, "He should be able to lie himself out of such a small matter with ease."

He acted as if he had just remembered a funny joke for he had Penny on his staff.

Up in the 727 Pan Am flight, over the South China Sea, the No Smoking signs went off. I closed my eyes and gave silent thanks to whomever looked down on me from above. I expected to enjoy great moments where nothing else would happen to me.

At that moment Penny's delicate scent engulfed me. There she stood next to me with two grinning airline stewardesses enjoying what they took to be the unfolding of a fairy tale romance. Many of the passengers also seemed to have expected that unfolding.

One of the smiling stewardesses said, "Penny, there are two vacant seats next to each other in first-class. One for you and one for this Green Beret master sergeant." A warm glow of well-being spread though me like the effect of a third very dry martini. Penny was in my arms where I held her so tight she could barely wiggle her body to let me know that again she wore no underwear.

Her first words to me were almost drowned out by the many hoots which came from the happy, homeward-bound soldiers, as they craned their necks over the seats to see the lovely Penny being overwhelmed by one of their own.

"I told you I'd get you, soldier," she said with happiness shining in her eyes. And well she might, for she surely had me wrapped up and exactly where she wanted me, and where I wanted to be.

"Who be gots who?" I asked, "seems I be gots me one boo coo be good, beautiful, sexy female, and to hell with the PX."

I almost lost sight of my mailbag, and would have, had a young Army captain close by not retrieved it for me and handed it to me.

"She's quite some lady. But Sergeant, don't let her make you forget that you are an Official Courier."

In the first class compartment, I took her into my arms and again felt all the things that I had wanted to do so badly for my own amusement and to shake the hell out of Booby Trap while we were in the hallway of MAGV Headquarters.

The airline stewardesses giggled like teenyboppers. They acted reluctant to leave us and tend to their other passengers. One very cute stewardess stood close by with the liquor pushcart, and hardly paid attention to a civilian who was trying to reach for a drink.

"Tony, I have 30 days leave, and I know your orders also authorize 30 days leave, plus travel time to Fort Bragg," Penny said, while holding on to my arm as we settled comfortably into our seats.

"We're going to love the world and everything in it — whoa, whoa! Don't stop this world, I love it," she cried with loud, gay laughter, while throwing her arms up and pulling a stewardess down to her and giving her a hug. It took three of those small airline bottles of scotch before I could fully grasp the situation and formulate an operational plan that would go into effect as soon as I felt the soil of our beloved country under my feet.

After the sixth little bottle of scotch, I did not care if rotten eggs were thrown at me, as had been done another time when I had returned to the United States.

Jim's words came to me, "This guy can fall into a bucket of shit and come out smelling like a rose."

I felt good, and if I had been told that I, indeed, did smell like a rose, I would have believed it.

"We have a lot of living to do when we get on the ground," I said to Penny when I managed to get her tongue out of my mouth.

"Yes," Penny answered sweetly. "That is why I am here."

Welcome to

Hellgate Press

Words of War
From Antiquity to Modern Times
by Gerald Weland   ISBN: 1-55571-491-9
176 pages, Paperback: $13.95

Words of War is a delightful romp through military history. Lively writing leads the reader to an understanding of a number of soldierly quotes. The result of years of haunting dusty libraries, searching obscure journals, and reviewing microfilm files, this unique approach promises to inspire many casual readers to delve further into the circumstances surrounding the birth of many quoted phrases.

Army Museums
West of the Mississippi
by Fred L. Bell, SFC, Retired   ISBN: 1-55571-395-5
318 pages, Paperback: $17.95

A guide book for travelers through 23 museums of the west. *Army Museums* contains detailed information about the contents of each museum and the famous soldiers stationed at the forts and military reservations where the museums are located. It is a colorful look at our heritage and the settling of the American West.

The Parrot's Beak
U.S. Operations in Cambodia
by Paul B. Morgan   ISBN: 1-55571-543-5
200 pages, Paperback: $14.95

By the author of *K-9 Soldiers: Vietnam and After,* Morgan's latest book divulges secret insertion techniques and information about Nixon's secret war that the government still refuses to acknowledge.

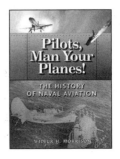
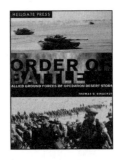
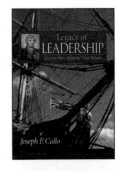